JAMES THOMSON

JAMES THOMSON

by William Aikman

JAMES THOMSON

Poet of 'The Seasons'

By

DOUGLAS GRANT

Associate Professor of English in the University of Toronto

LONDON
THE CRESSET PRESS
MCMLI

First published in 1951 by
The Cresset Press Ltd., 11 Fitzroy Square, London, W.1
and printed in Great Britain by
Western Printing Services Ltd., Bristol

PREFACE

I HAD written the first draft of this biography of James
Thomson before I was told that a collection of family
papers might contain some references to the poet. As I
turned those papers over, I sharply realized the truth of
Dr. Johnson's dictum, that 'nobody can write the life of a
man, but those who have eat and drunk and lived in social
intercourse with him'. I read in one letter how the poet was
writing a new play, but because my imagination was not
prompted by the personal knowledge which Johnson believed to be indispensable to a biographer, I could not feel,
as the contemporary recipient of the letter must have felt,
the immediacy of the poet's personality behind that casual
remark. The unique spirit of each man is sympathetically
transfused into the understanding of his friends, but it
remains as aloof and as indefinable to the later biographer as
the colour of the sky.

The best biographies are those which have been written
by friends and contemporaries, and, luckily for posterity, the
life of James Thomson has been written by some one who
knew and loved him well. Patrick Murdoch's memoir was
published in 1762 as the preface to a collected edition of the
poet's works, and, although it is unfortunately brief and un-
documented, it carries us directly into Thomson's presence.
It is among the best of those prefatory memoirs in which the
eighteenth century delighted, and it will always be the
primary source for an understanding of the poet's genius and
character.

Murdoch's memoir was soon augmented by more detailed
studies. Throughout the later eighteenth and early nineteenth centuries, when Thomson's reputation stood high,
various biographies appeared, usually as the prefaces to new

editions of his poetry, and each added some fresh and illuminating information. The work of Sir Harris Nicolas,
Allan Cunningham, and Peter Cunningham, scholars and
men of letters, is particularly valuable. It was not until 1895,
however, that a complete and critical biography was published, and it was left to a French scholar to undertake this
necessary task. Léon Morel's *James Thomson, sa Vie et ses
Œuvres*, is an exact and thorough piece of research, but his
bald narrative, bolstered up by a cumbrous array of notes, is
inadequate and unsatisfactory. Any later biographer, however, must be indebted to Morel for his industry.

I have attempted in this work only to tell the story of the
poet's life, and I have avoided criticizing his poetry in detail
or writing a history of his philosophical ideas. It is unlikely
that I could have improved upon the large body of criticism
that has already been published, and particularly upon G. C.
Macaulay's admirable analysis of Thomson's poetry, which,
since it is in the *English Men of Letters Series*, is easily acces-
sible. Nor could I urge further the rigorous examination of
the poet's philosophy which has been undertaken by several
American scholars, and it seemed unnecessary to repeat the
conclusions reached by Professor Alan Dugald McKillop in
The Background of Thomson's Seasons. I am indebted to Professor McKillop in many ways, and also to Professor
Marjorie Nicolson, whose study, *Newton Demands the Muse*,
a model of imaginative research, has prompted many of my
observations.

The chief contribution which this biography will make
towards an understanding of the poet is, of course, the publication of his remarkable correspondence with Miss Elizabeth Young. I am deeply indebted to Lady Gordon Cumming
of Altyre for her kind permission to publish these letters and
some hitherto unpublished poems. I felt that were I to print
all the letters in full in the text, the last part of my biography
would be greatly out of proportion to the first, and I have
therefore quoted only what I thought necessary to my
purpose in the text, and printed the remainder as an appen-

dix. The reader will easily be able to reconstruct their sequence.

Many of my friends have been ready with information and suggestions, and I should like to acknowledge the kindly help I have received from Professor W. L. Renwick, who spent some of his meagre petrol ration on driving me round the Borders and pointing out *en route* how the landscape influenced the poet's vision of nature; Mr. John Hayward, who read the manuscript and showed me how it could be improved in many places; Professor A. S. P. Woodhouse, who read the proofs and made some valuable suggestions; Mr. Edmund Blunden, M.C., who was naturally interested in a biography of a poet after his own heart; Professor John Butt; Professor Geoffrey Tillotson; Mr. John Woodward; Dr. J. C. Corson; Mr. E. C. Paton; and Mr. Gilbert Turner, the Librarian of Richmond Public Library, who courteously and effectively answered my many inquiries. I have particular pleasure in thanking Mrs. Joyce A. Bristow, a descendant of the poet's favourite sister Elizabeth, for information about her family which she put at my disposal. I am also indebted to the Chatsworth Estates Company for permission to print from Mallet's letter to Pope. The officials of the Bodleian, the British Museum, the National Library of Scotland, and the Register House, Edinburgh, showed me their traditional courtesy. Particularly, I must thank the University of Toronto, which granted me leave of absence to finish the work. I should add that the Librarian of the University Library, Edinburgh, questions whether the drawing by William Aikman, which I have reproduced as a frontispiece, is in fact a portrait of the poet. It was presented to the Library by the Earl of Buchan, who presumably knew its history, as a genuine resemblance. If it is compared with Slaughter's sketch, which Buchan also at one time owned, I think it can be accepted as a likeness taken shortly after the poet's arrival in London.

1949   D.G.

CONTENTS

ILLUSTRATIONS

CHAPTER I

CHILDHOOD AND FIRST POEMS

The Tweed, pure Parent-Stream,
Whose pastoral Banks first heard my Doric Reed,
With, Silvan Jed, thy tributary Brook.

THOMAS THOMSON[1] was born about 1666 in the
Border village of Ednam. The name of Thomson was
common in the district, and it would be a desperate attempt
to prove that Thomas sprang from other than common
stock; but his father, although only a gardener in the service
of Andrew Edmondstoune of Ednam, was able to arrange
that he should be educated at the College in Edinburgh.
There was nothing unusual in the son's apparent advancement from a low to a higher station. The distinctions between a gardener and his master were slight; peasantry and
gentry spoke the same tongue, 'braid Scots', and behaved
with the same uncouth manners; they were equally bigoted,
litigious, and independent; and, since the landlords had not
yet been taught how to extract value from their estates, they
both were poor.

There were other more vital reasons for the homogeneity
of this backward society. The Scottish consciousness at the
close of the seventeenth century was entirely preoccupied by
religion. Precept, dogma, and church government were
debated with furious determination, and the absorbing, un-
edifying dissensions of the sects excluded other thoughts.
This wasteful, tedious wrangling had at least a democratic
tendency. The Church, by admitting all its members to a
share in its direction, fostered independence and levelled
social distinctions. Master and man might be at the same

[1] See Hew Scott, *Fasti Ecclesiae Scoticanae*, 1917, ii, 139.

time elders of a church and at variance over a tenet, and the equality which reigned within the church could hardly be kept behind its doors. The traditions of Scottish education too were egalitarian. Each boy, no matter what his class, was offered the same opportunity, and Scotland's virility during the eighteenth century derived from this arrangement, which allowed arts, trades, and professions to recruit their strength from the whole people. The ministers in particular came from common stock. The Church of Scotland, unlike the Church of England, had no rich livings to attract into its service the gentry's younger sons at a loose end for a career; and those prepared to undertake a minister's duties in return for a pittance were those who knew greater hardship and poverty. The congregations, moreover, preferred rough sincerity to amiable civility. 'A large proportion' of these ministers, wrote a contemporary social historian, 'and these were the most acceptable to the common people, were regarded as hot-headed, morose, narrow-minded men, who had in general a very moderate stock of learning.'[1]

Thomas Thomson, whom his father intended for the Church, went to the College at Edinburgh to acquire this very moderate but necessary stock of learning; and, after he had laureated in August 1686, and continued on through the Divinity Class, he was licensed to preach, on 17 June 1691, by the Presbytery of Kelso. A year later, on 12 July 1692, through the influence of Andrew Edmondstoune and other well-disposed friends, he was inducted into the church of his native village, Ednam.

Ednam lies two miles to the north of Kelso. At the end of the seventeenth century the village was no more than a line of impoverished cottages which, running parallel to a stream, the Eden, from which it derived its name—Edenham shortened in pronunciation to Ednam—, led up to a church and manse, which have long since been replaced by more spacious if uninteresting buildings. The cottages have been improved, but the village's plan has remained unchanged until

---

[1] John Ramsay, *Scotland and Scotsmen in the Eighteenth Century*, 1888, i, 219.

to-day. The country in this part of Roxboroughshire is undulant and pastoral, and its summer air of secluded opulence is heightened by the numerous music of hidden brooks and the distant prospect of barren hills. The neighbouring market town of Kelso stands on the banks of the Tweed, which at that time was unbridged, and the traffic on the main road from Edinburgh to Newcastle, which crossed the river there, had to trust to a ferry and a good ford.[1] It was, and still is, a handsome, substantial town graced with the ruins of a great and magnificent abbey.

Thomas Thomson cannot have found that his charge exacted too much attention. The minister at Kelso, it is true, warned his congregation in what must have been a rousing sermon that, '*If there was a Town in the World like* Sodom, Kelso *was it*';[2] but his accusation should be dismissed as an adroit appeal to local patriotism. The young minister's time would be pleasantly preoccupied by religious controversy—although to which of the many possible sides he inclined is unknown—and by the censuring of the more natural sins. He was apparently liked as an amiable and righteous minister, and we can take on trust this comment upon his character: he was 'but little known beyond the narrow circle of his co-presbyters, and to a few gentlemen in the neighbourhood; but highly respected by them, for his piety, and his diligence in the pastoral duty'.[3]

It was not long before he married, and on 6 October 1693, 'Mr Thomas Thomson Minister of Ednam and Beatrix Trotter in the parish of Kelso gave up their Names for proclamation in order to Marriage'.[4] Beatrix Trotter was a daughter of Alexander Trotter of Fogo—a Berwickshire village about seven miles to the north of Ednam—and of Margaret Hume, a daughter of William Hume of Bassendean; and Beatrix could thus claim through her mother a

---

[1] See Defoe, *Tour thro' Great Britain*, 1753, iv, 149.
[2] Kirkwood, *Plea before the Kirk*, 1698, p. 38.
[3] *Works of James Thomson*, 1762, i, ii.
[4] *Ednam Parish Records*, Register House, Edinburgh.

distant connexion with the noble house of Hume.[1] She had
in addition to her birth the more solid attraction of being a
co-heiress to the small property of Widehope, or Wideopen,
on Kale Water. The date of their marriage is unrecorded,
but on 7 May 1695, 'Mr Thomas Thomson Minister had
a sone baptized called Andrew'. His second son, Alexander,
was baptised on 7 March 1697, and his first daughter, Isobel,
on 4 January 1699. His fourth child and third son was born
in 1700, and in the parish register the entry reads: 'M^r
Thomas Thomsons sone James Bapized [sic] Septr 15 day.'
This son was to become the Poet of the Seasons.

There is disagreement among the biographers about the
true date of his birth. Patrick Murdoch, his close friend,
stated that the poet was born on 11 September,[2] but because
the customs of the Church of Scotland demanded that eight
days rather than four should elapse between a birth and a
baptism, some later biographers have chosen 7 September
as the date of his birth.[3] But Murdoch must have known
which day the poet and his family chose to keep as his birth-
day, and 11 September is the more plausible date.

There is, equally, disagreement about the place of his
birth. An assiduous anecdotist who visited Ednam in the
middle of the nineteenth century to discover if any memories
of the poet had lingered on among the villagers, met a crone
who told him 'that her mother had lived at the old manse,
and frequently heard what had been told to inquirers. The
manse in which Thomson was born, she said, was of mud;
and he was born in the parlour, which had a bed in a recess
concealed by a curtain.'[4] This is circumstantial enough but a
rival tradition asserts that the poet was born in his mother's
house at Wideopen.[5] Wideopen lies less than a mile beyond
Morebattle, a village eight miles to the south-east of Kelso,
at the head of a narrow dene cut in the hillside by a burn
which flows down to pass under the road leading to

[1] See Scott, op. cit., and Léon Morel, James Thomson, 1895, p. 8.
[2] Works of Thomson, 1762, i, ii.   [3] See Morel, op. cit., p. 10.
[4] William Howitt, Homes and Haunts of British Poets, 1847, ii, 213.
[5] See History of the Berwickshire Naturalists' Club, 1916, xxii, 401–2.

Yetholm. The site of the house is now marked by a level green plot, which was once the garden, and by a fragment of masonry which has been included in a stone dyke. A visitor to the spot at the beginning of this century has left an account of what there was then to be learnt about its history. 'The House itself was pulled down about fifty years ago. An old man, John Scott, for years minister's man and beadle, who knew it well, and every inch of the hill round, showed me exactly where it stood. It was a small house, two storied and thatched, and well known as "Thomson's House". Its doorway, looking east, must have been dangerously near the edge of the burn, a thread almost in hot summer, but often brawling over its banks in time of spate. Close behind the house—there must have been the merest passage between —stood three cottages in a row, also dating back to Thomson's day. The last remaining one was pulled down forty years ago.'[1] The tradition is that James, in accordance with a custom of the time that children, if it were possible, should be born upon their own land, was born in this house. It is, however, most improbable that the mother and her child could be carried across the eleven rough miles from Wideopen to Ednam in time for a baptism on 15 September, and the tradition that this was so may be lightly dismissed. The poet must, however, have spent many of his childhood days at Wideopen, and the neighbouring scenery would deeply impress his imagination. The narrow dene, alert with the vital silence peculiar to the Border hills, leads into a glen that opens on to the spacious valley through which the quick delightful Kale runs to join the Tweed. The opulent, almost feminine, contours of Highside and Linton hills bound the prospect to the east, but to the north, from the rise on which Morebattle is sited, the landscape spreads out in a broad sweep where light and shadow can manœuvre unconfined. This and similar scenes became the stuff upon which the poet's imagination worked, and trained him to observe nature and its effects in a particular way.

[1] *Ibid.*

Although it can claim the honour of his birth, Ednam was
the poet's home for only two months. Thomas Thomson
accepted a call from the congregation of Southdean, and on
6 November 1700 he was admitted to his new charge.

Southdean parish lies to the south-west of Jedburgh at
the foot of Carter Fell. A survey of the parish was made
towards the end of the eighteenth century,[1] and from this
record we learn that it was about twelve miles long and seven
broad in extent, and consisted mainly of rough hill pasture
and a little arable land able to bear oats and barley. When
Thomas Thomson entered upon his ministry, the population must have numbered more than the seven hundred and
fourteen souls who were recorded as dwelling in the parish
in 1793. An observer remarked in that year: 'From tradition, as well as from innumerable vestiges and ruins of
houses, population must have been considerable a century
ago, and from general opinion, it is greatly diminished.'[2]
The peasantry who grazed their sheep on the moorland and
tilled the narrow fields would be even more primitive and
impoverished than their descendants whom Tobias Smollett
saw and described in 1772: 'The country people of North
Britain live chiefly on oat-meal, and milk, cheese, butter,
and some garden stuff, with now and then a pickled herring,
by way of delicacy; but flesh-meat they seldom or never
taste, nor any kind of strong liquor, except twopenny, at
times of uncommon festivity.—Their breakfast is a kind of
hasty-pudding, of oat-meal, or pease-meal, eaten with milk.
They have commonly pottage to dinner, composed of cale
or cole, leeks, barley or big, and butter; and this is reinforced
with bread, and cheese made of skimmed milk. At night they
sup on sowens or flummery of oat-meal.—In a scarcity of
oats, they use the meal of barley or pease, which is both
nourishing and palatable. . . . They are clothed with a coarse
kind of russet of their own making, which is both decent
and warm.—They dwell in poor huts, built of loose stones
and turf, without any mortar, having a fire-place or hearth

---

[1] John Sinclair, *Statistical Account of Scotland*, 1794, xii, 67–72.　　[2] *Ibid.*, p. 68.

in the middle, generally made out of an old mill-stone, and a hole at top to let out the smoke.'[1]

But in spite of poverty, and actual starvation in the years of famine (1709 was such a year), the parish, it was claimed, was healthy except for frequent epidemics of small-pox—a terrible scourge until innoculation was introduced later in the century—and 'rheumatisms, pains in the stomach and bowels, owing, likely, to the low and damp situation of the houses'.[2]

The parish church had been built only ten years before Thomas Thomson arrived, but the manse cannot have been either a solid or commodious building since it was found necessary to reconstruct it in 1736. The manse is situated at the foot of Southdean Law in a bend of the river Jed, which curves round the foot of the lawn before the house. It is remote from the world, and the bickering of the Jed and the disconsolate crying of the moor-birds emphasize rather than disturb its seclusion. Here James Thomson passed the first fifteen years of his life. There are few records of these years but it is possible to imagine from the little that we do know, and from the evidence in his own poetry, how his character developed. The centre of his life, the comfortable cocoon in which he grew, was the family; and since their isolation prevented them from mixing generally and intimately with other society, the effect of the father's and mother's characters upon those of their children would be far reaching. His father's piety and amiability have been touched upon; his mother drew this praise from an earlier biographer: 'She was . . . a person of uncommon natural endowments; possessed of every social and domestic virtue; with an imagination, for vivacity and warmth, scarce inferior to her son's, and which raised her devotional exercises to a pitch bordering on enthusiasm.'[3] James would, therefore, be instructed from his earliest days in religion, but because of his mother's imaginative temperament, it would be presented to

---

[1] Smollett, *Humphrey Clinker*, 1790, p. 304.   [2] Sinclair, *op. cit.*, p. 68.
[3] *Works of Thomson*, 1762, i, iv.

him not as a catalogue of doctrines and a dull code of behaviour but as a beautiful and powerful spirit eluding in its flight the scope of reason: 'Whatever advantage Mr. *Thomson* might derive from the complexion of his parent, it is certain he owed much to a religious education; and that his early acquaintance with the sacred writings contributed greatly to that *sublime*, by which his works will be for ever distinguished.'[1] This instruction must have been gently and persuasively given, because there is an entire absence in his work and mature character of that spiritual tension which is peculiar to those who, having been bred with religious strictness, revolt bitterly against the memory of their childhood.

Meanwhile the family grew apace; four more daughters, Margaret, Mary, Elizabeth, and Jean, and a fourth son, John, were born; and the household must have been always engaged in numberless tasks, which would make the long winter nights seem too short. The wildness without and the friendly warmth within the house were contrasted by the poet in his most famous sentimental picture, and had he not enjoyed a happy childhood, he could not have written so sensitively:

> The Fowls of Heaven,
> Tam'd by the cruel Season, croud around
> The winnowing Store, and claim the little Boon
> Which PROVIDENCE assigns them. One alone,
> The Red-Breast, sacred to the household Gods,
> Wisely regardful of th' embroiling Sky,
> In joyless Fields, and thorny Thickets, leaves
> His shivering Mates, and pays to trusted Man
> His annual visit. Half-afraid, he first
> Against the Window beats; then, brisk alights
> On the warm Hearth; then, hopping o'er the floor,
> Eyes all the smiling Family askance,
> And pecks, and starts, and wonders where he is:
> Till more familiar grown, the Table-Crumbs
> Attract his slender feet.

There would also be games and songs to beguile the time,

[1] *Works of Thomson* 1762, i, iv.

and particularly the Border ballads would be told. There are
no obvious traces of these traditional tales in his work, but
the poet cannot have been unaffected by their simplicity,
excitement, plaintiveness, and flashes of true poetry. A few
well-thumbed books, some easy lessons, and field-sports
would take their place in this ordered, simple, domestic life.

This withdrawn existence was entirely undramatic; but
beyond the manse there lay some of the most dramatic
country in Britain, and familiarity with it provided that
stimulus which the poet's young imagination required.
There stretches to the south of Southdean the great barren
range of the Cheviots. The broad hills rise round-shouldered
against the sky, and between them bends the idle desolation
of the moors. Coomb Edge, Dod Fell, The Trouting, Lamb
Rig, Knox Knowe, Scrathy Holes, Catcleugh, and Arks
Edge bulge from the desert of Carter Fell and Kielderhead
Moor. A desolate region, whose tufted marshes and spongy
hillocks are threaded by a network of streams which make
their way down through rocky channels into the glens. The
dried hue of these slopes, blotched by sour-green mosses in
the spring, and their hostile, almost animal, silence, which
seems to harass the traveller who attempts their recesses,
made them repulsive to the eighteenth century's sensibility.
They were a wilderness which man could not reclaim for
his use, and though they might be admired when distance
had subdued and tranquillized their horror, the century
interpreted them as a threat, which it had to repel, to an
admired social and natural decorum. When Thomson, in
obedience to this sensibility, stood upon the high places
about his home, and turned his back to the hills, he would
see laid out before him the long sweep of a delightful pastoral landscape. The English countryside owes its beauty to
the cloistered grace of many particulars, a brook, a coppice,
a beanfield, or a handful of primroses in a hedge, and its
poets approach nature through such details; but in the
Borders these particulars lose their identity in the panorama.
The eye moves down along a valley, follows it until it

widens and enters another, and continues on across a plain which is bounded only by the horizon. This landscape is ordered into foreground, middle distance, and distance, as deliberately as though it had been arranged by some great seventeenth-century artist, a Salvator Rosa or a Gaspar Poussin. The pictorial effect is heightened by the subsidiary hills which, branching out transversely from the Cheviot massif, contain the landscape as though in a frame. Green and brown, and their various tones, are the dominant colours; the others are submerged and must be sought out; but to compensate for this uniformity, the effects of light and shade are more vivid and impressive than those of any other district. From the heights the volatile interchange of sun-light and shadow can be followed across the plain; the clouds massing on the horizon before they extend throughout the wide air, and the rain scud which strikes before their advance, can be watched as though they were an army manœuvring; and the unstained clarity of a winter's day, when the air seems as solid but as lucent as crystal, can almost be touched. Each change of wind or weather is finely and immediately recorded in the variations of light.

This landscape trained Thomson to observe and describe nature in a particular way, and it will be found that its peculiarity is exactly reflected in his poetry. The effect of this secluded life upon his character is no less obvious. A home where love was expressed in undemonstrative kindliness does not create in even the most sensitive mind those psychological fractures which lead to intellectual subtlety and introspective questioning; it makes instead for simplicity and emotional tranquillity; and untroubled by perplexities, but stimulated by his mother's imaginative rendering of the Bible, James passed easily through his boyhood, receptive to the natural, but oblivious to the human, drama.

His education at home, or at a school which may have been held in the neighbouring village of Chesters, can have made few demands upon him; but about 1712 he was sent to the school at Jedburgh, eight miles from Southdean, and a decayed woollen town whose 'public Buildings, Bridges, Streets, and Works' were 'greatly out of Repair'.[1] The grammar school, which was held in some esteem, was kept in the aisle of Jedburgh Church. 'Dr. Somerville, formerly Minister of Jedburgh, wrote in a letter dated the 24th April 1795: "Of Thomson's having attended the school here, there is no doubt, for when I came here twenty years ago several survived who had been his companions, and some of them his class-fellows. When I made application for a new school-house to the heritors, in 1778, on account of the ruinous state of the old one, I was told by the person who was then the Provost, that he thought that the aisle of the Church might again be employed for that purpose; that greater men than any of the present generation had been educated there, for it was the place of the school when Mr. Thomson and himself attended it." '[2] The Provost, if he could have shielded his memory against the brightness of Thomson's posthumous fame, might have preferred his own juvenile promise to that of the poet, who gave but small indication of any ability at school. 'Mr. Thomson, in the early part of his life, so far from appearing to possess a sprightly genius, was considered by his schoolmaster, and those which directed his education, as being really without a common share of parts.'[3] This tale is echoed by every biographer, and another is told to illustrate his distaste for his school-work: one day he was heard by the schoolmaster to exclaim, 'Confound the Tower of Babel', and when he was asked for an explanation, he naturally if unoriginally replied, 'If it were not for the Tower of Babel, there would be no languages to learn'.[4] The slow, rigorous discipline of Latin exercises, the staple of all Scottish education at this time, even when taught by an able master, would not come easily to an immature and hesitant boy; but precocity does not always presume genius, and there were

[1] Defoe, *op. cit.*, iv, 148.
[2] *Poetical Works of Thomson*, ed. Harris Nicolas, 1847, i, vi *n*.
[3] Theophilus Cibber, *Lives of the Poets*, 1753, v, 190.
[4] *Poetical Works of Thomson*, ed. Bell, 1855, p. 7 *n*.

friends who recognized that under the superficial appearance of stupidity Thomson concealed the promise of future
abilities. He was lucky to be encouraged at this time by men
of taste who were prepared to take trouble over his youth.

The first person to be interested was a young farmer,
Robert Riccaltoun, or Riccarton, who, after studying at the
College in Edinburgh, returned to carry on his father's farm
at Earlshaugh, which lay in the parish of Hobkirk adjoining
that of Southdean. Although he did not take the Divinity
curriculum at the College, he at length decided to enter the
ministry, and after being licensed to preach in 1717, he was
presented to the living of Hobkirk in 1725. He must have
been a man of singular charm and intelligence. He was
possessed 'of such amazing powers, that many persons of
genius . . . who conversed with him, have been astonished,
that such great merit should be buried in an obscure part of
the country, where he had no opportunity to display himself, and . . . seldom an opportunity of conversing with men
of learning'.[1] Another witness to his merits was more
particular in his praise: 'A large portion of original genius,
rather than a cultivated understanding, together with
facetious manners, an ample store of observation and anecdotes, and a predilection for the society of young men,
characterized him . . . A benevolent heart, a rich imagination, a taste for what was beautiful and sublime in the works
of nature, expressed with simplicity and propriety . . .
procured the affection and esteem of all his intimate
acquaintances.'[2] Riccaltoun in his later years 'modestly
acknowledged that he had considerable influence in discovering and prompting the poetical talents of Thomson,
who, in his youthful days, had been his frequent visitor'.[3]
Murdoch went even further in his account of the poet, and
affirmed that Riccaltoun not only encouraged Thomson's
first poetical essays but undertook, 'with the father's appro-

[1] Cibber, *op. cit.*, v, 190.
[2] Thomas Somerville, *My Own Life and Times*, 1861, pp. 128, 129.
[3] *Ibid.*, p. 129.

bation, the chief direction of his studies, furnished him with the proper books, corrected his performances; and was daily rewarded with the pleasure of seeing his labour so happily employed'.[1] If Thomson was backward at school, Riccaltoun may have coached him during the holidays. He must certainly have encouraged his pupil to read the poets critically, to judge his own juvenile verses by their standard, and have fostered his love for nature and stimulated his ambition by talking enthusiastically. Such sympathetic tuition would give an apparently backward and awkward boy self-confidence, and help him to believe that his verses might reach excellence one day. We certainly know the manner in which Riccaltoun criticized Thomson's early work. When another young poet's efforts were later submitted to him for his opinion, he wrote: 'I have looked over the specimen which you sent me of his poetical talents; and, had I the same opportunities, I would treat him as I did Mr. Thomson, and still do all my friends in that way; viz. to discourage to the utmost of my power indulging that humour where it requires more judgment than everybody is master of to keep imagination and fancy to their proper province.'[2] This would imply that he advised Thomson not to attempt subjects which were obviously beyond his immature powers, and to avoid that luxuriance of diction which, if we can judge from his later work, was his peculiar temptation. But though Riccaltoun discovered that Thomson, 'so far from being without parts, really possessed a very fine genius, yet he never could have imagined, as he often declared, that there existed in his mind such powers, as even by the best cultivation could have raised him to so high a degree of eminence amongst the poets'.[3] The few juvenile verses which have survived, and these cannot be the worst, show that Riccaltoun must have been gifted with extraordinary prescience if he could have foretold from their quality his pupil's future eminence.

[1] *Works of Thomson*, 1762, i, ii. [2] *Works of Thomson*, ed. Bell, p. 12 *n*.
[3] Cibber, *op. cit.*, v, 191.

Among the other men of taste who distinguished some
ability in the boy was Sir William Bennet of Grubbat,
whose estate adjoined Mrs. Thomson's small property at
Wideopen. His house and grounds at Marlefield were often
visited by the poet Allan Ramsay, and Sir William is supposed to have helped him to compose his great pastoral of
The Gentle Shepherd. Ramsay celebrated Marlefield's beauty
in some verses, and described its owner as Phoebus's 'much-
dauted son'.[1] Sir William, who was 'well known for his gay
humour and ready poetical wit, was highly delighted with
our young poet, and used to invite him to pass the summer
vacation at his country seat: a scene of life which Mr.
Thomson always remembered with particular pleasure'.[2]
Among the earliest of Thomson's verses that have survived
there is *A Poetical Epistle to Sir William Bennet*, in which he
sincerely if uneasily adopts the conventional attitude of a
poet towards a patron:

> My trembling muse your honour does address,
> That it's a bold attempt most humbly I confess;
> If you'll encourage her young flagging flight,
> She'll upwards soar and mount Parnassus' height.

Verses written later in praise of Marlefield are rather better
than this *Epistle*, but their cracked veneer of conventional
diction cannot conceal the young poet's artlessness:

> O! what delight and pleasure 'tis to rove
> Through all the walks and alleys of the grove,
> Where spreading trees a checker'd scene display,
> Partly admitting and excluding day;
> Where cheerful green and odorous sweets conspire
> The drooping soul with pleasure to inspire;
> Where little birds employ their narrow throats
> To sing its praises in unlabour'd notes.

Sir William may not have inspired Thomson to write anything of real merit but his patronage must have contributed
a little towards his development.

Sir Gilbert Elliot of Minto, whose estate lay on the banks

[1] *Poetical Works of Ramsay*, 1800, i, 74.   [2] *Works of Thomson*, 1762, i, iii.

of the Teviot, is also supposed to have encouraged the poet. Thomson's uncle and cousin worked for Sir Gilbert as gardeners, and it may be imagined that he would be willing to help their relation if it lay in his power, but there is no reliable evidence that he did so. At Ancrum, however, a village close by Sir Gilbert's estate, Thomson had some friends nearer his own age, John and William Cranstoun, the sons of the local minister. Ancrum is on Ale Water, which, after passing beyond the village, flows beneath a high red sandstone cliff. A series of caves have been hewn out of this cliff, and in one of them, known as 'Thomson's Cave', the poet is popularly supposed to have written some of his verses. He more probably enjoyed climbing up the difficult, and now almost impassable, access to them.

Thomson, however, although he must have been flattered by the attention shown to him, at least recognized the true value of his juvenilia. Whatever he wrote during this time, either to entertain Sir William Bennet, or in obedience to Riccaltoun, or for his own amusement, 'he destroyed every new year's day; committing his little pieces to the flames, in their due order; and crowning the solemnity with a copy of verses, in which were humorously recited the several grounds of their condemnation'.[1] This anecdote illustrates his early determination to be a poet, and his recognition of real critical standards.

Verses, friendship with men who were willing to help him forward, the ever-present and persuasive influence of nature, and the luxury of a happy and united home, made up his life until he was fifteen. It was then decided that he should study at the College in Edinburgh with the intention of entering the ministry. His mother, an enthusiast in religion, probably encouraged him to agree to this career, and the attraction of living in the capital would help him to concur quietly in his parents' plans for his future.

[1] *Ibid.*

CHAPTER II

A STUDENT AT EDINBURGH

There studious let me sit,
And hold high converse with the MIGHTY DEAD.

T HE Jacobite rising of 1715, when an undisciplined
band wandering purposelessly about the Lowlands
inflicted suffering, particularly upon Jedburgh, may have
delayed James Thomson's journey to Edinburgh for a few
weeks. 'According to tradition, a servant of his father conducted him to the capital, seated behind himself on horseback; but such was his reluctance to forsake the country,
that he had no sooner been left to himself in the city, than
he set out on foot for home, and was back at his father's
manse (between fifty and sixty miles distant) as soon as the
man and his horse. When his parents remonstrated with
him respecting this disobedient conduct, he passionately
observed that "he could study as well on the haughs of
Sou'den as in Edinburgh".'[1] An improbable story which
may be, however, interpreted into truth, if it is accepted as
no more than a fictitious illustration of the poet's early
recognition that he would derive his strength from an
observation of nature rather than from the study of books.
If he did rebel, he was quickly commanded or persuaded
into obedience, and he matriculated in Professor William
Scott's Greek Class at the beginning of the academic
year.[2]

The curriculum of the College of Edinburgh—it did not
assume the title of University until a much later date—was
confused, but a number of radical reforms introduced in

[1] Robert Chambers, *Biographical Dictionary of Eminent Scotsmen*, 1835, iv, 346–7.
[2] *Matriculation Register*, Edinburgh University Lib.

1708, which modelled the teaching upon the Dutch universities of Utrecht and Leyden, laid the foundation of the College's future greatness.[1] The first year was devoted to Latin and the second to Greek, but because those boys who came from country schools usually had a poor grounding in these languages, the lectures were confined to their elements: 'But persons coming from other Universities, or who, on examination, showed the requisite proficiency, might pass over both the Humanity and Greek classes.'[2] Those students who were allowed to pretermit Latin or Greek or both languages were called *Supervenientes*, and since Thomson matriculated at once in the Greek class, it would appear that he became one of these privileged students, who 'were often very numerous'.[3]

The College buildings were undistinguished. A tolerant visitor in 1709 wrote, 'The College is a good building, with three courts',[4] but a later observer, who had an intimate knowledge of the College's real condition, left a very different description of its state in 1768, which, after allowance has been made for deterioration, probably corresponded to what Thomson saw when he began to attend his classes. 'A stranger, when conducted to view the University of Edinburgh might, on seeing such courts and buildings, naturally enough imagine them to be almshouses for the reception of the poor; but would never imagine that he was entering within the precincts of a noted and flourishing seat of learning. An area which, if entire, would have formed one spacious quadrangle, is broken into three paltry divisions, and encompassed partly with walls which threaten destruction to the passenger, and partly with a range of low houses, several of which are now become ruinous and uninhabitable . . . The teaching rooms of the Professors are, in general, mean, straitened, and inconvenient.'[5] The ruinous and uninhabitable 'low houses' had deteriorated from the 'neat Buildings for the Use of such Students as please to

---

[1] See Alexander Grant, *Story of the University of Edinburgh*, 1884, i, 262 ff.
[2] *Ibid.*, i, 264. [3] *Ibid.* [4] Quoted *ibid.*, ii, 190. [5] Quoted *ibid.*, i, 193–4.

C

lodge in them'[1] of Thomson's day, which were, however,
only used by students in poor circumstances. Those students
who could afford the small expense lodged in the town, and,
because there was no collegiate system at all, they qualified
for residence only by attending the lectures. Thomson,
whose parents, if not affluent, were certainly not in mean
circumstances, probably boarded in a house with a few
companions. The College did have some attractions: 'The
Library is neatly kept, well furnished with Books put in
very good Order, cloistered with Wire Doors, which none
but the Keeper can open, which is   re commodious, and
less encumbering, than Multitudes o Chains, commonly
used in other Libraries.'[2] The Library a. had a collection
of pictures and curiosities, the most 'curiou   of which was
'a crooked Horn, cut out of a Woman's Hea when Fifty
Years old, and who lived Twelve Years after it'.

Thomson's attendance at the Greek class was, however,
quickly and dramatically interrupted by his father's death
on 9 February 1716. The circumstances in which he died
make a remarkable story. 'The narrative is related by Dr.
Somerville, who states, from his intimate knowledge of the
traditions of the country, that the clergyman who, at the
beginning of the last century, should have ventured to treat
ghosts, witches, and fairies with incredulity, would have
been regarded as a heretic. It happened during the Rev. Mr.
Thomson's ministration of the parish of Southdean that an
apparition appeared which produced indescribable consterna-
tion, and which was called, from the place which it selected
for its exploits, the Woolie Ghost. This terrible phantom
spread so much alarm among all classes, that it was at last
considered necessary to call in the proper authority to lay
the spirit, and Mr. Thomson was required, in his clerical
capacity, to perform that function. The ceremony was
opened in due form at Woolie; but the minister had scarcely
begun to pray when a ball of fire struck him on the head,
and so effectually paralyzed him that he became incapable of

[1] Defoe, *op. cit.*, iv, 78.   [2] *Ibid.*   [3] *Ibid.*, p. 79.

uttering another word. In this condition he was carried home, and expired in great agony. The authenticity of the story, we are further informed, was vouched for by a person "of rank and education, above the vulgar"; and it was so implicitly credited in the neighbourhood, that when Dr. Somerville took charge of the parish, many years after the occurence, he found it necessary to speak guardedly on the subject, and more than once gave offence by maintaining silence when it was mentioned.'[1] However his father died, whether by diabolic interference or from natural causes, James, although he hurried home 'with all the diligence he could use',[2] did not arrive in time to receive his last blessing. 'This affected him to an uncommon degree' and 'some extraordinary instances of his grief and filial duty on that occasion' were long remembered.[3] His father was buried in Southdean churchyard, and his grave is marked by an inscribed metal plate placed over the earlier stone tablet whose inscription has been weathered away.

Thomson must have returned sadly to Edinburgh to continue his studies, but he would be comforted by the knowledge that his mother intended to move from the manse to the capital. She was helped in her affairs by Robert Riccaltoun and by another close friend, William Gusthart, who was minister to the neighbouring parish of Crailing and Nisbet until 1721, when he was translated to the parish of Tolbooth in Edinburgh. From there he could more immediately further the interests of the widow and her family whom he had taken under his protection. This friend advised Mrs. Thomson to mortgage her moiety of the farm at Wideopen, and by following this advice she was able to take a house in Edinburgh, 'where she lived in a decent frugal manner, till her favourite son had not only finished his academical course, but was even distinguished and patronized as a man of genius'.[4] The house which she took cannot have been large but it was tolerably furnished.

---

[1] *Works of Thomson*, ed. Bell, pp. 8–9. [2] *Works of Thomson*, 1762, i, iii.
[3] *Ibid.* [4] *Ibid.*, i, iii–iv.

Among the many beds which such a large family would need, there was 'an angel bed with blue curtains and blue covering all mounted with blue lace', and a similar bed 'mounted with white lace'; there were plenty of chairs, six of which, the most valuable, had 'timber backs and leather bottoms'; and among the miscellaneous furnishings there were '17 pair of blankets, 13 pair of sheets, 7 Table cloaths and two duzon and a half of Naprie'; but there was no china or silver ware, and the family ate off wooden trenchers and drank from wooden cups.[1] The furniture would, of course, be removed to Edinburgh from the manse, and its inventory affords little evidence of the family's present income. It cannot have been very much; a minister's widow received no pension at this time, and the mortgage on the farm can have brought in little; but the elder sons, of whom nothing is known, may have contributed something towards their mother's support. She must have had many difficulties to contend with in the effort to live within her means and yet to keep up appearances, and her son, in his fine verses upon her death, has vouched for the trials which beset her:

See! where the kindest, best of mothers lies,
And death has closed her ever watching eyes;
Has lodged at last in peace her weary breast,
And lull'd her many piercing cares to rest.
No more the orphan train around her stands,
While her full heart upbraids her needy hands!
No more the widow's lonely fate she feels,
The shock severe that modest want conceals,
The oppressor's scourge, the scorn of wealthy pride,
And poverty's unnumber'd ills beside.

The town of Edinburgh, which was to be Thomson's home for the next ten years, was at this time among the most remarkable in Europe; and to the contemporary Englishman, it was a foreign capital whose language, religion, customs, and society were entirely different from those of the sister kingdom. The backbone of the town was

[1] Register House, Edinburgh.

the High Street which ran for more than a mile from Holyrood Palace to the Castle, and which was described as 'perhaps the largest, longest, and finest Street, for Buildings, and Number of Inhabitants, in the World'.[1] As this street gradually rose from the Palace to the Castle rock, which dominated the whole town, narrow side-lanes branched off like ribs and curved down the steep, almost precipitous sides of the ridge, and proved 'very troublesome to those, who have not very good Lungs'.[2] The mountainous site determined the town's construction, and to pack the inhabitants safely within its walls, whose circumference was limited by the nature of the ground, the buildings had to be contiguous and many stories high. This compression made the town assume a geometrical pattern rather like that formed by sugar crystals which have accreted round a piece of string. On account of its situation, wrote a contemporary Englishman, 'the City lies under such Inconveniencies, as are made a Subject of Scorn and Reproach by some, as if the People delighted in Stench and Nastiness; whereas, were any other People to live under the same Unhappiness of a rocky and mountainous Situation, a Throng of Buildings from Six to Ten Stories high, a Difficulty of obtaining Water . . . we should find a *London*, or a *Bristol*, as dirty as *Edinburgh*, and, perhaps, less able to make their Dwelling tolerable, at least in so narrow a Compass; for, tho' many Cities have more People in them, yet, I believe, there is none in the World, where so many People live in so little Room'.[3] The 'nastiness' at which more happily situated foreigners mocked arose from the custom of getting rid of ordure by tossing it out of the windows after ten o'clock at night, and to walk the streets after that hour was to undertake a risky journey: 'It sounds very oddly in the Ears of a Stranger, to hear all Passers-by cry out, as loud as to be heard to the uppermost Stories of the Houses . . . *Hoad yare Hoand*; that is, *Hold your Hand, and throw not, till I am passed.*'[4]

[1] Defoe, *op. cit.*, iv, 67. [2] *Ibid.* [3] *Ibid.*, iv, 69. [4] *Ibid.*

The people who lived pent up within these narrow streets were still in the grip of a gloomy and intolerant religion which infected their character with its bile, and the Church's idea of good behaviour was strictly enforced by a vigilant magistracy. 'It is not to be wondered, that, among a sour and fanatick people, magistrates so well disposed to exercise authority, should pay particular attention to what they called the duties of religion. A rigorous attendance on public worship was enforced. People called, from their office, *seizers*, patroled the streets, and apprehended those found walking them during the times of sermons.'[1] Another Scot, but one who was safely expatriated, also condemned their religion and their unsociability. After denouncing 'their ignorance of the world' which rendered them 'unfit for entertaining sensible strangers', he continued: 'A gloominess in religion renders one part of them very barbarous, and an enthusiasm in politics so transports the genteeler part, that they sacrifice to party almost every consideration of tenderness. Among such a people, a man may long live, little known, and less instructed; for their reservedness renders them uncommunicative, and their excessive haughtiness prevents them from being solicitous of knowledge.'[2] This is a harsh judgement which, although a valid criticism of the generality, who were still demoralized by the previous century's bitter turbulence, did not allow, however, for the renascent culture which was gradually mollifying the national acerbity.

The reformation of the College's curriculum in 1708 slowly affected the nature and quality of the teaching, and engendered a new spirit of inquiry and tolerance, which was also fostered by the increasing social and cultural interchanges with England. After passing through the Humanity and Greek classes, the student continued on through the classes of Logic and Natural Philosophy. The Professor of Logic, Colin Drummond, still announced dull and antiquated doctrines, but the Professor of Natural Philosophy,

1 Hugo Arnot, *History of Edinburgh*, 1788, p. 192.   2 Cibber, *op. cit.*, v, 164–5.

Robert Stewart, although one of his students remarked that he 'never had excelled',[1] slowly discarded Cartesianism and became a cautious convert to Newtonianism. His lectures must have sown some of the seeds of James Thomson's deep interest in the modern scientific and philosophic changes which were altering man's whole conception of his universe. The students if they wished could also attend the classes taken by the Professors of Mathematics and Moral Philosophy. But because graduation had fallen into disregard, 'no such thing as a curriculum could really continue to exist [and] each student attended such classes as he or his friends might think advisable'.[2] This academic freedom indirectly encouraged the pursuit of learning by allowing the student to read those subjects to which he was particularly attracted.

But of greater significance than the education officially dispensed was that provided by the numerous literary clubs and societies which were formed at this time. Their purpose was to encourage the study of the works of the best English authors, and they were inspired by Richard Steele's and Joseph Addison's periodical papers, *The Tatler* and *The Spectator*, which were read as eagerly in Edinburgh as in London. All the contemporary Scottish historians insist upon the supreme importance of these papers in the development of Scottish taste and literature. 'Those admirable papers', wrote John Ramsay, 'prepared the minds of our countrymen for the study of the best English authors, without a competent knowledge of which no man was accounted a polite scholar.'[3] The papers encouraged the study and imitation of English authors, and Patrick Murdoch, Thomson's biographer and fellow-student, confirmed Ramsay's opinion when he wrote: 'About this time, the study of poetry was become general in *Scotland*, the best *English* authors being universally read, and imitations of them attempted. *Addison* had lately displayed the beauties of

---

[1] Alexander Carlyle, *Autobiography*, 1860, p. 46.
[2] Grant, *op. cit.*, i, 277.   [3] Ramsay, *op. cit.*, i, 7.

Milton's immortal work; and his remarks on it, together with Mr. *Pope's* celebrated *Essay [on Criticism]*, had opened the way to an acquaintance with the best poets and critics.'[1] The better to study these authors, those who wished to excel in science or literature formed clubs where they could discuss selected works and criticize one another's performances. 'In order to improve themselves and counteract conceit . . . societies were instituted wherein at stated times . . . ingenious paradoxes were started and assailed with equal ingenuity. There the members used to submit their first essays in composition to the friendly censure of their associates, which helped to lop away luxuriances and check presumption. Meanwhile the tribute of applause was not withheld from rising merit.'[2] The most important club was the Rankenian, named after the landlord of the tavern where it met, which, numbering among its members many who were to achieve fame, was 'highly instrumental in disseminating through Scotland freedom of thought, boldness of disquisition, liberality of sentiment, accuracy of reasoning, correctness of taste, and attention to composition'.[3]

Thomson belonged to the Grotesque Club, which would meet like the others in some tavern, the place where even the most sedate business was conducted at this time; and among the other members of this oddly named club was David Malloch—or Mallet, as he chose to call himself after he had emigrated to London—who was to play an important part in Thomson's career. We learn from Malloch that Thomson was considered the jest of the club, and that the poems which he submitted for criticism were treated with ridicule. The same apparent obtuseness and simplicity concealed now, as they had done from some of his earlier acquaintances, the genius which was cautiously seeking for self-expression. Perhaps his continuance at home as the favourite son of an emotional mother prevented him from yet attaining that independence without which nothing can be accomplished. He was emotionally immature, and he

---

[1] *Works of Thomson*, 1762, i, iv.   [2] Ramsay, *op. cit.*, i, 8, 9.   [3] *Ibid.*, i, 8 *n.*

continued to be so throughout his life; this eventually helped to destroy his happiness.

His verses may have been ridiculed by the club, but he succeeded in having three poems accepted for publication in 1720 in a volume entitled *The Edinburgh Miscellany*. The third of these pieces, 'Verses on receiving a flower from his mistress', is a very artless attempt to pay courtly compliments in a style which had long since been abandoned; the second, 'Upon Happiness', is a confused vision in which the vain attempts of mankind to secure happiness are surveyed by the poet from the hill of Contemplation, and concludes on an unconvincing pietistic note; and the first, 'Of a Country Life', by far the most successful, is interesting for what it foreshows rather than for what it achieves. The style is extremely laboured; neither the metre nor the vocabulary is handled easily; and the poet seems to fumble towards a meaning like a man in the dark. Unless we knew that these poems were written by a poet who was later to win a unique place in English literature, we should pass them by as the weak effusions of an untalented poetaster. They could be dismissed as worthless; but because they were written when Thomson was almost twenty, at a time when genius should have begun to throw off some intermittent rays at least, they must be more narrowly considered. The impression they give is that the poet was writing in a foreign language. The words are threaded on the metre, like beads on a wire, without any appreciation of their value or the order which they should follow, and appear to have been collected haphazardly from other poets and arranged in an arbitrary pattern. The poems are exercises pursued as methodically as though the poet had been writing in Greek or Latin; and although they clumsily attempt to adopt the airs and graces of contemporary English poets, the spirit of poetry has entirely vanished under this rough treatment. They are poor poems, but they should not have been so when the poet succeeded in writing a great poem only five years later. They can therefore be disregarded as the first attempts of

retarded genius, or their failure can be explained by reference
to the condition of Scottish literature at this time. Neither
Thomson nor his contemporaries knew English; they spoke
and thought in broad Scots; and when they wished to write
in English, they had to learn it as conscientiously as they
would have studied any other foreign tongue. John Ramsay
particularly emphasized the difficulties which they met with
in this literary attempt: 'These juvenile adventurers and
their counsellors would soon see the impossibility of making
a distinguished figure in the republic of letters without a
proper attention to the graces of composition . . . for more
than a century nothing of character had appeared in the
dialect usually called "broad Scots". To render it polished
and correct would have been a Herculean labour, not likely
to procure them much renown. Nothing, therefore, remained but to write classical English, which, though
exceedingly difficult to men who spoke their mother tongue
without disguise, was greatly facilitated by the enthusiastic
ardour with which they had studied the best English authors.
In all their essays at composition, it behoved them to avoid
everything that could be called a Scotticism or solecism,
while they endeavoured to catch the manner of their
favourite writers.'[1]

Inevitably, this sedulous but necessary imitation of
English poets resulted in a mechanical, unconvincing
manipulation of language, and inhibited Thomson from
expressing himself with ease. Because he had to learn his
vocabulary from books and not from conversation, his
diction acquired a strong literary flavour, and because the
themes which he adopted from contemporary English
authors were foreign to Scottish thought and society, his
poems were necessarily clumsy and unsatisfactory. His faults
are particularly obvious in a pastoral dialogue between
Thirsis and Corydon, another of his juvenilia. Corydon
bemoaning the death of their mutual friend Damon des-
cants:

---

[1] Ramsay, *op. cit.*, i, 9.

Ye birds, be mute, as through the trees you fly,
Mute as the grave wherein my friend does lie.
Ye winds, breathe sighs as through the air you rove,
And in sad pomp the trembling branches move.
Ye gliding brooks, O weep your channels dry,
My flowing tears them fully shall supply;
You in soft murmurs may your grief express,
And yours, you swains, in mournful songs confess.

The style, theme, and diction of these verses are but pale, though pleasant enough, reflections of the pastorals written by Ambrose Philips, Alexander Pope, and their imitators.

Thomson's first poem in *The Edinburgh Miscellany*, 'Of a Country Life', is notable, however, because he was attempting an original subject. The diction may be lifeless, the rhythm may move forward with a familiar monotonous beat, but the subject is treated with imagination and sensitivity. The delights of a country life are briefly touched upon in succession, each receiving its appropriate praise, and although no particular passage is outstanding, the poem shows that the poet was already beginning to realize what subjects would allow his genius an opportunity of proving its unique powers.

A year before the publication of *The Edinburgh Miscellany*, Thomson had finished his Arts course. He followed the fashion and did not take his degree; apparently believing with most of his fellow-students that laureation was a formality with which he could dispense. He then matriculated in Professor William Hamilton's Divinity class. The seriousness of his intention of entering the ministry at this time is shown by his election as Lowland Bursar by the Presbytery of Jedburgh.[1] This award was probably obtained for him through the representations of Robert Riccaltoun, William Gusthart, and other clerical friends of his mother, who would be anxious to help the widow as much as lay within their power. Thomson held this bursary for four years, and its annual renewal proves that neither his conduct nor his opinions made the Presbytery suspect him to be un-

[1] *Jedburgh Presbytery Records*, General Assembly Library, Edinburgh. See note on p. 282.

suited to such a profession in any way. A gradual change was taking place in the character of the Church at this time, which would make it more attractive to a young man who intended to continue literary pursuits. The sour fanaticism of the elder ministers, whose 'rustic and austere' manners were repellent to the younger generation, was being leavened by a new tolerance and catholicity. The rising clergy, who 'recommended a more liberal course of culture to their young friends', and 'professed to disclaim bigotry and gloom as bastard virtues';[1] and they gladly accepted, though with important reservations, the new philosophy announced by Lord Shaftesbury, whose deistic and philanthropic doctrines were tingeing the whole of contemporary thought and sensibility. The Church under their direction ceased to be an intellectual waste and became a cultural force which, radiating slowly and imperceptibly throughout society, humanized manners and encouraged intellectual curiosity. The old customs and behaviour were, however, rooted out only with difficulty, and when Thomson was a divinity student, although challenged, they were still securely entrenched.

The first letter by Thomson which we have was written from Edinburgh on 11 December 1720, to his friend William Cranstoun, now a doctor, whom he used to visit at Ancrum during his school-days. The poet, after welcoming a letter from his friend, wrote: 'I fondly embrace the proposal you make of a frequent correspondence this winter, and that from the very same principle you mention; and when the native bright ideas which flow from your good humour have the ascendant over those gloomy ones that attend your profession, I expect you will not be awanting.' The 'principle' which determined this correspondence would seem to have been a desire to practise English composition, and the letter which followed this salute is really an essay in the manner popularized by *The Spectator*. But it does allow us to see something of the poet's character at this time, and by its

---

[1] Ramsay, *op. cit.*, i, 220–1.

references to 'concerts, balls, assemblies, &c.'—of which
there were very few in contemporary Edinburgh—and
'Tippeny' cells—taverns which sold small beer—something
of the kind of life he knew. After his greeting, he continued:
'You will allege that I have the advantage over you, being
in town, where daily happen a variety of incidents. In the
first place you must know, though I live in Edinburgh, yet
I am but little conversant in the beau monde, viz. concerts,
balls, assemblies, &c. where beauty shines and coxcombs
admire themselves. If nature had thrown me in a more soft
and indolent mould, had made me a Shapely or a Sir Fopling
Flutter, if fortune had filled my pockets, (I suppose my
head is empty enough as it is,) had I been taught to cut a
caper, to hum a tune, to take a pinch, and lisp nonsense with
all the grace of fashionable insipidity, then I could—what
could I have done? hardly write; but, however, I might
have made a shift to fill up a half sheet with "rat me",
"damn me", &c. interspersed with broken characters of
ladies gliding over my fancy like a passing image over a
mirror. But if both nature and fortune had been indulgent to
me, and made me a rich, finished gentleman, yet would I
have reckoned it a piece of my greatest happiness to be
acquainted with you, and you should have had entertainment if it was within the circle of wit and beauty to afford
it; but alas! as it is, what can you expect from the Divinity
Hall or a Tippeny cell? It must be owned, indeed, that here
in Edinburgh, to us humble sons of Tippeny, if beauty
were as propitious as wit sometimes, we would have no
reason to complain of the superior fortune of the fluttering
generation; and O! ye foolish women, who have thus
bewitched you? is it not wit that immortalizes beauty, that
heightens it, and preserves it in a fresh eternal bloom? And
did ever a fop either justly praise or admire you? . . . but
whither am I rambling? What I am going to propose is,
and you see there is great need for it, that you would in your
next settle our correspondence into some order, and acquaint
me on what subject you would have me write to you, for

on news of any kind I shall soon run aground. . . . I designed
to have sent you a manuscript poem, but I have no time till
next week.'[1]

The infrequent amusements, at which he seems to have
cut such a poor figure, cannot have interfered with his
studies because the Divinity curriculum was hardly enforced at all. The classes in Hebrew were optional and since
the professor, James Crauford, joined the subject to a class
in Chemistry, even conscientious students were unlikely to
attain to more than a nodding acquaintance with Oriental
languages.[2] The Church History class was also optional and
it cannot have been well attended; only a good lecturer
could hope to attract an audience, and we know that the
professor, Matthew Crauford, was addressing only 'six or
seven hearers'[3] in 1731. Matthew Crauford had been appointed to the chair in 1720, and it is improbable that
Thomson attended the classes held by a man who would do
nothing 'but for money'.[4] His time would be more profit-
ably spent with the sons of Tippeny. The only classes which
he had to attend were those taken by the Professor of
Divinity, who was at this time William Hamilton, 'a man
exceedingly beloved and respected'.[5] His kindliness and
sincerity, morality and liberality, exercised a great influence
upon his students, who 'professed through life the highest
veneration for the memory of this excellent man, whom
they took for their model';[6] and we know that Thomson
always mentioned him with respect.[7]

All the evidence shows, however, that Thomson was
much more concerned to acquire a literary reputation than
to prepare himself for the ministry, but it was proving difficult to convince the Edinburgh critics of his ability. The
Grotesques had joined to ridicule familiarly those poems
which he had laid before them, and more portentous critics,
'learned gentlemen', were not at all impressed by his per-

---

[1] Quoted *Works of Thomson*, ed. Nicolas, i, ix–xi.   [2] See Grant, *op. cit.*, ii, 289.
[3] *Ibid.*, ii, 308.   [4] *Ibid.*   [5] Ramsay, *op. cit.*, i, 227.   [6] *Ibid*, i, 228.
[7] Cibber, *op. cit.*, v, 192.

formances: 'Some inaccuracies of style', wrote Patrick Murdoch, 'and those luxuriances which a young writer can hardly avoid, lay open to their cavils and censure; so far indeed they might be competent judges: but the fire and enthusiasm of the poet had entirely escaped their notice.'[1] Briefly, the intellectual climate of Edinburgh was not propitious to poetry. A contemporary critic, who it is to be hoped was guilty of some exaggeration, wrote: the citizens of Edinburgh are such lovers of decorum, 'that they will admit of no infringement upon it; and were a man with more wit than Pope, and more philosophy than Newton, to appear at their market place negligent in his apparel, he would be avoided by his acquaintances who would rather risk his displeasure, than the censure of the public, which would not fail to stigmatize them, for associating with a man seemingly poor; for they measure poverty, and riches, understanding, or its opposite, by exterior appearance.'[2] This opinion is confirmed and amplified by a contemporary Edinburgh versifier, Joseph Harvey, who, in the preface to a collection of verses published in 1726, condemned the capital's literary taste: 'There is a Set of young Gentlemen amongst us', he wrote, 'who are Masters of as polite and elegant a Stile, either in Prose or Numbers, as some, perhaps, even celebrated Writers elsewhere. But such an extraordinary Bashfulness possesses them, that 'tis next to impossible to prevail with them, to favour One with a Sight of any Production of theirs, if it is not a very particular, intimate Friend. This is a vicious Kind of Modesty indeed! . . . But perhaps there is one Way to account for this deplorable Distemper, and that is, the byass'd Taste of some, even grave and judicious People, of our Nation. They have got a Tradition among them, which they stick too close to in all Conscience, and 'tis this, If a Man writes out of the common Road, in Prose or Numbers (but especially in Numbers) Why, he's Airy or Pedantic, or Light i' th' Head; which is all one as to say, he's a Fool or a Madman. Now, 'tis cer-

---

[1] *Works of Thomson*, 1762, i, v.   [2] Cibber, *op. cit.*, v, 165.

tainly no Wonder, if a Gentleman should be afraid to
expose the politest Performance, since he's, in a Manner,
sure to meet with such a Character for his Pains. And this,
I think, may be one Reason, why our best Productions of
this Kind ly stiffled and unknown.'[1]

There is no reason to believe that Harvey was guilty of
exaggeration; and if a young Scot was eager to succeed in
literature, Edinburgh was obviously not the place for him
to stay. Allan Ramsay, poet, publisher, and wigmaker, it is
true, did achieve some success, but his Scots poems, excellent though they are, were written for the popularity, and
never stra_ _d from the common road. Thomson could—
and a nati_ _alist might plausibly argue, should—have written in br__d Scots and helped Ramsay to revive a literary
tradition which, despite his injections, was dying; but
Thoms_ n and his ambitious contemporaries were only
anxio_ s to e__ulate and excel the admired English authors,
and _re__ _d by an unsympathetic public at home, they
nat___ _y turned towards London for encouragement.

_homson, we know, was not depressed by the unfavour-
_e criticisms which were generally passed on his verses.
Mr. *Thomson*, however,' wrote Patrick Murdoch, 'conscious
of his own strength, was not discouraged by this treatment;
especially as he had some friends, on whose judgment he
could better rely, and who thought very differently of his
performances';[2] and an earlier biographer affirmed, that he
had 'private approbation for several of his pieces . . .
before he quitted his native country'.[3] One poem, a paraphrase on the hundred and fourth Psalm, after it had been
approved by Riccaltoun, was transcribed by the poet's
admiring friends, and a copy somehow reached the hands
of the critic, politician, and generous patron of literature,
William Benson. Benson admired the full diction and dis-
tinctive thought of these verses, which, despite faults and
occasional lapses, rise far above a literary exercise:

---

[1] Joseph Harvey, *Collection of Miscellany Poems and Letters*, 1726, iii–vi.
[2] *Works of Thomson*, 1762, i, v.   [3] Cibber, *op. cit.*, v, 194.

How many are thy wondrous works, O Lord! . . .
Out of thy boundless goodness thou didst fill
With riches and delights both vale and hill:
E'en the broad ocean, wherein do abide
Monsters that flounce upon the boiling tide,
And swarms of lesser beasts and fish beside:
'Tis there that daring ships before the wind
Do send amain, and make the port assign'd.

After he had read the poem Benson remarked, 'that he doubted not if the author was in London, but he would meet with encouragement equal to his merit. This observation of Benson's was communicated to Thomson by letter, and, no doubt, had its natural influence in inflaming his heart, and hastening his journey to the metropolis.'[1]

We do not know when Benson commended these verses but in 1724 Thomson received another recognition of his ability from London. Aaron Hill—who was later to become Thomson's friend—printed in the forty-sixth number of his periodical paper, *The Plain Dealer*, Thomson's verses on *The Works and Wonders of Almighty Power*. Hill had already printed in the same paper David Malloch's fine ballad of *William and Margaret*, and it is probable that Thomson submitted his verses to Hill through the same channel of communication used by his friend. The poem,[2] which is a clever versification of a passage from Lord Shaftesbury's work, *The Moralists, a Philosophical Rhapsody*—proving, incidentally, how early the poet responded to that philosopher's doctrines—begins:

Gladly, I would declare, in lofty Strains,
The Power of Godhead, to the Sons of Men.
But Thought is lost, in its Immensity!
Imagination wastes its Strength in vain:
And Fancy tires, and turns within itself,
Struck, with the amazing Depths of Deity!

Hill ostensibly printed the poem to illustrate how learning was flourishing in Edinburgh, and he introduced it with

[1] *Ibid.*, v, 194.
[2] This poem is discussed by Herbert Drennon in *Modern Philology*, xxxii (1934–5), 33–6.

D

this encomium: 'To how surprising a Degree these fine
Spirits have succeeded, in their noble *End*, let the following
Sentiments declare; conceiv'd and express'd, with all the
Clearness, Depth, and Strength, of an *experienc'd Philosopher*,
by a Member of this *Grotesque Club*, who was in his *Four-
teenth Year only*, when he compos'd, in Blank Verse, a Poem,
now in my Hands; and founded on a Supposition of the
Author's sitting a whole Summer Night, in a Garden, looking upward, and quite losing himself, in Contemplation on
the Works, and Wonders, of Almighty Power.—If this was a
Subject, naturally above the Capacity of so very a Boy, to
what a Degree does it increase our Wonder, when we
find it treated, in this Masterly Manner!' Other poets had
tampered later with their juvenile verses, and if Thomson
did compose this poem at so early an age, he undoubtedly
improved upon it before he submitted it to Hill.

Hill's public recognition of the poet's merit, joined to
Benson's private praise, would be enough to encourage
him, confident as he was in his own powers, to venture upon
a literary career; but about this time another incident
weakened his determination to stay in Edinburgh and enter
the ministry. He had matriculated in the Divinity class in
1719, and during the next four years he performed the public
exercises in the Divinity Hall which Professor Hamilton
required. His name appears in the list of exercises, 'prescribed to be delivered', which the Professor carefully
kept, and on 2 March 1723, he had prescribed to him a lec-
ture on the ninety-eighth Psalm.[1] His friend, Patrick
Murdoch, who had matriculated in the Divinity class in
1721, has left an account of how the poet performed this or
a similar exercise. Murdoch, unfortunately, is not very
particular in his information. He said that the exercise was
delivered 'about a year' after Thomson had begun to attend
Hamilton's lectures, and he did not give the number of the
Psalm, merely referring to it as one 'in which the power and
majesty of God are celebrated'. The ninety-eighth Psalm,

---

[1] *List of Theologues in the University of Edinburgh*, Edin. Univ. Library.

however, is a triumphant pæan of praise, in which the Psalmist calls upon the whole earth to 'make a joyful noise', and it may be to Thomson's exercise upon this Psalm that Murdoch vaguely referred. But though many details appear to have slipped his memory, his account of what happened at the exercise is vivid and particular enough. 'Of this psalm he gave a paraphrase and illustration, as the nature of the exercise required; but in a stile so highly poetical, as surprized the whole audience. Mr. *Hamilton*, as his custom was, complimented the orator upon his performance, and pointed out to the students the most masterly striking parts of it; but at last, turning to Mr. *Thomson*, he told him, smiling, that if he thought of being useful in the ministry, he must keep a stricter rein upon his imagination, and express himself in language more intelligible to an ordinary congregation.'[1] Another biographer embroidered this plain tale by making the poet deliver the exercise in blank verse, but he agreed with Murdoch that the audience were 'astonished' and that the Professor rebuked him for the luxuriance of his language.[2] The kindly Professor perhaps took the poet to one side later in the day and, after praising his ability, reminded him that his interests as well as those of the Church required that his expositions should be adapted to the dour popular intelligence. Both biographers agree that the effect of this friendly remonstrance was to deflect the poet from his intention of entering the ministry, a career in which 'his expectations . . . might be very precarious'.[3]

Thomson, however, did not immediately withdraw from the Divinity class after he had performed his exercise upon the ninety-eighth Psalm. He was prescribed a homily on Matthew, xxvi, xxix, on 23 March 1724, and in that year Hill printed his poem and, perhaps, Benson's encouraging remark was forwarded to him. He now decided to forsake a profession for which he knew himself to be unsuited. He had not freely chosen the Church, and the clerical

[1] *Works of Thomson*, 1762, i, v–vi.   [2] Cibber, *op. cit.*, v, 193.
[3] *Works of Thomson*, 1762, i, vi.

poverty and severity which ruled at this time in Scotland would be repellent to a man of his temperament; 'it seldom happens, that a man of great parts can be content with obscurity, or the low income of sixty pounds a year, in some retired corner of a neglected country'.[1] He determined therefore to try his fortune in London. The later evidence of his letters shows that he did not abandon at once his intention of entering the ministry, but that his ordination depended upon his literary success or failure. He succeeded, and he was never required to return into bondage. Had he failed, he would have been baffled and oppressed in a Church with whose doctrines he had little sympathy and with whose clergy he was temperamentally at variance. The Church of England was always prepared to provide a comfortable niche for such men, but the Church of Scotland had neither time nor use for those whose imaginations drove them abroad into spiritual territories where its authority could not run.

His decision to try his fortune in London would cause little surprise in Edinburgh, which was witnessing at this time the firm establishment of Scotland's greatest eighteenth-century industry—the export of men. Whatever may have been the material benefits of the Act of Union, and that they were great no one could deny, the psychological effect of that Act had been to destroy a nation's polarity. The government removed to London, the Scotsman's *active* attachment to his country was weakened; his language declined into a dialect spoken only by the lower classes; and those who were ambitious in either politics or literature, or who were eager to make a career in the army, or trade, or the professions, removed to the south. Alert, intelligent, and determined, they went to London in their thousands, and there they were supported and promoted by the interest of earlier emigrants, who had already established themselves in an angry but amused metropolis. David Malloch vividly described the appearance of his impoverished countrymen

---

[1] Cibber, *op. cit.*, v, 193.

upon their arrival and how he rallied to help them in their initial plight: 'Our country pours forth her annual swarms, increasing, inexhaustible. Good Lord! what strange, unseemly creatures they are too! I have seen three and twenty of my own acquaintances, who, I believe, will not be provided for these three and twenty years. But all the poor service I can do shall never be wanting.'[1]

Thomson did not set out upon this adventure unprepared. He 'received some encouragement from a lady of quality, a friend of his mother's, then in *London*',[2] who has been identified as Lady Grizel Baillie, a courageous and talented woman, and a very distant relation of Mrs. Thomson's. 'And although this encouragement ended in nothing beneficial, it served for the present as a good pretext, to cover the imprudence of committing himself to the wide world, unfriended and unpatronized, and with the slender stock of money he was then possessed of.'[3] This is, however, an exaggerated statement of his unpreparedness. He arranged for several letters of introduction to prominent Scotsmen in London. He had almost completed his arrangements by the beginning of 1725, and he then wrote to his friend William Cranstoun about some difficulties which were still perplexing him: 'I received yours', he wrote, 'and can never sufficiently resent the regard for my welfare that you show in them. You are so modest as to desire me to correct any thing I see amiss in your letter to Mr. Elliot, and you will transcribe it again but I assure you I am not so vain as to attempt it: if there was no other thing to bind me to a good behaviour but our recommendation and character of me, I could go great lengths of mortification to answer them. Your letter to my cusin, I do not doubt, will be considerably useful to me, if I can find him out. I remember I heard that Mr. Colden's letter was very serviceable to George Brown. I do not doubt but if Mr. Colden was advertised, I might have one too, and there will be time

---

[1] Mallet to Kerr, 29 December 1725; *Edinburgh Mag.*, ii (1793), 171.
[2] *Works of Thomson*, 1762, i, vi. [3] *Ibid.*

enough, for our ship sails not this fortnight, yet during that time, if it can contribute any thing to your diversion, and when I go to London, you may lay your account of paying out some sixpences. If you have leisure, I could wish to hear from you before I go away, notwithstanding your apostolical conclusion, which I believe is as sincere, and will be as effectual, as the best of them.'[1]

He addressed another letter to Cranstoun a week or so later, immediately before the boat was due to sail from Leith, and we learn from it that Mr. Colden forwarded his prayers for the poet's success instead of the required letter of introduction. His reference to a good-humoured fellow student reveals his attitude to the study of Divinity. It is a simple, sincere, tolerant, and determined letter: 'I received yours by which I find you have been as much concerned as Mr. Colden indifferent about me—he, good man, recommends me to God Almighty; very well—but I wish he had exerted something more of the Layman on that occasion for (to be deeply serious) the merciful Father of Mankind beholds all his needy offspring with a melting eye, and needs none to prompt him to acts of Goodness, so that I can't conceive for what purpose people's prayers for one another are, unless it be to stir up humane and social dispositions in themselves.—I have gotten several recommendations and am promised more afterwards when I am fixed to any particular view, which would make them more pointed and effectual.—I shall do all that's in my power; act, hope, and so make something out, or be buried in obscurity. There is, and I'm persuaded of it, I triumph in it, another life after this, which depends as to its happiness on our Virtue, as this, for the most part, on our fortune: my spirits have gotten such a devious turn by these reflections that altho' I be thinking on Mess John, I declare I'll hardly force a laugh before we part (for this I think will be my last letter from Edinburgh, for I expect to sail every day). Well since I was speaking of that merry soul, I hope he's as

---

[1] Quoted *Works of Thomson*, ed. Nicolas, i, xiii–xiv.

bright, as easy, as dégagé, as suceptible of an intense laugh as he used to be.—Tell him when you see him that I laugh in imagination with him. Ha! Ha! Ha! Mess John! how in the name of wonder dragged you so much good Humour along with you, thro' the thorny paths of Systems and School Divinity considering the many hardy attempts you have had to epitomize Turrentine? and so forth.—Whenever I began to rust in these damp exercises, the Doctor cleared me.—Well—may Wit, Humour, and everlasting Joy surround you both, and if I but at any time could kindle up the laugh from London, I'll be sure to have it returned upon me with greater force.'[1]

James Thomson embarked from Leith in a ship sailing to London soon after he had written this letter to Cranstoun. He was but scantily provided with money and necessities, but he was determined to succeed. It was a dark rough night and his mother, saddened at the departure, though ambitious for the success, of her favourite son, attended him to the quay. He was never to see her or Scotland again, and in some moving verses upon her death, he remembered how she had last appeared before him:

> But ah! that night . . .
> When on the margin of the briny flood,
> Chill'd with a sad presaging damp I stood,
> Took the last look, ne'er to behold her more,
> And mix'd our murmurs with the wavy roar;
> Heard the last words fall from her pious tongue,
> Then, wild into the bulging vessel flung,
> Which soon, too soon, convey'd me from her sight,
> Dearer than life, and liberty, and light!

This remembered scene, however, is darkened by sorrows which, when the ship sailed, still lay hidden in the future. The poet's sadness at parting from his home and its familiar life would be quickly forgotten in the contemplation of his prospects as the ship made its slow and careful way down the coast.

[1] Quoted *ibid.*, i, xiv–xv.

CHAPTER III

LONDON AND LITERARY FRIENDS

O THAMES,
Large, gentle, deep, majestic, King of Floods!

LONDON in 1725 was a small town mainly contained within its ruinous walls. Beyond the walls, squares and crescents were being run up in the pleasant fields to house the nobility and the rising middle classes, who either wished to retreat into a town-house from the rural winter's unsociability, or to escape from the dirt and noise of the City. But this construction, which has continued with mad acceleration down to our day, had hardly begun to dint the countryside, and twenty minutes' walk from Charing Cross would take the curious stroller into shady lanes, wooded retreats, and tranquil hamlets, whose peasantry's rustic manners proved that they were as yet unaware of the neighbouring metropolis's fashions and expansive threat. Within the walls, the people, swarming like bees in a hollow rotten tree, worked with unceasing, tireless energy to confirm the commercial supremacy which the nation was assuming in every market of the world; and wagons and coaches, masters and carters, passed and repassed in the dangerous, unpaved alleys, which ran like devious arteries to the river and its warehouses. John Gay, in his delightful poem, *Trivia*, reflected upon the frightening, bewildering traffic with which the foot-passenger had to contend; beware how you cross the street, he warned his reader, or else

> on either Hand
> Pent round with Perils, in the midst you stand,
> And call for Aid in vain; the Coachman swears,
> And Carmen drive, unmindful of thy Prayers.

Where wilt thou turn? ah! whither wilt thou fly?
On ev'ry side the pressing Spokes are nigh.

But despite dangers, dirt, and poverty, for the wealth did not seep very far down into society, the air of the people, coarse and boisterous in their behaviour, was alert and vigorous. The city was aware of its greatness.

James Thomson landed in London at the beginning of March, and, if one biographer—who implied that he had this story from the poet himself—is to be believed, he made his way through the crowded streets bewildered and fascinated by the strange scenes which each turning presented. His little money and letters of introduction were closely wrapped in a handkerchief, and as he walked slowly on it was picked from his pocket. The conclusion of this anecdote suggests that it was not an invention: 'This accident would have proved very mortifying to a man less philosophical than Thomson; but he was of a temper never to be agitated; he then smiled at it, and frequently made his companions laugh at the relation'.[1] A confirmation of the truth of this story is to be found in his first letter from London to William Cranstoun; he thanks his friend in it for an introductory letter to a Mr. Elliot; but we have already seen him acknowledging in an earlier letter an introduction to Elliot, and this second letter was probably sent to him at his request to replace the one which had been stolen.

His first thought was to call upon David Malloch, or—to give him the name which he had begun to assume—David Mallet, who was living in Hanover Square as tutor to the Duke of Montrose's sons. Mallet, a dapper, quick-witted, talented but unscrupulous man, had quickly made himself at home in London, and he would be able both to explain the capital and to advance his friend's interests through his connexion with the Montrose family. After he had found lodgings, Thomson would begin to present his letters of introduction. Among the first Scotsmen whom he visited was Duncan Forbes, who was at this time repre-

[1] Cibber, op. cit., v, 195.

senting Inverness in Parliament. He had already seen some
of Thomson's verses, and he received him 'very kindly'.[1]
Forbes, one of the greatest Scotsmen of his century, joined
friendliness and shrewdness, hard-drinking and sobriety,
and not only enjoyed and ably criticized the arts, but
generously patronized the artists; and he would be an invaluable ally to a young man who was attempting to establish himself in London. He took the trouble to introduce the
poet to many of his acquaintances and among these was the
Scots painter, William Aikman. Aikman, who had the
reputation of being 'a very ingenious portrait painter and a
modest, good man',[2] became a close friend of the poet, and
through the position which he held in 1724 of Steward to
The Society of Virtuosi of St. Luke, a group of 'men of the
highest character in arts, and gentlemen lovers of art',[3] he
was able to introduce him further into influential company.

Thomson was eager to take advantage of every opportunity to advance himself, and he would persuade people to
favour him by his prepossessing manner and appearance. He
became in his later years corpulent and ungainly and almost
sullen in his expression, but in his youth 'he had been
thought handsome'.[4] The sketch Aikman made of him at
this time shows a broad, open, intelligent, and sensitive
face. The forehead is finely modelled, the nose determined,
and the mouth full and sensual. His eyes were, however, the
index of his character. Murdoch described how even in later
life, when his features had become gross, his expression
would brighten when he was greeted by a friend and his
eyes would dart 'a peculiar animated fire'.[5] The eyes in this
sketch are quiet and observant but quick with suppressed
excitement. The whole countenance gives the impression of
reflective sensibility, good-nature, and friendliness. Such a
man, helped forward by willing friends, can have had little
difficulty in achieving success.

---

[1] *Works of Thomson*, 1762, i, vi.
[2] Quoted W. T. Whitley, *Artists and their Friends in England 1700–1799*, 1927,
i, 60.   [3] *Ibid.*, i, 76.   [4] *Works of Thomson*, 1762, i, xvi.   [5] *Ibid.*

His introduction into London life could not be completed in a few days, and from the tenor of his first letter to William Cranstoun, written on 3 April, we can gather that he was depressed by the apparent difficulty of eventually realizing his ambition, and by his failure to find immediately some position which would provide him with necessities. He even suggested that he might return to Scotland and enter the ministry. 'If I should not succeed, in your next, advise what I should do: Succeed or not, I am firmly resolved to pursue Divinity as the only thing now I am fit for.—Now if I can't accomplish the design on which I came up, I think I had best make Interest and pass my tryals . . . [ms. defective] . . . to return soon to Scotland again, I may not return no better than I came away: and to be deeply serious with you, the more I see of the Vanity and Wickedness of the World, the more I am inclined to that sacred office.' After these melancholy remarks, he continued to describe the plays and the actors which he had seen at Drury Lane Theatre: 'Mills and Johnston are pretty good actors.— Dicky Norris that little comical toothless Devil will turn his back, and crack a very good joke yet. There are some others of them execrable. Mrs. Oldfield has a smiling jolly face, acts very well, in comedy, but best of all, I suppose, in Bed, she twines her body and leers with her eyes most bewitchingly.—Mrs. Porter excels in tragedy, has a sharp piercing voice and enters most into her characters, and if she did not act well she could not be endured, being more disagreeable in her appearance than any of them . . . These are a few of the observations I have made at Drury-lane Theatre hitherto, to which I have paid five visits, but have not been at the New house [Covent Garden Theatre] yet; my purse will not keep pace with my inclinations in that matter.'[1]

His melancholy and discouragement would be rendered more intolerable by the news that his mother had died on

[1] A transcript of this letter, which I have used here, is in the *Forster Coll.*, 48. E.4; Victoria and Albert Museum.

12 May, and the poet in his moving verses on her death showed how deeply he felt his loss. But soon after this sad event, the representations of Mallet and other friends on his behalf were successful, and he secured the position of tutor to Lord Binning's son. It is not known when he took up this appointment, but he was certainly residing with the family in the country on 20 July, and from a letter addressed to Mallet on 10 July—in which he wrote, 'If you knew the satisfaction the sight of your hand gives me, you would not spare me frequent letters'[1]—it would appear that he had been acting as tutor for some time before this last date. Mallet claimed the credit of finding this position for him,[2] but since Charles Hamilton, Lord Binning, the son of the Earl of Haddington, was the son-in-law of Lady Grizel Baillie, who had originally encouraged Thomson to try his fortune in London, it is probable that she was more instrumental than Mallet in securing this appointment for the poet. Lord Binning also wrote verses of some merit—one stanza from a song will illustrate his pleasant touch:

> Ah! woe is me, poor Willy cry'd,
>   See how I'm wasted to a span:
> My heart I lost, when first I spy'd
>   The charming, lovely milk-maid Nan.
> I'm grown so weak, a gentle breeze
>   Of dusty Roger's winnowing fan
> Would blow me o'er yon beachy trees,
>   And all for thee, my smirky Nan.

—and his readiness to accept Thomson as a tutor to his son would be a friendly gesture to a brother poet as well as an act of compliance to the representations of the Duke of Montrose, stirred into action by Mallet, and of his mother-in-law. The tutorship can have been worth little, but it at least gave him temporary security and an opportunity to meet people able to dispense other patronage. Thomson himself recognized that it was neither a suitable nor a secure

---

[1] Peter Cunningham, *Correspondence of Thomson and Mallet; Philobiblon Soc.*, 1859, iv, 6. [2] Joseph Spence, *Anecdotes*, 1858, p. 249.

position, and he did not relish the task of teaching his young charge: 'Now I'm pretty much at ease in the country', he wrote to Cranstoun on 20 July from Lord Binning's house at East Barnet, 'ten miles from London, teaching Lord Binning's son to read, a low task, you know, not so suitable to my temper, but I must learn that necessary lesson of suiting my mind and temper to my state . . . the business of a Tutor is only precarious, and for the present'.[1]

During the summer and autumn of this year, however, he was also occupied in writing his first great poem of *Winter*. It is the tradition that this poem was composed in the Borders before he ever decided to emigrate to London; and one version of this tale actually gives the particular hill—it lies close to Widehope and was once appropriately called Parnassus—on which he was supposed to have found inspiration.[2] But although this tradition is wrong, its persistence points out a more important truth than a mere matter of fact. The poet wrote *Winter* in England, but all the time he was engaged on the poem he remembered those wild scenes which had deeply impressed him in his childhood. When he raised his head from the desk, he would see through the windows of the house at East Barnet the gentle Hertfordshire landscape, but his imagination passed across its contented breadth to reach and recapture the memory of the barren wildernesses about his early home, where winter reigns with irresistible power and grandeur. The poem is an evocation of his childhood and the countryside in which it was passed. The description of the thaw will show how deep an impression that scene must have made upon him as a child:

> At last, the muddy Deluge pours along,
> Resistless roaring; dreadful down it comes
> From the chapt Mountain, and the mossy Wild,
> Tumbling thro' Rocks abrupt, and sounding far:
> Then o'er the sanded Valley floating, spreads,

[1] *Forster Coll.*, 48. E.4; V. & A.
[2] *Hist. Berwick. Naturalists' Club*, 1916, xxii, 402.

Calm, sluggish, silent; till again constrain'd,
Betwixt two meeting Hills, it bursts a Way,
Where Rocks and Woods o'erhang the turbid Stream.
There gathering triple Force, rapid, and deep,
It boils, and wheels, and foams, and thunders thro'.

It is hardly surprising that the first season he described
should be winter. He was homesick at East Barnet for his
own country: 'This country I am in', he wrote, 'is not very
entertaining; no variety but that of woods, and them we
have in abundance; but where is the living stream? the airy
mountain? and the hanging rock?'[1] He would therefore
remember the Borders in that season when their character is
most impressive and memorable. The sadness of the season
was also suited to his own melancholy forebodings about
his future prospects and his grief for his mother's death,
and the poem must be considered not only as an objective
description of nature but as a subjective expression of his
spiritual condition at this time.

Winter was not written straight through from beginning to end. The poet began by writing 'detached pieces, or
occasional descriptions'[2]—'single winter pieces', Mallet
called them[3]—and as he finished them, he forwarded them
to Mallet for his criticisms—'You may take what liberties
you please with my poem,' he wrote to Mallet on 10 July
1725, 'and I will thank you for it'.[4] But as these detached
pieces grew in number, he and Mallet decided that they
should be collected into a single poem.[5] Mallet certainly
deserves praise for so successfully encouraging the despondent poet at this time. Another friend also played an
important part in the genesis of *Winter*; this was Robert
Riccaltoun, who had earlier written some verses on the
winter storms in the Borders, which have been identified
with a poem entitled *A Winter's Day*, that was published

---

[1] Letter to Cranstoun, September 1725; quoted *Works of Thomson*, ed. Nicolas,
i, xxii.   [2] Cibber, *op. cit.*, v. 195 *n*.   [3] Spence, *op. cit.*, p. 249.
[4] Cunningham, *op. cit.*, p. 6.
[5] See Spence, *op. cit.*, p. 249; and Cibber, *op. cit.*, v, 195 *n*.

in a miscellany compiled by Richard Savage in 1726.[1] Thomson frankly acknowledged his indebtedness to Riccaltoun: 'Mr. Riccaltoun's Poem on Winter, which I still have', he wrote to Cranstoun, 'first put the design into my head. In it are some masterly strokes that awakened me.'[2]

His position as tutor obviously allowed him time to write his poem but it did not provide him with sufficient money to maintain himself in necessities; and at last he had to request a small loan from his faithful friend, William Cranstoun. He exactly described the difficulties which he had had to encounter. 'There is a little business I would communicate to you before I come to the more entertaining part of our correspondence', he began; 'I am going, hard task! to complain, and beg your assistance. When I came up here I brought very little money along with me, expecting more upon the selling of Widehope, which was to have been sold that day my mother was buried. Now it is unsold yet; but will be disposed of as soon as it can be conveniently done, though indeed it is perplexed with some difficulties. I was a long time here living at my own charges, and you know how expensive that is; this, together with the furnishing of myself with clothes, linen, one thing and another, to fit me for any business of this nature here, necessarily obliged me to contract some debts. Being a stranger here, it is a wonder how I got any credit; but I cannot expect it will be long sustained unless I immediately clear it. Even now, I believe, it is at a crisis. My friends have no money to send me till the land is sold, and my creditors will not wait till then: you know what the consequences would be. Now the assistance I would beg of you, and which I know, if in your power, you will not refuse me, is a letter of credit on some merchant, or such like person in London,

---

[1] The poem was reprinted in *Gent. Mag.*, 1740, p. 256 as 'A Winter's Day written by a Scotch Clergyman, corrected by an eminent Hand'—the 'eminent Hand' was Mallet. See also Morel, *op. cit.*, p. 18 *n.* 2.

[2] Letter to Cranstoun, September 1726; quoted *Works of Thomson*, ed. Nicolas, i, xxiii.

for the matter of twelve pounds, till I get money upon the selling of the land.'

After this 'little business'—and Cranstoun probably responded to his appeal—he continued with a nostalgic evocation of his early home, and a reference to the poem he was writing: 'Now I imagine you seized with a fine, romantic kind of a melancholy on the fading of the year; now I figure you wandering, philosophical and pensive, amidst the brown, withered groves, while the leaves rustle under your feet, the sun gives a farewell parting gleam, and the birds

> Stir the faint note, and but attempt to sing.

'Then again, when the heavens wear a more gloomy aspect, the winds whistle, and the waters spout, I see you in the well-known Cleugh, beneath the solemn arch of tall, thick, embowering trees, listening to the amusing lull of the many steep, moss-grown cascades, while deep, divine contemplation, the genius of the place, prompts each swelling awful thought . . . There I walk in spirit, and disport in its beloved gloom . . . Nature delights me in every form, I am just now painting her in her most lugubrious dress for my own amusement, describing Winter as it presents itself.' Yet, he continued, 'being only a present amusement, it is ten to one but I drop it whenever another fancy comes across'.[1]

He did not, however, drop the idea, and the separate winter-pieces had been brought together in a single poem by the end of the year. It was now necessary to find a publisher prepared to gamble on the success of an unknown poet. Mallet, who must again claim credit for his friendly initiative, actively canvassed the booksellers without success,[2] but at last J. Millan, a small bookseller, 'without making any scruples, printed it'.[3] It has been said that Millan bought the work for three pounds[4] but, as later evi-

---

[1] Letter to Cranstoun September 1725; quoted *Works of Thomson*, ed. Nicolas, i, xxi–xxiii. [2] See Cibber, *op. cit.*, v, 196. [3] *Ibid.*
[4] *The Seasons*, ed. Wright, 1770, pp. viii–ix *n.*

dence will show, Thomson did not part with the copyright; and it is probable that he reached some agreement with Millan whereby they shared the profits from the work.

Mallet's industry did not stop when a publisher had been found. He wrote with his ready pen the fulsome dedication to Sir Spencer Compton, the Speaker of the House of Commons, which introduced the poem.[1] Sir Spencer had a fine house at Chiswick, and his well laid-out gardens had won him the reputation of being 'by much the best Gardener in England',[2] and he might have been expected to take under his patronage a poet who could write so ably upon nature. It was certainly wise to attempt to win his favour because he wielded considerable influence. Mallet, after making his friend venture to approach the chosen patron with 'a modest cheerfulness', excused his inability to draw Sir Spencer's character in its full glory: 'I am conscious of my Want of Strength, and Skill for so delicate an Undertaking: And yet, as the Shepherd, in his Cottage, may feel and acknowledge the Influence of the Sun with as lively a Gratitude, as the Great Man, in his Palace, *even I* may be allowed to publish *my Sense* of those Blessings, which, from so many powerful Vertues, are derived to the Nation they adorn'. It may be thought that such praise would have been enough to draw a reward from the most miserly politician, but it will be seen that Sir Spencer's purse remained tightly closed.

The poem was published in a fine folio at the beginning of April 1726, and its appearance was thus announced in the press: 'WINTER. A Poem. Dedicated to the Rt. Hon. Sir Spencer Compton. By James Thomson, A.M. pr. 1s.'[3] Thomson had never troubled to take his degree and he was not entitled to use it after his name in either the advertisements or on the title-page of the poem itself, but he cannot

---

[1] See Spence, *op. cit.*, p. 249.

[2] Sir John Clerk, *Journey to London in 1727* (M.S.); *Clerk of Penicuik Papers*, Register House, Edinburgh.

[3] Murdoch said the poem was published in March, but the first advertisement I have found is that quoted from *The Flying-Post*, 5–7 April 1726.

E

be blamed for having tried every device to attract as many readers as possible. But neither the degree nor the dedication to Sir Spencer was immediately successful. 'For some time', wrote a biographer, 'Mr. Millan had reason to believe, that he should be a loser by his frankness; for the impression lay like as paper on his hands, few copies being sold.'[1] This neglect is hardly surprising; the poet was entirely unknown; the public are never alert to pick out from the countless books and pamphlets the one work of genius from the worthless remainder; and the poet's theme and style were original enough to deter those whose taste expected poetry to be written only in the accepted fashion. But the delay between the poem's publication and its recognition as an original work was comparatively short. It quickly fell into the hands of Thomas Whateley, the author of a treatise on landscape gardening[2]—'a man not wholly unknown among authors', is Dr. Johnson's brief comment upon his character[3]—who at once appreciated and advertised its merits: 'One Mr. Whatley, a man of some taste in letters, but perfectly enthusiastic in the admiration of any thing which pleased him, happened to cast his eye upon it, and finding something which delighted him, perused the whole, not without growing astonishment, that the poem should be unknown, and the author obscure. He learned from the Bookseller the circumstances already mentioned, and, in the extasy of his admiration of this poem, he went from Coffee-house to Coffee-house, pointing out its beauties, and calling upon all men of taste, to exert themselves in rescuing one of the greatest geniuses that ever appeared, from obscurity.'[4] This may not be an exaggerated description of Whateley's missionary zeal, but if he was among the first, he was not the only critic to acclaim the poet and to advance his fame.

[1] Cibber, *op. cit.*, v, 196.
[2] There is some confusion as to whether it was Thomas Whately or a Robert Whately who first advertised *Winter*, but the former seems to have the better claim to this distinction; see Morel, *op. cit.*, pp. 49–51.
[3] Johnson, *Lives of the English Poets*, ed. G. B. Hill, 1905, iii, 284.
[4] Cibber, *op. cit.*, v, 196–7.

Among the poets and wits whose acquaintance Mallet had made in London was Aaron Hill, who had earlier printed some verses both by Mallet and Thomson, and a copy of *Winter* was of course sent to him for his approval. Hill's fame withered after his death, and his contemporary reputation has come down to us as desiccated and as faintly coloured as a flower pressed between the pages of a book; but he attained to an enviable position in literature in his day, which he could not have supported unless he had been gifted with real talents. Handsome in appearance, well-mannered and familiar in society, and widely travelled, he had engaged with remarkable versatility in a host of projects besides that of literature. He was ever eager to pursue any scheme, no matter how impracticable, if he thought the country would benefit; the extraction of oil from beech-mast occupied his earlier years, and the attempt to reintroduce the commercial cultivation of the vine into southern England his later. His real passion, however, was for literature and particularly for the stage. He was more than a competent dramatist and a talented poet, and many of his verses can still be read with pleasure. He was too often diffuse or crabbed in his style but these lines from his poem, *The Wedding Day*, show how simply and well he could write on occasion:

> 'AURELIA, thou art mine,' I cry'd—and she
> Sigh'd soft—'Now DAMON, thou art lord of me.
> But, wilt thou', whisper'd she, 'the knot now ty'd,
> Which only death's keen weapon can divide,
> Wilt thou, still mindful of thy raptures past,
> Permit the summer of love's hope to last?
> Shall not cold wint'ry frosts come on too soon?
> Ah, say! what means the world, by honey moon?'

Unfortunately, his careful manners were tinged with pomposity, and the rotund style of phrase and compliment which he adopted in his correspondence, gave the impression of a greater conceit than he probably possessed. He certainly had the right to be conceited, however, if he believed the adulation with which his works were generally received; and if his contemporaries hailed him as 'one of the greatest Poets that ever grac'd the *English* Nation',[1] he could not be expected to doubt whether posterity would show him the same respect. He was a man whose friendship was worth winning, and he was 'of so amiable a disposition, that whoever cultivated an intimacy with him, was sure to be a gainer'.[2]

Hill was genuinely impressed by the quality of *Winter*, and he wrote to Mallet a letter praising the poem which, if we may judge from Hill's usual epistolary style, would be enough to turn any young poet's head. The letter was shown to Thomson who wrote to thank Hill for his compliments, and a correspondence was begun between the two which was conducted by Thomson in terms of the grossest flattery. Dr. Johnson succinctly described this correspondence when he wrote: 'Thomson obtained likewise the notice of Aaron Hill, whom, being friendless and indigent, and glad of kindness, he courted with every expression of servile adulation'.[3] But this servility can be excused if we remember that Thomson would not only be grateful for opportune praise and excited to some demonstration by the approval of so eminent a critic, but he would see that his adulations were received with pleasure. It was common for other literary figures of the age to lavish excessive praises upon each other, and those who would blame Thomson must extend their condemnation to include most of his contemporaries.

Thomson wrote his first letter to Hill on 5 April, and he received an answer to which he quickly replied on 18 April. Two paragraphs from this second letter are enough to show the level on which the ensuing correspondence was conducted: 'I Receiv'd yours with a Soul awaken'd all to Joy, Gratitude, and Ambition. There is such a noble Excellence of Mind, so much uncommon Goodness, and Generosity of

[1] *British Journal*, 1 October 1726.   [2] Cibber, *op. cit.*, iv, 349.
[3] Johnson, *op. cit.*, iii, 284.

Heart, in every thing you say, as at once charms and astonishes me.

'As you think, imagine, and write, with a diviner Warmth, superior to the rest of Mankind; so the very Praises, you bestow, bear the Stamp of Eminence, and reflect stronger on yourself.'[1]

Meanwhile, other critics had begun to take notice of the new poet, and only eight weeks or so after the first publication of the poem, a correspondent in the newspapers praised it roundly and called for a second edition. 'I here send you some Observations on a POEM, lately published in *Blank Verse*;' wrote this anonymous correspondent, 'which, if you please, you may communicate to the Publick . . . They are writ with the Design to make a *fine Poem* more generally known, than I am afraid it is, by there not being yet a *Second Edition* of it. And in doing this, I intend the paying a Compliment to the *Publick*, rather than to the Poet himself; who is to me, as by his Name he seems likewise to be to the World, unknown. I shall be glad indeed, if I could be any way subservient to his *Fame*, by any Thing I shall say of his *Performance*: But it is not *That* which I have principally in View, but a more general Good; to make a Work more read, the Perusal of which will give a most entertaining, rational, instructive Delight and Satisfaction, to every one whose Mind is capable of receiving it. I would likewise congratulate the Age on the *Appearance* of a *Writer*, who, as far as may be collected from his *first Attempt*, is likely to be so great an Ornament to it. And such a one, I dare predict, will be the *Author* of *WINTER, a Poem*; lately publish'd, and inscribed to a very worthy Patron, the present *Right Honourable* SPEAKER *of the Honourable House of Commons*: A Patron worthy of such a Performance; and, I may add, a Performance, in all respects, worthy so great a Patron!'

After this initial flourish of careful periods, the correspondent continued to praise the theme and diction of the poem, and the poet's '*good Heart*', which lent a 'true

---

[1] Aaron Hill, *Collection of Letters*, Dublin, 1751, p. 49.

Sublimity to *Reflection*'. He concluded by recommending the
great men of the age not to be niggardly in their patronage
of such a genius, and by affirming, that were he to quote
from the poem the reader would lose 'that particular
Beauty which each Part reflects on the others; and above
all, you lose that great Excellency of the Piece, I mean, the
new and *masterly manner* in which he has introduced his
Reflections, and made them to succeed his several Descriptions throughout the whole Performance. All the several
Parts are indeed beautiful in themselves; but all combined
together, like a Cluster of Jewels, while each shines with its
proper Lustre, produce a more exquisite Brightness by the
Harmony of their Rays.' At length, to clinch his argument,
the correspondent ended with, 'he must be allow'd to have
the genuine Spirit of sublime Poetry in him, and bids fair
to reach at length the Heighth of *Milton's* Character;
beyond which I think he need not aspire'.[1]

The patron had, unfortunately, not proved himself
'worthy of such a Performance'. If he had glanced at the
dedication, he had not thought it worth a fee, and angered
by his neglect, Thomson, with the aid and encouragement
of Hill and Mallet, decided to take his revenge in the second
edition of the poem. Both Hill and Mallet agreed to write
commendatory verses for this edition and to satirize Sir
Spencer's ingratitude in them. The verses were written and
Thomson was enthusiastic about their quality: 'Pleasing is
your Praise,' he wrote to Hill, 'but severe is your Satire:
'Tis particularly mark'd with exalted Sentiment, and
generous Contempt. There is a Force in it, that strikes thro'
the Heart; and a Majesty, not to be express'd. In a Word, it
is unaffected Resentment of a great Mind.'[2] But suddenly Sir
Spencer, reminded of his duty, sent for the poet and presented him with twenty guineas. Thomson wrote to Hill on
7 June describing the interview: 'I hinted to you in my
last, that, on *Saturday* Morning, I was with Sir *Spencer*
Compton. A certain Gentleman, without my Desire, spoke to

[1] *London Journal*, 4 June 1726.   [2] Hill, *op. cit.*, p. 52.

him concerning me; his Answer was, that I had never come near him: Then the Gentleman put the Question, if he desir'd that I should wait on him, he return'd, he did: On this, the Gentleman gave me an introductory Letter to him. He receiv'd me in what they commonly call a civil Manner, ask'd me some Commonplace Questions, and made me a Present of Twenty Guineas. I am very ready to own, that the Present was larger than my Performance deserv'd; and shall ascribe it to his Generosity, or any other Cause, rather than the Merit of the Address.'[1] The poet after this generous acknowledgement could only curse his hasty enlistment of Hill's and Mallet's satirical talents. He obviously could not print their attacks on Sir Spencer, but neither did he wish to lose their admirable panegyrics upon his own merit. At last, after many appeals and adroit flattery, he persuaded them to alter their verses so that although patrons in general were satirized, Sir Spencer was carefully excluded from their attacks. He only achieved his purpose with difficulty: 'Twenty guineas, twenty curses on them!' he exclaimed in a letter to Mallet on 13 June, 'if they serve me that trick. I expected that our names should have lived together, there, when money and all its lovers shall perish. All the first page might still stand entire, and the others filled out a thousand ways. If you will have satire; a remedy the age much wants, and which may be executed with a good design, a public spirit, and success, I need not mention to you the avarice, little-ness, luxury, and stupidity of our men of fortune; the general barbarous contempt of Poetry—that noblest gift of Heaven! our venal bards as you have lashed them already, our lewd, low, spiteful writers; hornets of Parnassus, Operas, Masquerades, Fopperies, and a thousand things. You might make a glorious apostrophe to the drooping Genius of Britain—have Shakespeare and Milton in your eye, and invite to the pursuit of genuine poetry.'[2] Neither Hill nor Mallet could refuse their compliance, and the prefa-

---

[1] *Ibid.*, p. 55. [2] Cunningham, *op. cit.*, pp. 10–11.

tory verses to the second edition of *Winter* were relieved of their sting.

Thomson had meanwhile become thoroughly dissatisfied with his position of tutor to Lord Binning's son, and in May 1726, he left to take up a position in London. 'I go, on *Saturday* next,' he wrote to Hill on 24 May, 'to reside at Mr. *Watt's* Academy in *Little Tower-street*, in Quality of Tutor to a young Gentleman there.'[1] We can learn exactly from an advertisement what this Academy taught and the principles on which it was conducted. It was announced in *The Post-Boy* for 28–30 April 1726, that:

'At the Academy in Little Tower-street is to be learned every Qualification necessary for Business or Accomplishment, after a peculiar and approved Method; there being retain'd several Professors, capable to answer for their respective Trusts, to teach Writing, Arithmetick, and Merchants Accounts; all Parts of Mathematicks; and to give Courses of Experimental Philosophy, also the Classicks and Modern Languages; and to Foreigners and others, not well inform'd therein, the English Language, Drawing, Dancing, &c. There are also proper Accomodations for Boarding; and those that do not Board, may be taught either in Publick or Private, the Pupils being under proper Regulations, and the whole Education so calculated, as to answer the Ends of those whose Fortunes are not abounding, as well as of the Rich, the Charge increasing only with the Number of Qualifications to be attain'd; as may be seen at large in the Account of the Conditions and Terms, to be had at the said Academy. Letters are directed to Messieurs Tho. and W. Watts: And from this Academy Noblemen, Gentlemen, and Merchants, may be always likely to be supply'd with Stewards, Clerks, or Book-Keepers, duly qualify'd, and capable to give Security for their Fidelity.'

An announcement of a later date shows that this liberal Academy was carried on by 'Mr. William Watts, Mr. James Stirling, F.R.S. and Mr. John Bland, late of the Custom-

---

[1] Hill, *op. cit.*, p. 53.

house'; and that these Professors had added to the establishment's equipment 'a curious and compleat Apparatus for giving COURSES of GEOGRAPHY, ASTRONOMY, and EXPERIMENTAL PHILOSOPHY'.[1]

The names set out in the second advertisement show at once that this was no ordinary school. John Bland was a most accomplished penman, specimens of whose work were often used to illustrate contemporary text-books on calligraphy. James Stirling was a considerable mathematician who had to retire from Oxford in 1715 after becoming involved in Jacobitical activities. He withdrew to Venice, where he learnt the secret of Venetian glass-making—the knowledge of which, it is said, brought him into some danger—,but returned to London about 1725. He was the friend and correspondent of Sir Isaac Newton, and the correspondent of many Continental mathematicians of reputation.[2] Thomas and William Watts, the principals of this Academy, were also scientists and mathematicians of some standing and they appear to have fully understood and taught the new philosophy enunciated by Newton. Stirling and William Watts delivered a course of lectures on mechanical and experimental philosophy in 1727, and three of the seven parts into which this course was divided were devoted to discussions on 'The *Galilean* and *Newtonian* Philosophy', 'Opticks, Explaining the Nature of Vision, of Reflecting and Refracting Glasses, and of Light and Colours, according to Sir *ISAAC NEWTON'S* Theory', and 'Astronomy; or the System of the Universe more particularly Explain'd'.[3] They were helped in this course by a Peter Brown and a William Deam, 'Mathematical Instrument-Maker, . . . by whom the principal Instruments of the Apparatus were made'. The course was held 'over the *Bedford* Coffee-House, *Covent-Garden*, and at the Academy in *Tower-Street*'. Thomas Watts, helped by Benjamin

[1] *London Evening-Post*, 5–7 December 1728.
[2] See Charles Tweedie, *James Stirling; a Sketch of his Life and Works*, 1922.
[3] *A Course of Mechanical and Experimental Philosophy, consisting of Seven Parts.* n.d.

Worster, A.M., delivered an independent course of lectures upon experimental philosophy about this time, which was also held at the Academy.[1]

It is therefore clear that the Academy was a centre for the popular study of Newton's revolutionary philosophy, and that every facility, from competent professors to proper instruments, was made available. Thomson's intense interest in Newtonianism—an interest which profoundly affected the whole direction of his thought and the nature of his poetic imagery—must be dated from the time of his employment at the Academy. He may have picked up some smattering of knowledge in Edinburgh but that would be infinitesimal compared with what he would learn in Little Tower Street, where he had every opportunity of conversing upon the subject with men who could readily and lucidly expound and demonstrate Newton's discoveries.

It is not known to whose son Thomson was tutor after he entered the Academy, nor the subjects in which he instructed the boy; but he was capable of teaching him the classical languages and of generally supervising his education. The duties were probably not very onerous, and he would be left with time to write his poetry and to cultivate a friendship with men of genius in the capital. The second edition of *Winter* was published in the first weeks of July. It was advertised on 23 June, that 'Next Week will be published the 2d Edition of WINTER. A Poem';[2] and on 16 July, that '*This Day was publish'd, in 8vo, upon a Superfine Paper, the* SECOND EDITION *of* WINTER, a Poem. By *James Thompson*. Price One Shilling.'[3] He added to this edition some further lines describing an Alpine winter scene —thereby beginning the series of additions to his poems which eventually transformed them into very different works —and a preface setting out his opinion of contemporary poetry. He roundly condemned those poets who chose trifling subjects and consequently debased the spirit of

<hr>

[1] *A Course of Experimental Philosophy. . . . To be perform'd by Benj. Worster, A.M. and Tho. Watts*, n.d.   [2] *Whitehall Evening-Post.*   [3] *London Journal.*

poetry: 'To be able to write on a dry, barren Theme, is looked upon, by some, as the Sign of a happy, fruitful Genius—fruitful indeed! like one of the pendant Gardens in Cheapside, water'd every Morning by the Hands of the *Alderman* himself. And what are we commonly entertain'd with, on these Occasions, save forced, unaffecting Fancies; little, glittering Prettinesses; mixed Turns of Wit, and Expression; which are as widely different from Nature POETRY, as Buffoonery is from the Perfection of human Thinking?' Let poetry, he demanded, 'once more be restored to her antient Truth and Purity; let Her be inspired from Heaven; and, in Return, her Incense ascend thither: Let Her exchange Her low, venal, trifling Subjects for such as are fair, useful, and magnificent; and, let Her execrate these so as, at once, to please, instruct, suprize, and astonish.' He then continued to praise Nature as a subject worthy of any poet's pen: 'I know no Subject more elevating, more amusing, more ready to awake the Poetical Enthusiasm, the philosophical Reflection, and the Moral Sentiment, than the *Works of Nature*'. He ended by praising the poets whose verses introduced his poem. The first verses were by Hill, who advised the poet to keep clear of patrons:

> Firm in your native strength, thus nobly shown,
> Slight such delusive props, and stand alone;
> Fruitless dependance oft has found too late
> That greatness rarely dwells among the great.

The last were by Mallet, who began to sing Thomson's praises with the couplet:

> Charm'd and instructed by thy powerful song,
> I have, unjust, withheld my thanks too long.

The second of these complimentary poems, addressed 'To Mr. Thomson, on his blooming Winter', was signed 'Mira' —'the fictitious name', wrote Dr. Johnson, 'of a lady once too well known'.[1] This lady was a Mrs. Martha Sansom who had already attained notoriety under the name of 'Clio',

---

[1] Johnson, *op. cit.*, iii, 286.

and Mallet, her intimate friend, revised her tribute to
Thomson as in the past he had revised her other effusions.[1]

Before the second edition of *Winter* appeared, Thomson
was encouraged by the growing chorus of approval to begin
the description of a second season, *Summer*. He complained in a letter of 11 June to Aaron Hill, 'Shall I languish
out a whole Summer, in the same City with you, and not
once be re-inspir'd with your Company? Such a Happiness
would much brighten my Description of that Season';[2] and
'to fill out' his letter, he transcribed a passage from the new
poem upon which he was engaged. After praising some of
Mallet's verses in a letter of 13 June to him, he continued:
'How wild you sing, while I here warble like a city linnet in
a cage. If my beginning of "Summer" please you, I am sure
it is good. I have writ more which I'll send you in due time.'[3]
The two friends during the following summer submitted to
each other passages from their respective poems for criticism
—Thomson forwarding extracts from *Summer* and Mallet
replying with extracts from his poem, *The Excursion*, a work
similar in both style and theme to *Summer*—and it is
possible to follow in some detail the composition of this
second 'Season'. The tone of the correspondence was one of
mutual adulation; Thomson did not hesitate to compare
Mallet to Milton, and, on one occasion, to Shakespeare; and
Mallet—whose letters are lost—doubtless replied in the
same vein.

We learn from a letter of 2 August, that Thomson proposed to confine his description of Summer to the natural
progress of one day: 'In the enclosed sheets of "Summer",'
he wrote, 'I raise the sun to nine or ten o'clock; touch lightly
on his withering of flowers; give a group of rural images;
make an excursion into the insect kingdom; and conclude
with some suitable reflections. I have written a good deal
more; you will be notoriously guilty of poetical injustice, if
you make me not a proper return.'[4] Mallet at first agreed

---

[1] See *Athenaeum*, 1859, p. 78.   [2] Hill, *op. cit.*, p. 57.
[3] Cunningham, *op. cit.*, p. 13.   [4] *Ibid.*, pp. 29–30.

with this plan but he later criticized its conduct, and Thomson had to answer the objections which he raised: 'Prythee make no apology for your friendly sincerity, know you not that it is not in your power to disoblige me? Why did you not object against my method, with regard to "Summer", when I first gave you an account of it. I told you then expressly that I resolved to contract the season into a day. The uniform appearances of nature in summer easily allow of it. But not to dispute which of the schemes is most preferable, I am so far advanced, having writ three parts of four, that I cannot without the most painful labour alter mine. Let me tell you besides that we entirely agree from the noonday retreat to the evening. I have already written of shade and gloom, and woodland spirits &c. exactly as you hint, more than a week ago. Verdure and flowers belong to the Spring; and fruits to the Autumn; and therefore not to be anticipated. I design towards the end of my poem to take one short glance of corn fields, ripe for the sickle, as the limit of my performance. I thank you heartily for your hint about personizing Inspiration, it strikes me. Next post I will send you a sheet or two more.'[1] We learn from a subsequent but undated letter that he was drawing towards the end; and a phrase, 'I make an excursion to Africa', points out the effect of the Watts's 'geographical apparatus' upon his imagination. He enclosed some more sheets of the poem in this letter, which contained 'a Panegyric on Britain, which may perhaps contribute to make my Poem popular. The English people are not a little vain of themselves and their country. Britannia too includes our native country Scotland. After this I make an excursion to Africa; which I intersperse and conclude with some reflections. What remains of my Poem is a description of thunder and the Evening, Thunder I have writ, and am just now agreeably engaged with the Evening. The beginning of the sheets I have sent you at this time, connects with the cataract; but methinks I am very talkative about myself.'[2]

[1] Letter of 11 August; *ibid.*, pp. 17–19.   [2] *Ibid.*, pp. 20–1.

The self-confidence of these letters provides a remarkable contrast to the diffidence of those written to Cranstoun in the previous year. The poet no longer doubted his chance of success, or suggested that he would return to Scotland to enter the ministry. He had already achieved some fame and the prospect ahead was bright. He summarily rejected Mallet's suggestion that he should alter the plan of 'Summer', and he showed in an aside that he was equally quick to refuse other advice which he thought unsuitable to his genius. 'Mr. Aikman', he wrote, 'did me the honour of a visit yesternight. . . . We were in the Tavern and drunk your health. His reflections on my writings are very good; but he does not in them regard the turn of my genius enough, should I alter my way I would write poorly, I must choose what appears to me the most significant epithet, or I cannot with any heart proceed.'[1] Despite his flattery of Hill and Mallet, he did not defer to opinions if he believed they ran counter to his originality. He was determined to write as he wished, and the reception given to his first poem had proved that the public were prepared to welcome what he wrote. He needed no longer to fear that he would fail in his 'grand project'.

[1] Letter of 11 August 1726; *ibid.*, p. 19.

CHAPTER IV

THE POET OF THE SEASONS

Nor, ye, that live
In Luxury and Ease, in Pomp and Pride,
Think these lost Themes unworthy of your Ear.

THE success of *Winter* won James Thomson the
respect and applause of contemporary men of letters
and connoisseurs, who were eager both to be associated
with rising merit and to claim friendship with so pleasant
and humane a person. While he was teaching at the
Academy in Little Tower Street and writing *Summer*, he was
making a circle of friends who were to consider him with
constant affection. Many years later a young poet called him
'that right friendly bard', but the tribute might have been
paid by any one of his earlier acquaintances. They loved and
admired his frankness, his lack of all affectation, his un-
restrained good-humour, his conviviality and his enthusiasm for poetry. Literature was not then the polite and
respectable affair into which it has since been tamed by better
manners, but a violent and unscrupulous war conducted by
protagonists who never spared outrageous abuse, and sometimes descended to more hurtful tricks and even physical
violence. There were few poets, and very few of prominence,
who came through that general conflict with unquestioned
characters, but Thomson throughout his life was almost
entirely exempt from jealous attacks and retained to the last
an immaculate reputation. His character and abilities con-
ciliated even those literary pests who made abuse a career,
and kept the friendship of those whom chance led into
hostile camps.

His friends were, at first, Mallet, and those to whom

Mallet could introduce him. David Mallet had quickly made
himself familiar in London and assiduously cultivated a
friendship with any one who might advance his career. He
also adopted other devices to ensure his success. He purged
his speech of its Scottish dialect, and this reformation—by
no means an easy one—was so effective that David Hume,
the philosopher, later submitted his writings to him with
the request that he would prune his style of its Scotticisms.
He changed his name from discordant Malloch to eupho-
nious Mallet because, he said, the English would not
pronounce the original correctly;[1] but his enemies averred
that he jested so much against the Christian religion in the
coffee-houses, that Malloch became corrupted to Moloch
and shame at being so known made him get rid of the
original.[2] His linguistic and cognominal improvements
were matched by his sartorial; he was publicly mentioned in
1726 as 'a dapper *Scotch* gentleman';[3] Dr. Johnson slight-
ingly called him 'the prettiest drest puppet about town';[4]
and we know that his 'favourite dress was a suit of black
velvet'.[5] Johnson, who disliked him intensely, said that he
was the only Scotsman of whom other Scotsmen did not
speak well,[6] and satirized him in his *Dictionary* by defining
alias as 'A Latin word signifying otherwise; as Mallet, alias
Malloch; that is otherwise Malloch'. He was instinctively
regarded with distrust but his conversation, his polite manner, and his real abilities gained him admittance everywhere
and restrained his critics to whispers. But despite his faults,
he served Thomson well during his crucial first year in
London, and their correspondence shows that they were on
intimate terms. Mallet's support of his friend, however, was
not disinterested: 'Mr. Thomson's Winter', he wrote, 'has
met with a great deal of deserved applause, and was written

---

[1] Mallet to Kerr, 15 September 1724; *Edinburgh Mag.*, ii (1793), 2.
[2] *Correspondence and Memoirs of Wilkes*, ed. Almon, 1805, i, 77 *n.*
[3] *British Journal*, 24 September 1726.
[4] Boswell, *Tour to the Hebrides*, 1785, p. 201.
[5] Thomas Davies, *Life of Garrick*, 1780, ii, 47 *n.*
[6] Boswell, *Life of Johnson*, ed. Birkbeck Hill and L. F. Powell, ii, 159.

by that dull fellow, whom Malcolm calls the jest of our club. The injustice I did him then, in joining with my companions to ridicule the first, imperfect essays of an excellent genius, was a strong motive to make me active in endeavouring to assist and encourage him since; and I believe I shall never repent it. He is now settled in a very good place, and will be able to requite all the services his friends have done him in time.'[1] This friendship continued throughout Thomson's life, but there is reason to believe that it was Mallet, rather than Thomson, who cultivated it. One who knew them well, replying to a question about Mallet, said: 'Sir, that person's name was properly "Malloch"; but I used to call him "Moloch" in our festive moments, and Thomson enjoyed the jest. Sir, he had not Thomson's heart; he was not sound at the core; he made a cat's-paw of Thomson, and I did not like the man on that account.'[2] Mallet probably thought that Thomson's popularity could very well be extended like an umbrella to include himself; but his initial encouragement of Thomson should not be belittled.

He also made the acquaintance of other members of the Scottish colony in London, who would naturally rally to help their countryman; but one, also a poet, showed little desire to encourage a rival. This unfriendly person was Joseph Mitchell. He too had found his way from Edinburgh to London in search of literary success, and upon his arrival in the south he had engaged so warmly in support of Sir Robert Walpole and his administration that he became known as 'Sir Robert Walpole's Poet'. His literary efforts were, however, of little service to his patron. Mitchell also scraped up a living by composing elegies upon the recently dead which he presented to their mourning relatives. A curious letter exists in which he begged Sir John Clerk of Penicuik to accept some verses upon the death of his son 'as a Token of my Respect to the Memory of the Youth I so much valued. Such as they are, they wait on you: and, believe

---

[1] Mallet to Kerr, *n.d.*; *Edin. Mag.*, ii (1793), 338.
[2] Hone, *Table-Book*, 1830, ii, 110.

F

it, my Muse was hearty in the Sorrow, that inspir'd them, however unworthy they are of your dear Son's Merit, and your own Perusal.'[1] This effusion must have earned him a pound or two. London improved neither Mitchell's fame nor his character, and, 'a slave to his pleasures, and governed by every gust of irregular appetite',[2] he was treated with scant respect by his fellow Scots. Thomson, however, presented him with a copy of *Winter* upon its publication, and received in acknowledgement these lines:

> Beauties and faults so thick lye scattered here,
> Those I could read, if these were not so near.

'To this Mr. Thomson answered extempore,

> Why all not faults, injurious Mitchell; why
> Appears one beauty to thy blasted eye;
> Damnation worse than thine, if worse can be,
> Is all I ask, and all I want from thee.

Upon a friend's remonstrating to Mr. Thomson, that the expression of blasted eye would look like a personal reflexion, as Mr. Mitchell had really that misfortune, he changed the epithet blasted, into blasting.'[3] Thomson later referred to Mitchell as 'that Planet-blasted fool'.[4]

Other and better poets than the truculent and barren Mitchell were among his early acquaintances. Alexander Pope, ever ready to discover and promote merit, became his friend, and Thomson introduced into *Winter* a fine compliment to him:

> First of your kind! society divine!
> Still visit thus my nights, for you reserv'd,
> And mount my soaring soul to deeds like yours.
> Silence, thou lonely power! the door be thine;
> See on the hallow'd hour that none intrude,
> Save *Lycidas* the friend, with sense refin'd,
> Learning digested well, exalted faith,
> Unstudy'd wit, and humour ever gay.

[1] *Clerk of Penicuik Papers*, Register House, Edinburgh.
[2] Cibber, *op. cit.*, iv, 347.   [3] *Ibid.*, v, 197-8.
[4] Letter to Mallet, *n.d.*; Cunningham, *op. cit.*, p. 27.

Or from the muses' hill will *Pope* descend,
To raise the sacred hour, to make it smile,
And with the social spirit warm the heart:
For tho' not sweeter his own *Homer* sings,
Yet is his life the more endearing song.

Pope and Thomson liked and admired each other from the first, but their real intimacy belongs to a later day. John Dyer, whose delightful poem of *Grongar Hill*, among the finest of all the eighteenth-century's many landscape-poems, was published in 1726, had been asked to write some satirical verses upon Sir Spencer Compton for the second edition of *Winter*, but 'luckily' he had 'very handsomely excused himself'[1] before it had become necessary to disarm those prefatory verses. Dyer had trained and practised as a painter but became discouraged by his lack of success and later entered the Church of England. Another poet who sought out Thomson was Dr. Edward Young. He had succeeded on the stage with his two tragedies of *Busiris* and *The Revenge*, and during the years of his early friendship with Thomson, he was publishing the series of satires which were printed collectively as *The Love of Fame*. His greatest work, the sombre and astonishing *Night Thoughts*, was not written until many years later. The Doctor was known as a fashionable parson, a notorious tuft-hunter, and a seeker after church preferment, which, in spite of the fantastic adulation he lavished on the great, for ever eluded him. He did not impose upon Thomson, who denounced as rubbish his verses entitled *The Instalment*, in which Sir Robert Walpole was acclaimed in lines like these:

See, *Britain*, see thy WALPOLE shine from far,
His azure ribbon, and his radiant *star*:
A *star* that, with auspicious beams, shall guide
Thy vessel safe, thro' fortune's roughest tide.

'I have not seen these reflections on the Dr.'s Installment', he wrote to Mallet on 2 August 1726, 'but hear they are as

[1] Letter to Mallet, 13 June 1726; *ibid.*, p. 12.

wretched as their subject. The Dr.'s very buckram has run short on this occasion; his affected sublimity even fails him, and down he comes with no small velocity.'[1]

Perhaps the oddest of Thomson's literary acquaintances was that strange, unhappy creature Richard Savage, who was later to introduce Samuel Johnson to the alleys and by-places of London. His claim to be the illegitimate child of the Earl of Rivers and the Countess of Macclesfield had been made public by Aaron Hill in *The Plain Dealer* in 1724, and the story of his suppositious mother's cruel and un-natural rejection of him won him much sympathy and charity. A man of distinguished appearance, with the airs and tastes of a gentleman, he easily persuaded people to believe in his concocted story, but those who were gulled quickly discovered that his fair outside hid a rotten and unscrupulous heart. His dissipation and chicanery made everyone distrust him, and his real literary talents, neglec-ted and addled by loose living, were forgotten in the desire to avoid his company. Thomson had no illusions about Savage. He met him in company with Aaron Hill on 26 April 1726, and the next day he wrote to Hill a letter which joined criticism of Savage to adroit flattery: 'Nothing is, to me, a stronger Instance of the unimprovable Nature of that unhappy Creature of whom you speak so compas-sionately, notwithstanding the barbarous Provocation he has given you, than his remaining bleak and wither'd under the Influence of your Conversation—a certain Sign of a Field that the Lord has curs'd.'[2] Later in this year, he again wrote about Savage, this time to Mallet: 'How came you to be so unreasonable as to expect regularity from S—? as well might you hope for poetry from a satchel of rhymes, writhed lines and hard words. What in the name of Incon-sistency has he to do with being punctual, would you bring the wild ass from the range of the desert, he who cries Bray! Bray! and laughs at the letter writing throng? why, he has given me as many promises of a letter this summer as he has

---

[1] Letter to Mallet, 13 June 1726; *ibid.*, pp. 30–1.   [2] Hill, *op. cit.*, p. 51.

writ lines, nay repeated lines; and yet it is well known, it
never entered into his head but when he promised to perform—if then. I shall have that letter from him when he is
made the Laureate; I am out there too for that may happen.'[1]
Savage later failed in his application for the laureateship,
but Queen Caroline in return for an ode upon each of her
birthdays gave him a pension, and the grateful Savage
assumed the title of 'volunteer laureate'. Thomson probably
never received the letter.

Other and more influential people than poets, however,
sought Thomson's friendship. George Bubb Dodington, a
time-serving politician, wit, and small poet, was so impressed by *Winter* that he made it known to Thomson
through Edward Young that he would be glad to accept
the dedication of his next poem. Thomson had intended
dedicating *Summer* to Lord Binning, but when Binning
learnt that Dodington was anxious to appear as the poet's
patron, he refused to accept the dedication and advised
Thomson to give it to Dodington, a man of much greater
influence than he could command. Dodington was a vain,
ostentatious, almost ludicrous, character, but he had both a
quick intelligence and a real appreciation of poetry, and
was prepared to patronize well any poet who would make
his taste in the arts better known. Pope certainly had him in
mind when he wrote:

> Proud, as *Apollo* on his forked hill,
> Sate full-blown *Bufo*, puff'd by ev'ry quill;
> Fed with soft Dedication all day long,
> *Horace* and he went hand in hand in song.

Dodington promised to be a much more appreciative and
generous patron than Sir Spencer Compton, and Thomson
did not delay accepting his offer of patronage.

The publication of *Summer* was announced at the
beginning of 1727. An advertisement in the *London Journal*
on 7 January for the third edition of *Winter* carried a post-
script, '*N.B.* In the Press, and will speedily be published by

---

[1] Cunningham, *op. cit.*, p. 26.

the said *John Millan*, SUMMER, a POEM. By *James Thomson*.' The poem was promised for 'next week' on 11 February, and its publication was announced in the *St. James's Evening-Post* for 14–16 February. *Summer* was much more widely and impressively advertised than *Winter*, and Millan had obviously found that his investment in the young, unknown poet had paid a good interest. The poem was introduced by a dedication to Dodington which must have delighted the great man. The poet declined the superfluous task of describing his patron's character in a fine sentence: 'And when I consider that a character in which the virtues, the graces, and the muses join their influence as much exceeds the expression of the most elegant and judicious pen, as the finished beauty does the representation of the pencil, I have the best reasons for declining such an arduous undertaking'. Dodington rewarded the poet not only with a gift, which was no doubt substantially greater than Sir Spencer's reluctant twenty guineas, but with his friendship, and Thomson lived on terms of intimacy with him for many years and was a frequent visitor in his house.

Thomson undoubtedly intended to continue at once with the composition of a third 'season', but soon after the publication of *Summer* there occurred an event which turned his attention from this purpose. Sir Isaac Newton died on 20 March, and after his body had lain in state, it was buried in Westminster Abbey on 28 March. Eighteenth-century poets were quick to celebrate national occasions, and the death of so good and great a man, the glory of his country, offered a subject worthy of any poet. Many took advantage of Newton's death to publish elegiac verses but the quality of these was so low that they dishonoured the poets rather than honoured the philosopher. Thomson also wrote a poem upon his death, which was advertised in the *Post-Boy* for 29 April–2 May: '*This Week will be publish'd*, A POEM. Sacred to the Memory of Sir *Isaac Newton*. By J. Thomson, Author of *Summer* and *Winter*.' The poem passed through four editions in the first year of publication, and the public recognized that it was not an occasional work written to take advantage of national regret at the loss of a great man, but a noble poem inspired by genuine love and sorrow. James Stirling, the mathematician who also taught at the Academy in Little Tower Street, was the friend of Sir Isaac Newton, and there can be little doubt that he had at some time introduced Thomson to him; otherwise it would be impossible to explain the feeling of personal loss which burns keenly throughout the poem, and elevates the poet's imagination above philosophical and scientific facts. He began the poem with the question,

> Shall the great soul of *Newton* quit this earth,
> To mingle with his stars; and every muse,
> Astonish'd into silence, shun the weight
> Of honours due to his illustrious name?

And he continued in fine verse and with imaginative scope to set out the extent of Newton's genius and the natural glories which he had revealed to men. The harmonious marriage of scientific accuracy and poetic imagination makes the poem a remarkable achievement, and puts it among the finest of its kind in our language. This is how he described the philosopher's discovery of the nature of light:

> Even *Light itself*, which every thing displays,
> Shone undiscover'd, till his brighter mind
> Untwisted all the shining robe of day;
> And, from the whitening undistinguish'd blaze,
> Collected every ray into his kind,
> To the charm'd eye educ'd the gorgeous train
> Of *Parent-Colours*. First the flaming *Red*
> Sprung vivid forth; the tawny *Orange* next,
> And next delicious *Yellow*; by whose side
> Fell the kind beams of all-refreshing *Green*.
> Then the pure *Blue*, that swells autumnal skies,
> Ethereal play'd; and then, of sadder hue,
> Emerg'd the deepen'd *Indigo*, as when
> The heavy-skirted evening droops with frost.
> While the last gleamings of refracted light
> Dy'd in the fainting *Violet* away.

He concluded by calling attention to the moral example which Newton's life provided, and thus he succeeded in firmly uniting science to humanity:

> O'er thy dejected country chief preside,
> And be her *Genius* call'd! her studies raise,
> Correct her manners, and inspire her youth.
> For, tho' depraved and sunk, she brought thee forth,
> And glories in thy name; she points thee out
> To all her sons, and bids them eye thy star:
> While in expectance of the second life,
> When Time shall be no more, thy sacred dust
> Sleeps with her kings, and dignifies the scene.

Thomson was apparently helped in the composition of this poem by John Gray, who was later to become Rector of Marischal College, Aberdeen, where he founded two mathematical bursaries, 'a gentleman well versed in the *Newtonian Philosophy*, who, on that occasion, gave him a very exact, though general, abstract of its principle'.[1] But he may also have been helped by James Stirling and the Watts brothers. The poem was dedicated to Sir Robert Walpole, who cared not a rush for poets, and it is difficult to explain why Thomson should have chosen a patron with whose foreign policy he disagreed and which he was soon to attack openly. He may have been advised in the choice by Bubb Dodington—who was at this time himself showering Sir Robert with bad verses in the hope of being rewarded with a place in the administration—or by William Aikman. Sir Robert commissioned several pictures from Aikman, and appreciated that able artist's talents. 'This day I had the honour of a visit from Sʳ Robert Walpool,' wrote Aikman to Sir John Clerk on 15 July 1725, 'and I am to beginn another Pictur for him very soon.'[2] It is not known whether Thomson was rewarded or not for this dedication, but if he was, it was not sufficient to make him a loyal supporter of Sir Robert.

---

[1] *Works of Thomson*, 1762, i, ix.
[2] *Clerk of Penicuik Papers*, Register House, Edinburgh.

Thomson had by now won an enviable reputation, and he was recognized to be among the best of the young poets of the day. Sir John Clerk of Penicuik met Mallet and Thomson in London on 30 April 1727, and his brief memorandum of the meeting shows the estimation in which these two poets were held: 'at night on my return I met with Mr Maloch & Mr Thomsone two young Lads of my Country & justly esteam'd at present the best poets in Britain'.[1] Other patrons, with brighter reputations than George Bubb Dodington, were attracted to the poet, and among these was the Countess of Hertford. Frances Thynne, the granddaughter of the first Viscount Weymouth of Longleat, had married in 1715, when she was barely sixteen, Algernon Seymour, Earl of Hertford. She was appointed in 1723 a Lady of the Bedchamber to Princess Caroline, who became Queen in 1727, and through her royal mistress, whom she loved and admired, she was able to exercise considerable influence at Court. She herself wrote verses of some merit, and her correspondence reveals a vivacious and sensitive mind. She was also anxious to gather around her contemporary poets who reflected in their work those emotions which she herself felt deeply but was unable to express fully, and they did not refuse the proffered favours of an influential patron and an attractive and considerate woman. Lady Hertford's attention had been called to Thomson soon after the publication of *Winter*. Her friend and correspondent Mrs. Elizabeth Rowe, a woman 'famous for both poetry and piety', wrote to her in 1726: 'There is a Poem in blank verse lately printed call'd Winter by Mr. Thomson. 'tis very fine so I am perswaded will please the Justice of your taste. I must copy this description:

> The year yet pleasing but declining fast
> Soft, o'er the secret Soul, in gentle Gales,
> A Philosophic Melancholly breathes,
> And bears the swelling Thought aloft to Heaven.
> Then forming Fancy rouses to conceive,

[1] Clerk, *op. cit.*; *Clerk of Penicuik Papers*, Register House, Edinburgh.

What never mingled with the Vulgar's dream:
Then wake the tender Pang, the pitying Tear,
The Sigh for suffering Worth, the Wish prefer'd
For Humankind, the Joy to see them bless'd,
And all the Social Off-Spring of the Heart!'[1]

This recommendation was sufficient to make Lady Hertford both read the poem and seek the friendship of a poet who added to ability a 'good heart'. It was her practice to invite some poet down to the country every summer, and Thomson received an invitation in 1727 to stay with her at Marlborough Castle, the seat of the Seymours. Dr. Johnson's account of this visit is too good to be true; Lady Hertford, he wrote, used 'to invite every summer some poet into the country, to hear her verses and assist her studies. This honour was one summer conferred on Thomson, who took more delight in carousing with lord Hertford and his friends than assisting her ladyship's poetical operations, and therefore never received another summons.'[2] This tale was probably told to Johnson by his lying friend Richard Savage, who was pleased to spread as much poisonous gossip as he could, and it was not of course true. If Thomson caroused with the Earl, he did not offend her Ladyship, and he continued to be her correspondent and visitor for many years.

Savage was incapable of gratitude or else he would have suppressed this lie. His dissipation almost brought him to a timely end in this very year. He killed a man in a drunken brawl on 20 November 1727, and was tried for murder and found guilty. Many people, who had been persuaded that his history was true, pitied him and tried to secure his pardon. Foremost among these friends was Lady Hertford who, engaging 'in his support with all the tenderness that is excited by pity, and all the zeal which is kindled by generosity',[3] successfully represented Savage's case to her mistress the Queen, and secured a pardon for him. There

---

[1] Quoted H. S. Hughes, 'Thomson and the Countess of Hertford', *Mod. Philology*, xxv (1927–8), 443.   [2] Johnson, *op. cit.*, iii, 287.   [3] *Ibid.*, ii, 352.

can be little question that Lady Hertford was prompted to this generous activity by James Thomson.

While he stayed at Marlborough Castle enjoying the Earl's masculine society and her Ladyship's literary conversations, Thomson composed part of the next 'season', *Spring*, which he had determined to dedicate to his new patroness. The fame which the poet had won in so short a time is shown by the welcome accorded to the announcement of the new poem. An important article was published in the *Whitehall Evening-Post* for 16–19 March 1728, which introduced extensive quotations from the forthcoming poem with this eulogy:

'It has been a frequent Complaint among our Writers, of late Years, that the *British* Taste was never so universally depraved as at present. Nothing, they say, can draw the Attention of the Public, but Entertainments of mere *Sound*, and *Show*: the unmeaning Softness of *Operas*, and the pompous Absurdity of *Farce*. But, notwithstanding this Clamour, perhaps the general Taste is not at so low an Ebb, as those Gentlemen would have us believe. I chuse to say nothing of our modern Dramatic Representations, because I would not willingly offend those, whom it may most nearly concern: but I may be allowed to observe, from that favourable Regard which has been shewn to several late Attempts in other Kinds of Poetry, that the present Age is very well disposed to relish whatever is truly valuable in fine Writing.

'If an Author, altogether unknown to the World, and unsupported by any thing but the native Force of his own Genius, should make his first Attempt in Poetry, on a Subject which can only please by its genuine Worth and Beauty, without gratifying either the ill Nature, irregular Passions, or Levity of Mankind: if he should venture beyond this, and lay aside the favourite Mode of writing in Rhyme; I think the *general Encouragement* of such a Performance would be a very good Proof of my Assertion.

'And yet this is exactly true with regard to the Poems of *Winter* and *Summer*, which, tho' introduced into the World under all the Disadvantages I have been supposing, in a little time came to be universally read and approven. The Public, without dwelling on such minuter Faults as they might have found in them, distinguished, with a just Indulgence, that strong and fertile Imagination, which animates the several Representations of Nature they contain.'

This was the first of the articles which welcomed in *Spring*, and the praise was taken up later in the month in the periodical, *The Present State of the Republick of Letters*: 'Mr. Thomson, the ingenious Author of the admired Poems *Winter* and *Summer*, and that upon Sir Isaac Newton's death, is now publishing *The Spring*. This gentleman excels in the real sublime, in a strength and justness both of thought and expression, in such beautiful, natural, and affecting descriptions, as are rarely to be met with in any of our Countrymen since Shakespear and Milton. But the judicious and well-placed reflexions of piety, virtue and humanity which run through his works, are the strongest recommendations of them to me, and ought to be so to all. Without these, poetry of any kind is but an idle and a fruitless amusement, whereas the true design of it should be

> To wake the Soul by tender strokes of art,
> To raise the genius, and to mend the heart.

'This is what Mr. Thompson aims at more than any of our modern Poets, and succeeds in it very happily. But I want such language as his own to do him justice.'

This heralded poem was advertised for publication in *The Craftsman* for 25 May 1728: 'In a few Days will be published, SPRING. A POEM. By Mr. *Thompson*. London printed, and sold by *A. Millar* at *Buchanan's* Head against St. Clement's Church in the Strand.' This advertisement shows that a new publisher had taken over John Millan's interest in the poet. Andrew Millar, one of the most celebrated booksellers in the eighteenth century, was a stout patriot who treated generously those Scottish authors whose works he published, and he became not only Thomson's publisher but a close friend, to whom the poet was indebted for many kindnesses.

The laudatory article in the *Whitehall Evening-Post* had been followed by proposals for printing by subscription the four *Seasons* in one volume. The announcement read:

'Proposals for Printing by Subscription the FOUR SEASONS, with a Hymn on their Succession. To which will be added a Poem sacred to the Memory of Sir Isaac Newton. And an Essay on Descriptive Poetry will be prefixed to the Whole. By Mr. THOMSON.

'I. This Work is proposed to be printed in one Volume in Quarto, on a Superfine Royal Paper, and adorned with Copper-Plates adapted to the Subject.

'II. The Price of the Book in Sheets to Subscribers is One Guinea, to be paid at the time of Subscribing.

'III. The Names of Subscribers to be printed before the Work, which is in great Forwardness, and will be published with all possible speed.

'*N.B.* The Pieces already published, *viz*. Winter, Summer, and a Poem on the Death of Sir *Isaac Newton*, will be corrected and enlarged in several Places.

'Subscriptions are taken in by the Author, at the Smyrna Coffee-House in Pall-Mall; and by Mr. STRAHAN and Mr. WALTHOE, overagainst the Royal Exchange in Cornhill; Mr. MILLAR at Buchanan's Head, overagainst St. Clement's Church in the Strand; and Mr. MILLAN, at the Anchor in Pall-Mall.'

It is apparent from these proposals that Thomson did not intend at first to publish *Spring* as a separate poem but to include it in this subscription volume; but, as we will see, subscriptions came in slowly, and Millar probably advised him to print *Spring* by itself and to include only one new poem, the unwritten *Autumn*, in the collected volume.

The article in the *Whitehall Evening-Post* also hinted at another of the poet's plans. The anonymous author told the public: 'May I have leave just to hint that the *present* En-

couragement of so good a Genius may prove *their future*
Entertainment in a nobler way; when the Author shall rise
from the *still Life* of Poetry, to represent the Passions of
Mankind, those great Springs of Action; and the Distresses
flowing from them, which, by exciting our Compassion and
Fear, move and delight so exquisitely in the *Scene*.' The
public were intended to gather from this circumlocution
that the poet intended not only to complete *The Seasons* but
to produce a play, which had been planned already.

Among those who made Thomson's acquaintance after
the publication of *Winter*, Thomas Rundle, a prominent
ecclesiastic and the intimate friend and adviser of Charles
Talbot, the Solicitor-General, was one of the most important. Rundle, whose career was later to be blighted by the
suspicion of heresy, was a man of considerable intelligence,
personal charm, and dignity. His name is to be found in the
correspondence of Pope and Swift, and it is mentioned
there in terms of the greatest respect. He was always ready
to further the interests of those poets by whom he had been
impressed, and 'upon conversing with Mr. *Thomson*, and
finding in him qualities greater still, and of more value, than
those of a poet, received him into his intimate confidence
and friendship; [and] promoted his character every where'.[1]
He helped the poet to obtain subscriptions to his volume of
poems, and he wrote to his cultured correspondent, Mrs.
Barbara Sandys in March 1729: 'But to refresh you,
Madam, with chit chat more agreeable than this, I have
taken the liberty to put you into the list of subscribers for
Thompson's Poems, for which I beg your pardon; but
I know your taste, and am sure you will give it me. When a
man of genius employs his muse to make virtue agreeable,
the singularity is merit. And why should not we be as zealous to encourage the honest labour, as others are to reward
the muses when prostituted to indulge the passions, and be
bawds to dishonest pleasures. He hath certainly a genius, his
numbers are harmonious; his language strong, but in-

---

[1] *Works of Thomson*, 1762, i, viii.

accurate; his sentiments just, short and touching, because only the dictates of the heart, which even the vicious feel to be true, in spite in their labour to quench the light and natural inspiration in their souls . . . But now the muses are grown coquettes; and boys and rakes have been their only minions . . . If he reforms these amiable dames, and gives them once more a taste above delighting in trifles, and persuades them no longer to be the dishonourable hand-maids of dissoluteness, he will deserve our esteem, and what we esteem, we should reward; as far at least, as by giving such a man the countenance of our names, in a subscription.'[1]

Lady Hertford was no less anxious to help the poet than Rundle, and Mrs. Rowe at once complied with her request that she should subscribe to *The Seasons*: 'you could not more oblige me, Madam,' she wrote to Lady Hertford, 'then putting a subscription for me to Mr. Thompson's Poems wch I hope will meet, as they deserve, great encouragement'.[2] The poet, however, was not content to rely upon the activity of these solicitous friends, nor to wait at the Smyrna Coffee-house for subscriptions to come in; he went afield to win subscribers by personal appeals. He was helped by letters of introduction, and Edward Young gave him one to Joseph Spence, the Professor of Poetry at Oxford, who became Thomson's firm friend and admirer. Young wrote to Spence on 1 April 1729: 'I promised my Friend Mr. Tompson who is now finishing his Subscription in Oxford, all the advantages I could give him; for which reason I beg leave to introduce him to so valuable an acquaintance as yours. Which freedom I hope You will pardon'.[3] Unfortunately, there is no record of Thomson's visit to Oxford but it must certainly have been pleasant and perhaps profitable. Thomson made a very thorough canvas, and he could spare no time to criticize Sir John Clerk's poem, *The Country Seat*, which had been forwarded to him through Aikman for his opinion. Aikman excused his dilatoriness

---

[1] *Letters of Thomas Rundle*, 1789, ii, 75–9.
[2] Quoted Hughes, *op. cit.*; *Mod. Phil.*, xxv, 445.
[3] Quoted Spence, *op. cit.*, p. 298.

by referring it to his anxiety about his subscription: 'Thomson is so strong about his Subscription', he wrote to Clerk, 'that he minds nothing else.'[1]

He passed the summer and early autumn of 1729 in a visit to Bubb Dodington's seat at Eastbury, in Dorsetshire, which had been designed by the dramatist and architect, Sir John Vanburgh. The house has long since been destroyed but its appearance, Dodington's taste in furnishings, and the style of his house-parties are well known. Richard Cumberland, the dramatist, has left a vivid description of his own visit to Eastbury. The mansion, he wrote, 'was magnificent, massy and stretching out to a great extent of front with an enormous portico of Doric columns ascended by a stately flight of steps; there were turrets and wings that went I know not whither . . . Vanburgh seemed to have had the plan of Blenheim in his thoughts, and the interior was as proud and splendid as the exterior was bold and imposing. All this was exactly in unison with the taste of its magnificent owner, who had gilt and furnished the apartments with a profusion of finery, that kept no terms with simplicity, and not always with elegance or harmony of style . . . when I proceed to enquire into those principles of good taste, which should naturally have been the accompaniments and directors of that magnificence, I fear I must be compelled by truth to admit that in these he was deficient. Of pictures he seemed to take his estimate only by their cost; in fact he was not possessed of any; but I recollect his saying to me one day in his great saloon at Eastbury, that if he had half a score pictures of a thousand pounds apiece, he would gladly decorate his walls with them, in place of which I am sorry to say he had stuck up immense patches of gilt leather shaped into bugle horns upon hangings of rich crimson velvet.'[2]

Dodington's manner and appearance were fitted to his surroundings. He hung his corpulent, impressive figure with heavy, brilliant cloths, decorated with elaborate gold

---

[1] *Clerk of Penicuik Papers,* Register House, Edinburgh.
[2] Cumberland, *Memoirs,* 1806, pp. 140–3.

embroideries; and 'he had all the courtly and profound devotion of a Spaniard' towards the ladies, 'with the ease and gaiety of a Frenchman towards the men'.[1] The amusements which he provided for his guests excluded such trivialities as cards, and consisted of conversation, which allowed the host to show his genuine wit and scholarship, and readings from the poets and novelists, in which he also excelled. As Thomson walked the grounds, or surveyed from a distance the mansion's impressive façade, or strolled down its ornate corridors, he must have thought with amusement of the poor manse in which he had been bred. He repaid Dodington for his invitation by including in *Autumn*, which he was writing at this time, a fine description of Eastbury and the delightful countryside:

> In this glad season, while his last best beams
> The sun sheds equal o'er the meeken'd day;
> Oh lose me in the green, majestic walks
> Of, *Dodington*! thy seat, serene, and plain;
> Where simple Nature reigns; and every view,
> Diffusive, spreads the pure *Dorsetian* downs,
> In boundless prospect, yonder shagg'd with wood;
> Here rich with harvest; and there white with flocks.
> Mean time the grandeur of thy lofty dome,
> Far-splendid, seizes on the ravish'd eye.
> New beauties rise with each revolving day;
> New columns swell; and still the fresh spring finds
> New plants to quicken, and new groves to green,
> Full of thy genius all! the muses seat;
> Where in the secret bower, and winding walk
> They twine the bay for thee.

Thomson wrote to Mallet from Eastbury on 20 September, and we learn from his letter that he had not found as many subscribers as he could have wished to the collected edition of *The Seasons*. 'I have heard of an agreement among some of our modern Goths (who by the bye are even unworthy of that name)', he wrote, 'by which they bind themselves not to encourage any subscription whatever under a certain

---

[1] *Ibid.*, p. 140.

G

penalty. Methinks all tolerable authors in this age, all who can give honour and entertainment to it, should in opposition to this, and the general discouragement they labour under, enter into an association not to write at all; or if they do write, for their own pleasure and that of their particular friends, yet never to publish.' After elaborating this impracticable proposition, he continued with a reference to some girl, who appears to have been one in a succession of anonymous ladies who charmed his susceptible heart by turn:

'To turn my eyes a softer way, I am really touched with a fair neighbour of yours—you know who.—Absence sighs it to me. What is my heart made of? A soft system of love-nerves, too sensible for my quiet, capable of being very happy or very unhappy; I am afraid the last will prevail. Lay your hand upon a kindred heart, and despise me not. I know not what it is, but she dwells upon my thought, in a mingled sentiment which is the sweetest, the most intimately pleasing the soul can receive, and which I would wish never to want towards some dear object or other.

'To have some secret darling idea, to which one can still have recourse amidst the noise and nonsense of the world, and which never fails to touch us in the most exquisite manner, is an Art of Happiness that Fortune cannot deprive us of. This may be called romantic, but whatever the cause is, the effect is really felt. Pray when you write tell me when you saw her, and with the pure eye of a friend; and when you see her again whisper that I am her most humble servant. But my paper comes to an end: I wish for a walk with you upon the serene downs, to talk of a thousand things. There is nobody's company gives me greater pleasure, I will assuredly see you before I leave the country. I have been in dead solitude here for some days by past.'[1]

While Thomson stayed at Eastbury during this summer, he was completing the fourth and last 'season', *Autumn*, and his tragedy, to be called *Sophonisba*, which the town had been warned to expect. He also wrote some complimentary

[1] Cunningham, *op. cit.*, pp. 34-8.

verses, *The Happy Man*, addressed to Dodington, which James Ralph printed in his miscellany of poems, published in this year. However, before either *The Seasons* or *Sophonisba* was finished, Thomson published an occasional poem which, although by no means among his best work, appearing opportunely, achieved a certain success.

Britannia reveals one of the poet's most obvious and constant sources of inspiration, his patriotism. The history of *Britannia* is confused by Thomson's attempts to hide his authorship. The title-page carried the legend, 'Written in 1719', but the poem, which was a passionate appeal to the British people to assert their naval power against a Spanish threat to their security, clearly referred to events which had occurred in 1727; a year in which Spain's hesitant show of hostility against Gibraltar and her menacing attitude towards English merchants had raised a popular demand for war, and forced the Government to send a fleet to the West Indies, under the command of Admiral Hosier, to blockade the Spanish galleons. But the pacific minister, Sir Robert Walpole, had diplomatically avoided a declaration of war, and good relations with Spain had been slowly restored. Thomson undoubtedly wrote *Britannia* in this year, 1727, but refrained from publishing it at the time because, after publishing a panegyric on Walpole and his policy in the dedication to his poem on the death of Sir Isaac Newton, he could hardly turn at once against his new patron. But the popular dislike of Walpole's conciliatory policy had not yet died away in 1729, and Thomson no doubt felt that he could now safely, if secretly, print this appeal to national senti-ment. To conceal the author's identity, not only did the title-page carry a deceptive legend, but the poem was published by a bookseller who only this once appears to have been connected with the poet. The poem was advertised in the *St. James's Evening-Post* for 18–21 January 1729/30: 'This Day was publish'd BRITANNIA. A POEM. . . . Printed for T. Warner, in Pater-noster-Row. Price 1s.' The piece immediately appealed to the popular mood, and recommendations appeared in the newspapers; *Fog's Weekly Journal*, for 1 February, printed this eulogy: 'The *Daily Journal* of last Tuesday having presented us with a Transcript in Praise of PEACE, from an excellent Poem just publish'd, intitled, BRITANNIA; I hope you will oblige your Readers with the following Verses, from the same inimitable Piece; for tho' 'tis probable 'tis by this Time in the Hands of almost every Man of Taste and Judgment, yet I am confident, no one will think his Time ill-bestow'd to read a Part of it over again in your Paper. I hardly know where to chuse in the whole Piece, 'tis everywhere so excellent;—But e'en take it at the Beginning, and where I leave off, let the Reader peruse and wonder.'

The poem, like most verses which ride to success on a wave of popular emotion, is worth little; but there is one admirable passage in which the goddess Britannia describes the defeat of the Spanish Armada:

> The bolts of fate
> Resistless thunder'd thro' their yielding sides;
> Fierce o'er their beauty blaz'd the lurid flame;
> And seiz'd in horrid grasp, or shatter'd wide,
> Amid the mighty waters, deep they sunk.
> Then too from every promontory chill,
> Rank fen, and cavern where the wild wave works,
> I swept confederate winds, and swell'd a storm.
> Round the glad isle, snatch'd by the vengeful blast,
> The scatter'd remnants drove; on the blind shelve,
> And pointed rock, that marks the indented shore,
> Relentless dash'd, where loud the Northern Main
> Howls thro' the fractur'd *Caledonian* isles.

Meanwhile, Thomson's tragedy of *Sophonisba* had been finished and accepted for representation at Drury Lane Theatre. Rumours of its quality had gone about the town, and it was generally expected that it would be a great success. William Aikman gave some news about its production in a letter of 13 January 1729/30, to Sir John Clerk: 'You desir'd to know what Thomson & Malloch are about, they have both finish'd the Tragedies they were about this Summer and both are presented to the Old Playhouse; Thomson's which is call'd Sophonisba was first presented & is now upon rehearsal, it bears a very great character amongst the Virtuosi. Mr Dodington is extravagant in its praise as is Mrs Oldfield and several of the players. I wish they may not raise peoples expectations to a height about it that cannot be satisfied. Mr Malloch's Periander is much approv'd of by Mr. Pope, Dr. Arbuthnot and most that have seen it, but am afraid it will be too late to act it this winter as there are two already accepted before it.'[1] The hopes which the Virtuosi had raised were luckily not disappointed.

The story of the play, which had been used by earlier dramatists, was simply told by Thomson. Sophonisba, the Queen of Carthage, is shown as a woman prepared to sacrifice both herself and her lovers to her selfless patriotism. She uses Syphax, the King of Masaesylia, who is infatuated with her beauty, to defend her kingdom against an invading Roman army under the generalship of Scipio. But when he is defeated, she seduces from his allegiance a young prince, Masinissa, her earlier lover, who is serving under Scipio. He is torn between his revived love for Sophonisba and his loyalty to Scipio, whom he admires beyond all other men; but at last, in obedience to his duty, he sends Sophonisba a phial of poison. Eager to escape the humiliation of captivity, she drinks the poison, and the action closes with Masinissa, broken by grief and remorse, and the other characters gathered round her dead body.

It is not a good play. The action is too bald and uninteresting, and the characters are too devoid of individuality; Syphax is all malignity, Scipio nobility, Sophonisba patriotism, and Masinissa sentimentality; but the play was saved from failure by the finely resonant speeches, and the vigorous thought which informed the whole work. Thomson was quick to take every opportunity to show his poetic power, and there are many passages comparable with this one spoken by the self-tortured Masinissa:

[1] *Clerk of Penicuik Papers*, Register House, Edinburgh.

What dreadful havoc in the human breast
The passions make, when unconfin'd, and mad,
They burst, unguided by the mental eye,
The light of reason; which in various ways
Points them to good, or turns them back from ill.
    O save me from the tumult of the soul!
From the wild beasts within!—For circling sands,
When the swift whirlwind whelms them o'er the lands;
The roaring deeps that to the clouds arise,
While thwarting thick the mingled lightning flies;
The monster-brood to which this land gives birth,
The blazing city, and the gaping earth;
All deaths, all tortures, in one pang combin'd,
Are gentle to the tempest of the mind.

But rhetoric and touching sentiments would not have made the play a success if the actors had not been capable of seizing the advantages which they were offered. Thomson was lucky in having an admirable cast. Masinissa was played by Robert Wilks, among the greatest of eighteenth-century actors, who particularly excelled in expressing passion; and Syphax was taken by John Mills, whose voice was strong enough to command the necessary jealous rage. But it was Mrs. Oldfield's performance as Sophonisba which won for the play an enthusiastic reception. This actress, who attracted Thomson's attention when he visited the theatre upon his arrival in London, was well described by Thomas Davies: 'Mrs Oldfield was, in person, tall, genteel, and well shaped; her countenance pleasing and expressive, enlivened with large speaking eyes, which, in some particular comic situations, she kept half shut, especially when she intended to give effect to some brilliant or gay thought. In sprightliness of air, and elegance of manner, she excelled all actresses; and was greatly superior in the clear, sonorous, and harmonious tones of her voice.'[1] Sophonisba offered her many chances to prove her power, and it is recorded that she spoke the line

    Not one base word of Carthage, for thy soul!

[1] Thomas Davies, *Dramatic Miscellanies*, 1785, iii, 461–2.

'with such grandeur in her action, a look so tremendous, and
in a voice so powerful, that it is said she even astonished
Wilks, her Masinissa; it is certain the audience were struck,
and expressed their feelings by the most uncommon
applause'.[1] Thomson recognized his indebtedness to her in
the preface to the published edition of the play: '*Whatever
was designed as amiable and engaging in* Masinissa *shines out in
Mr.* Wilks's *action. Mrs.* Oldfield, *in the character of* Sophonisba, *has excelled what, even in the fondness of an author, I could
either wish or imagine. The grace, dignity, and happy variety of her
action have been universally applauded, and are truly admirable.*'

The play was first performed on Saturday, 28 February
1730, and the early nights were not without incident. One
story is told about the poet's nervous solicitude for his play's
success: 'Mr. Thomson who could not but feel all the
emotions and solicitudes of a young author the first night of
his play, wanted to place himself in some obscure part of
the house, in order to see the representation to the best
advantage, without being known as the poet.—He accordingly placed himself in the upper gallery; but such was the
power of nature in him, that he could not help repeating the
parts along with the players, and would sometimes whisper
to himself, "and now such a scene is to open", by which he
was soon discovered to be the author, by some gentlemen,
who could not, on account of the great crowd, be situated in
any other part of the house.'[2] An incident occurred during
the first two performances which would have been enough
to distress any dramatist. The wit and actor, Colley Cibber,
who excelled in comedy, was always anxious to play in
tragedy, for which he mistakenly believed himself to be
peculiarly suited. He had seized on the part of Scipio for
himself during the play's rehearsals, but the audience, tired
at last of his tragic experiments, would not tolerate him in
the part. 'For two nights successively, Cibber was as much
exploded as any bad actor could be. Williams, by desire of
Wilks, made himself master of the part; but he, marching

---

[1] *Ibid.*, iii, 465–6.   [2] Cibber, *op. cit.*, v, 210.

slowly, in great military distinction, from the upper part of
the stage, and wearing the same dress as Cibber, was mistaken for him, and met with repeated hisses, joined to the
music of catcalls; but, as soon as the audience were un-
deceived, they converted their groans and hisses to loud and
long continued applause.'[1] The performances thereafter
proceeded smoothly enough.

Richard Savage told Dr. Johnson, 'that of the Prologue
to *Sophonisba*, the first part was written by Pope, who could
not be persuaded to finish it, and that the concluding lines
were added by Mallet'.[2] It is, however, very unlikely that
Pope, whose dislike for this kind of writing was pronounced,
could have been persuaded to write even the first lines of a
prologue, and, since Savage is always to be suspected, it is
more probable that Mallet composed the whole. The
Epilogue, written 'By a Friend', was spoken by Mrs.
Cibber, who was to play an important part in the success of
Thomson's later plays.

The high hopes which Thomson's friends had raised
among the public before the production of *Sophonisba* were
not disappointed. One newspaper reported after the first
performance that the 'Tragedy is allow'd, by the best
Judges, in its Poetry, to be hardly inferior to any Piece the
Stage has produc'd for many Years: The Habits and
Decorations are very magnificent, and Mrs. Oldfield's Performance surprizing'.[3] The Royal Family took an immediate interest in the play, and the *Daily Post-Boy* for 6 March
carried the news that 'Last Night his Royal Highness the
Prince of Wales, the Princesses Amelia and Carolina, went
to the Theatre Royal in Drury-lane, and saw the Tragedy of
Sophonisba'. The author's benefit, which arrived on the sixth
night, was well advertised: 'By his Royal Highness's Command,' read the announcement in the *Daily Post-Boy* for 9
March, 'The Sixth Day. For the Benefit of the AUTHOR,
by his Majesty's Company of Comedians, At the Theatre

[1] Davies, *Dramatic Miscellanies*, iii, 471.   [2] Johnson, *op. cit.*, iii, 288.
[3] *London Evening-Post*, 5–7 March 1729/30.

Royal in Drury-Lane, this present Monday, being the 9th Day of March, will be presented a new Tragedy call'd SOPHONISBA. With new Habits. Tickets are deliver'd out by Mr. Cook, the Box-Keeper; and Mr. Millar, Bookseller at Buchanan's Head.' The theatre would be crowded, and the Prince of Wales, who was later to become Thomson's patron for many years, was there to applaud the patriotic sentiments which Mrs. Oldfield so harmoniously pronounced. His visit was briefly announced in the *St. James's Evening-Post*: 'Last Night his Royal Highness the Prince and Princess Royal, and others of the Royal Family, went to the Theatre-Royal in Drury-Lane, and saw the Tragedy of *Sophonisba*.' There was, however, a greater honour still to come. The poet, probably through the intercession of Lady Hertford, received the royal permission to dedicate the play to the Queen, and on Thursday, 12 March, it was announced, that 'Yesterday Mr. Thomson was introduced to her Majesty by the Right Hon. the Earl of Grantham, and presented his Tragedy of *Sophonisba*, which is acting at the Theatre-Royal . . . and was graciously received'.[1] It was typical of the poet that he should take the opportunity the Dedication offered to celebrate his country's commercial genius: 'The notice Your MAJESTY has condescended to take of the following *Tragedy*', he began, 'emboldens me to lay it, in the humblest manner, at Your MAJESTY's Feet. And to whom can this illustrious *Carthaginian* so properly fly for protection, as to a QUEEN, who commands the hearts of a *People*, more powerful at sea than *Carthage*? more flourishing in *commerce* than those *first Merchants*? more secure against conquest? and, under a *Monarchy*, more free than a *Commonwealth* itself?'

The readers of the printed play were no less delighted than the spectators had been with its performance. Mrs. Elizabeth Rowe exclaimed in a letter to Lady Hertford: 'Mr Thomson has furnisht me with some of the most agreeable lines in the world to express my thoughts,

[1] *Daily Post-Boy*, 13 March 1729/30.

I want to be alone, to find some shade,
Some solitary gloom, there to shake off,
This weight of Life, this tumult of mankind,
And there to listen to the gentle voice,
The sigh of Peace.

'Tis a noble Tragedy, I can't help prefering it to Mr.
Addison's Cato; the language and Sentiments have all a
peculiar Grandeur. The following lines give me a very good
opinion of the author:

>   Ye misterious Powers,
> Whose ways are ever Gracious, ever Just,
> As ye think best Dispose of me;
> But whether thro' your gloomy depths I wander,
> Or in your mountains walk; give me the calm,
> The steady, smiling Soul;

In reading this, a sort of Divine Contentment Spreads on
the Mind; I seem to want nothing but to be wiser and
better.'[1] Thomas Rundle no less enthusiastically commended *Sophonisba* to Mrs. Sandys, and his judgement
reflected that of contemporary men of taste: 'I send you
Sophonisba, which I think a reasonable entertainment becoming virtue herself to behold with tears of approbation
. . . The story is a bad one, and its being true is the only
justification of it; the writing is incomparable, though the
pleasure it affords is not that popular kind, which can draw
crouded audiences . . . When it was acted, however, the
sentiments of virtue and honour were universally felt with
pleasure; and the audience was hurried, by the divine enthusiasm of nature, to honor, by the praise of their hands,
those moral beauties, which they cannot forbear loving,
even when they refuse to enjoy them . . . There are some
roughnesses in the numbers; some poetical extravagancies,
as nearly related to nonsense, as a note raised to the highest
pitch, by a fine singer, is to a scream; some aukward
odnesses of expression, which may be observed by one, who
is of a taste cold enough to attend to such minute transgres-

---

[1] Quoted Hughes, *op. cit.*; *Mod. Phil.*, xxv, 452.

sions, when his reason and fancy ought to be fired by good sense, harmony, and nature.'[1]

All the tributes to the successful dramatist, however, were not paid in prose; one at least was given the other harmony of verse. Samuel Boyse, a perverse, degenerate creature, 'of all men the farthest removed from a gentleman', who was at this time existing in Edinburgh, congratulated Thomson in some verses which he published in the following year. He asked him to

> Forgive the Muse, that with unpractis'd String,
> And fond Ambition dares thy Praise to sing;
> Pleas'd who beholds thy tow'ring *Genius* rise,
> And sees thy Merit shine in *Southern Skies*.

When Boyse arrived in London in 1733 he may have claimed Thomson's acquaintance on the strength of this panegyric, and the good-natured poet probably lent him some money, which he would learn had been squandered by Boyse in dissipation.

Sophonisba, however, did not escape uncriticized. There exists a curious letter from Mallet to Pope, written about the end of 1729, in which it is affirmed that a 'Mr. D.' publicly laid claim 'to a share in the Writing' of *Sophonisba*, at which Thomson was 'most divertingly angry'.[2] Shortly after the production of the play, an author, who signed himself with the initials 'T.B.', published a pamphlet, entitled *A Criticism of the New Sophonisba*, in which he commented with heavy wit upon all the faults he could discover in the work. He asserted that Thomson had been present at a performance of Benjamin Martyn's tragedy of *Timoleon*, which had been produced a few weeks before *Sophonisba*, and that he 'could not stifle his Envy, which burst into Expressions very unbecoming a Brother Adventurer'. Such behaviour would be very uncharacteristic of Thomson, and the remark must have been inspired by literary jealousy. The malicious pamphleteer also attributed *Sophonisba*'s success to '*Scotchmen* with tune-

---

[1] *Letters of Rundle*, 1789, ii, 107–9.
[2] Library, Chatsworth, Bakewell. I am unable to suggest the identity of 'Mr. D.'

ful Hands and merry Feet', who attended the performances
in force. This attack may have been written or inspired by
the 'Mr. D.' who claimed to have written part of the play,
but it did not spoil the play's success or smirch the poet's
reputation. The pamphlet, however, did contain one happy
parody of Thomson's occasionally bombastic style; the
exclamation 'Oh Sophonisba! Sophonisba Oh!' was altered
to 'Oh Jemmy Thomson! Jemmy Thomson Oh!', and the
joke took the town's fancy. Another story affirmed that
some wag in the pit called out the parody immediately
after the line was spoken on the stage,[1] but since Thomson
did not cut the line out of the printed edition of the play it is
more probable that the parody was begun by the pamphleteer. Henry Fielding also mocked at this unfortunate exclamation in the later editions of his farce, *The Tragedy of
Tragedies, or the History of Tom Thumb the Great*, where it
appeared as 'Oh Huncamunca, Huncamunca Oh!' Thomson was defended against the attack in another pamphlet,
entitled *A Defence of the New Sophonisba*, which appears to
have settled the controversy.

The subscription edition of *The Seasons*, which had been
promised for so long, was at last ready to be delivered to
the subscribers by the middle of this year. The following
advertisement appeared in the *Daily Post-Boy* for 4 June
1730: '*On Monday next will be ready to be delivered to the Subscribers*, *** The SEASONS, a HYMN on the Seasons, and a
POEM to the Memory of Sir *Isaac Newton. By Mr*. THOM-
SON. This Work is printed in Quarto, on a superfine Royal
Paper, with Four Prints of the Seasons, and Sir *Isaac
Newton's* Monument, all designed by Mr. *Kent*, and engraved by the best Hands. Several Additions are made to
those Pieces which have been publish'd before in Octavo,
and particularly WINTER is inlarged one half. The Copies
unsubscribed for will be sold by Mr. Millar, Bookseller
overagainst S. Clement's Church in the Strand, and Mr.

---

[1] Cibber, *op. cit.*, v, 209–10.

Brindley, Bookseller in new Bond street, at the Subscription Price of One Guinea.' It is a noble volume and the designs by William Kent, the painter, sculptor, architect, and land-scape-gardener, who was probably introduced to the poet by their mutual friend, William Aikman, are worthy of the poetry. 'Spring' is symbolized by shepherds and shepherdesses piping amorously to their flocks in the foreground of a landscape overarched by a rainbow; 'Summer' by a representation of Damon covertly watching Musidora, and her friends Sacharissa and Amoret, bathing in a stream—Kent in this case improved upon the poet by introducing a fourth naked beauty; 'Autumn' by huntsmen chasing a bounding stag across the landscape while the un-concerned peasantry continue to reap the corn, or to make love; and 'Winter' by a storm which raises a tempestuous sea and compels men and beasts to cower for shelter beneath the leafless trees.

The names of the subscribers were set out at length, and after 'THE QUEEN' there followed an impressive list of nobility and men of letters. The Duke of Argyll, the Duke of Beaufort, the Earl of Burlington—he was the patron of Kent and therefore took five copies—Lord Bolingbroke, the Earl of Chesterfield, the Duke of Hamilton, the Duke of Kent, the Earl of Oxford, the Duke of Roxborough, and the Earl of Westmorland were only some of the nobility who subscribed. William Aikman, John Arbuthnot, Alex-ander Pope—who took three copies—Allan Ramsay, William Somerville, Richard Savage, and Edward Young were among the artists and men of letters who subscribed. There were altogether three hundred and eighty-seven sub-scribers, and they took between them four hundred and fifty-six copies—Bubb Dodington, with typical ostentation, took twenty, and the Lord Provost of Edinburgh, who was obviously proud of his fellow-citizen, took half that num-ber. There were longer subscription lists to other contem-porary publications, but few in which so many men of birth or genius were brought together. Thomson's conscientious canvassing had clearly proved successful.

Autumn was first published in this volume, but later in the month it was printed separately as an octavo pamphlet. It was dedicated to the new Speaker of the House of Commons, Arthur Onslow, whom the poet's Muse addressed in this fashion:

> Thy noble cares she knows,
> The patriot-virtues that distend thy thought,
> Spread on thy front, and in thy conduct glow;
> While listening senates hang upon thy tongue,
> Devolving thro' the maze of eloquence
> A rowl of periods, sweeter than her song.

The Seasons, the *Hymn on the Seasons*, the *Poem to the Memory of Sir Isaac Newton*, and *Britannia* were also collected in an octavo volume and sold at seven shillings. This edition, which was advertised as published in August 1730, was decorated '*With a beautiful new Set of Cuts design'd by the famous* PICART',[1] drawn from 'Marble Statues in the Garden of Versailles 7 foot high', which, representing each season in the character of a single figure, made simple but impressive frontispieces to the poems.

It is difficult to discover exactly how much profit the poet made from his works while he retained the copyright; according to one account he made about a thousand guineas. It would appear that he sold *Spring* and *Sophonisba* to Andrew Millar on 16 January 1729 for one hundred and thirty-seven pounds and ten shillings; and that he sold the rest of *The Seasons*, *Britannia*, *A Poem Sacred to the Memory of Newton*, and an *Essay on Descriptive Poetry*, which was never published, to John Millan, on 18 July of the same year, for one hundred guineas. Millar bought the copyrights in Millan's possession on 16 June 1738 for the original price which Millan had paid to the poet. If these figures are correct, and the proceeds arising from the subscription must be added to the moneys which the poet received, Thomson

---

[1] *London Evening-Post*, 1–4 August 1730.

was reasonably remunerated by both the public and his publishers.[1]

While these editions of *The Seasons* were appearing, Thomson entered into an arrangement which was to lead to a great change in his fortunes. Thomas Rundle had persuaded his intimate friend Charles Talbot, the Solicitor-General, to ask Thomson to accompany his son, Charles Richard Talbot, on a Continental tour, and Thomson, who wished for nothing more than to travel abroad, gladly accepted this offer. He was not a tutor but a companion to the young man, and he was given a very generous allowance. William Aikman wrote to Sir John Clerk on 18 November 1730 to tell him about Thomson's appointment: 'Thomson is gone abroad with M[r] Talbot the Solicitor General's son and has 200£ per year allowed him for attending him only as a companion.'[2] Thomson announced his imminent departure for the Continent in a letter of 17 October to his friend Valentine Munbee, and it is an admirable picture of his character at this time.

'Dear Sir,
'I have been long in your debt, and am indeed afraid that I shall never get out of it. Your civilities to me dwell upon my mind in a very agreeable manner, and I heartily wish I could have added to their number by passing some part of the season with you according to your kind Invitation. Mr. Upton and I much desired, and often designed it, but what

---

[1] Andrew Millar brought an action against another bookseller in 1769 for pirating *The Seasons*, and the jury found in their special verdict that the work was 'at first published and printed by James Thomson for his own use and benefit at several times between the beginning of the year 1727 and 1729', and that Andrew Millar, 'in the year 1729, purchased this work called the Seasons for a valuable consideration, of James Thomson the author and proprietor'. A note to the account of this case added that Thomson 'reaped about a thousand guineas profit while the work was his own property; he sold it in 1729 to Millar for 160 pounds'. *Speeches and Arguments of the Court of King's Bench . . . in the cause Millar against Taylor*, 1771; quoted Morel, *op. cit.*, pp. 47 and *n.* 2, 48 *n.* 1. Nicolas published in the *Works of Thomson*, 1847, i, cx *n.*, the original documents by which Thomson assigned his rights in *The Seasons* and other poems in 1729 to Millar and Millan for £137 10*s.* 0*d.* and £105 respectively. These documents were also examined by Peter Cunningham, who vouched for their authenticity; see *Works of Thomson*, ed. Nicolas, revised by Cunningham, 1862, i, cxxiii.

[2] *Clerk of Penicuik Papers*, Register House, Edinburgh.

prevented him I know not, and what hindered me I cannot exactly tell. It was, it seems, predestinated that I should not be so happy. For him, who denies predestination, he must own it to be the fault of his free-will, or, if he pleases, of his platonic passion and attachment to some Ladies here in town. Now he innocently luxuriates amidst the Fair and Quadrille at Bath, which was lately to me for a few days the Limbo of vanity. The truth is I have been pretty much confined by studying of french and some other things proper for travelling. I travell along with Mʳ Talbot the solicitor's son, and we propose to set out for Paris in about ten days hence. When we are fixed for some time at any place I shall be very glad to exchange a letter with you and sustain an acquaintance which tho' but young yet is not a little valuable to me.

'All is as dull here as wit had never been; and the great platonic year predicted by the Dunciad in the following six fine lines, the millenium of dullness seems to be fast approaching.

> As one by one, at dread Medea's strain,
> The sickening stars fade off th' etherial plain;
> As Argus' eyes, by Hermes' wand opprest,
> Clos'd one by one to everlasting rest:
> So at her felt approach and secret might,
> Art after art goes out, and all is night.

Happy he who can comfort himself amidst this general night; and in some rural retirement, by his own intellectual fire and candle as well as natural, may cultivate the muses, inlarge his internal views, harmonize his passions, and let his heart hear the voice of peace and nature. As you can both relish and command this happiness it must be your's; and that it may always continue so is the sincere wish of,

'Dear Sir,

'Your most affectionate

'humble servant,

'James Thomson.'[1]

---

[1] Quoted Alan Dugald McKillop, *Background of Thomson's Seasons*, 1942, pp.177–8.

If he paused after signing his name to this letter to consider the past, he must have felt reasonably content. Only five years earlier he had arrived in London friendless and unknown; yet in the brief interval between his arrival and his departure for the Continent, he had written a great and appreciated poem, had produced a successful tragedy, which augured well for his future as a dramatist, and had become the friend of every important man of letters in contemporary England. There are few poets who have enjoyed a similar success. He must have set out on his travels at the beginning of November with a light and eager heart.

H

CHAPTER V

THE SEASONS

Come, Inspiration! from thy hermit seat
By mortal seldom found.

AT the close of the eighteenth century, fifty years after
James Thomson's death, two young men of genius
passed some days of the pleasant summer in walking along
the coast of North Devon. The inspired conversation of the
one, S. T. Coleridge, was remembered and recorded by the
other, William Hazlitt. Once they stopped at an obscure
country alehouse, and Coleridge, picking up a little worn-
out copy of *The Seasons* which lay in the parlour, exclaimed,
'*That* is true fame!' This simple remark is worth most of
the criticism that has ever been written on *The Seasons*. It lays
bare at once the secret of Thomson's greatness. Other poets
have been widely read; other poets have decisively affected
the progress of poetry; but no other poet has been so taken
to the nation's heart. *The Seasons* was once to be found in
every household. The alehouses had a duodecimo or octavo
from the press of the local printer, and another replaced it
when it was worn out by the casual fingering of chance
travellers; poor families had a similar edition ranged on the
kitchen shelf beside the Bible and *The Pilgrim's Progress*, and
its verses were the first that many children read; the middle
classes had elaborately gilt and bound editions, illustrated
by some popular and sentimental artist, a Stothard or a
Westall, lying upon a table in their front-rooms; and the
noble libraries boasted a royal quarto, which stood in impressive and unread state among the other furniture. A
glance through any catalogue will show that it is impossible to exaggerate the popularity of *The Seasons*. A glance
through any book of poetry written after its publication

will show that every considerable poet thereafter was affected either directly or indirectly by this extraordinary work. '*That* is true fame!' Coleridge was not speaking for effect; he was uttering a self-evident truth.

Why did *The Seasons* attain to such an unrivalled popularity? Why did it appeal from the first to all classes and conditions of men? Dr. Johnson has briefly answered this question: 'The reader of *The Seasons* wonders that he never saw before what Thomson shews him, and that he never yet has felt what Thomson impresses'.[1] Thomson chose as his theme Nature in all its variety, and he thus made common ground at once with his readers. The countryside lay only twenty minutes' walk away from Charing Cross—less from the centre of any other large town —and when they strolled that distance on an autumn afternoon or a spring morning, his readers would see spread out before them in all their plenitude those scenes which the poet had so accurately and felicitously described. His poetry was immediately familiar to them because it was concerned with what they had known but disregarded for so long. They would read it, however, not only with interest, but with excitement, because such a theme had never been attempted before in English verse. As they turned over the pages of *Winter*, a poem by an entirely unknown poet, they would recognize with pleasure the truth and beauty of its descriptions, and be unable to withhold their praise from such passages as this one upon the frost:

> This of the wintry Season is the Prime;
> Pure are the Days, and lustrous are the Nights,
> Brighten'd with starry Worlds, till then unseen.
> Mean while, the Orient, darkly red, breathes forth
> An Icy Gale, that, in its mid Career,
> Arrests the bickering Stream. The nightly Sky,
> And all her glowing Constellations pour
> Their rigid Influence down: It freezes on
> Till Morn, late-rising, o'er the drooping World,
> Lifts her pale Eye, unjoyous: then appears

[1] Johnson, *op. cit.*, iii, 299.

> The various Labour of the silent Night,
> The pendent Isicle, the Frost-Work fair,
> Where various Figures rise, the crusted Snow,
> Tho' white, made whiter by the shining North.

They were as familiar with this scene as they were with time, but until Thomson touched it, it was 'till then unseen'.

Thomson was the first modern poet to make Nature his theme. Earlier poets of course had not disregarded Nature; they had all delighted in its beauty; and the pastoral tradition can be exactly traced from Theocritus and Virgil down to Thomson. Chaucer, Spenser, Shakespeare, and Milton had observed and described its variety—even to mention this is to labour the obvious—and Thomson's contemporaries, Alexander Pope, Ambrose Philips, and John Gay, had happily used the countryside as a background for their pastorals. But earlier poets had made Nature subsidiary to humanity; it was the inferior support upon which the moral dramas with which they were concerned were played; and they only introduced it to give point and substance to imagery whose purpose it was to disclose human nature. The reader of Milton's famous and sublime description of Eden was intended by the poet to understand it as the physical reflection of a moral purity, and not to delight in it for its own sake. When the later poets, Thomson's contemporaries, introduced Nature, they arranged it carefully to provide a backcloth to throw into relief the insubstantial figures of the shepherds and shepherdesses who winsomely paraded rustic loves and sorrows in their verse. A tree, a cluster of roses, a sweet gale, and a swelling hill were but traditional properties which they could introduce where they willed, and although they were often admirably employed and prettily described, they were too obviously divorced from the reality. When Ambrose Philips, whose knowledge of British fauna was uncertain, let loose wolves in his pastorals—a mistake at which Pope rightly sneered—he only made ridiculous what had always been unnatural. Thomson, however, described Nature for its own sake. He shifted the interest of poetry from mankind to it, and lightened his descriptions of any artificiality.

He did not of course introduce this change alone; every poet is in accord with the spirit of his age; and some of his contemporaries had earlier and hesitantly attempted what he accomplished. Samuel Croxall, a forgotten but once popular poet, clearly influenced Thomson, and his work may be quoted to illustrate the general but indefinite interest which had been taken in Nature poetry before *The Seasons* was written. Croxall had published in 1715 a poem entitled *The Vision* in which this passage occurred:

> On various themes I spent the tedious night,
> And sleepless saw the morn's new dawning light;
> Then rose, and issueing forth with early day,
> Down to the woodland glade I bent my way;
> Where gentle Mole rolls on his silent streams,
> Through Surrian dales to meet the silver Thames.
> Here in the covert of a lonely grove
> Retired alike for poetry or love,
> Pensive beneath a spreading oak I stood,
> That veil'd the hollow channel of the flood;
> Along whose shelving banks the violet blue
> And primrose pale in lovely mixture grew.
> High over-arch'd the bloomy woodbine hung,
> The gaudy Goldfinch from the Maple sung;
> The little warbling minstrel of the shade
> To the gay morn her due devotion paid;
> Next the soft Linnet echoing to the Thrush
> With carols filled the smelling briar bush;
> While Philomel attuned her artless throat,
> And from the hawthorn breathed a trilling note.
> Indulgent nature smiled in every part,
> And fill'd with joy unknown my ravish'd heart. . . .
> Here every flower that Nature's pencil draws
> In various kinds a bright enamel rose:
> The silver dazy streak'd with ruddy light,
> The yellow cowslip, and the snow-drop white;
> The fragrant hyacinth, Apollo's flower,
> The fresh Narciss, that love the streamy shore.
> There crowfeet did their purple bells unfold,
> And the smooth king-cup shone with leaves of gold.

The imagery of these lines is as worn as the nap of ancient velvet, but their spirit is still fresh enough to show that Croxall deeply felt the nature which he has described; and their interest is that they illustrate a more direct approach to Nature than that of his better-known contemporaries. Thomson was familiar with Croxall's works. Croxall published in 1720 a poem, taken from the Song of Solomon and entitled *The Fair Circassian*, which became very popular and was reprinted a number of times. He appended some verses to this poem entitled 'On Florinda seen Bathing', and their story was retold by Thomson in *Summer* as the tale of Damon and Musidora. Damon, like Croxall's hero, covertly watches his mistress and her friends bathing naked in a stream, and in the original version of the tale he drew from this scene

> Such draughts of love and beauty to the soul,
> As put his harsh philosophy to flight.

Croxall's more natural hero, however, to quench his impulsive and amorous flame, dived into the water and put the nymphs to flight.

The introduction of this notorious tale of Damon and Musidora points out another element in *The Seasons* which contributed not a little to its success. A continued description of Nature would quickly have become tedious, and to relieve his readers and to make the description more effective, Thomson introduced into the poem short stories, sentimental anecdotes, and moral reflections. Thomas Rundle in a letter to Mrs. Barbara Sandys, admirably explained the intention of these incidental verses: 'The poet describes the various scenes of the year with all its contrast of landskip agreeably; and now and then inserts a digression of a short story, which relieves from the uniformity of the prospect, and seems as figures in the works of that sort of painters, to give life and action to what is in itself merely inanimate; the rocks, and groves, and streams, are indeed the principal and intended part of the performance. But those other beauties hinder the eye from being fatigued, and heighten and recommend the parts which are first and chief in designs of this nature.'[1] Rundle pronounced this opinion so authoritatively that he must have been repeating the poet's own explanation of his purpose. The perennial interest taken in these stories by successive generations of readers is proved by Wordsworth's remark, that all well-thumbed copies of *The Seasons* opened at the slightly salacious tale of Damon and Musidora. They are too insipid and sentimental for our taste, but they were fresh and surprising revelations of the human heart to Thomson's contemporaries. Nor has their lustre yet been entirely worn away; the unsophisticated reader may still feel a pang for the fate of the peasant lost in the winter snows, who at last, tired out, sinks down

> Beneath the shelter of the shapeless drift,
> Thinking o'er all the bitterness of death,
> Mix'd with the tender anguish nature shoots
> Thro' the wrung bosom of the dying man,
> His wife, his children, and his friends unseen.

Moreover, the poet sometimes rose in these tales to true poetry, before which the sentimentality melted away; the description of the shipwrecked mariner is one example of this occasional power:

> Unhappy he! who from the first of joys,
> Society, cut off, is left alone
> Amid this world of death. Ceaseless he sits,
> Sad on the jutting eminence, and views
> The rowling main, that ever toils below;
> Still fondly forming in the farthest verge,
> Where the round ether mixes with the wave,
> Ships, dim-discover'd, dropping from the clouds.
> At evening, to the setting sun he turns
> A mournful eye, and down his dying heart
> Sinks helpless; while the wonted roar is up,
> And hiss continual thro' the tedious night.

The illustrators of the expensive editions of *The Seasons* of

[1] *Letters of Rundle,* 1789, ii, 77–8.

course took the opportunity which these tales offered them to show their skill, and susceptible hearts could not remain unimpressed by the reiterated emotions begun by the poet and continued by them.

The sentimental reflections with which the poem is richly strewn are, however, of much greater interest than the stories. The stories could be skipped but the reflections are so embedded in the verse that no reader could hope to escape their persuasive influence. Thomson continually aimed to rouse 'the tender emotions', and he infused both mankind and Nature with sentiment. He wished to liberate the heart from the harsh imposition of reason and custom which rendered impotent the reviving springs of spontaneous feeling. Marriage, at this time a matter largely of commerce and convenience, naturally received his attention, and he praised that union which is not an inhuman legal bond

> but harmony itself,
> Attuning all their passions into love;
> Where friendship full-exerts his softest power,
> Perfect esteem enliven'd by desire
> Ineffable, and sympathy of soul,
> Thought meeting thought, and will preventing will,
> With boundless confidence; for nought but love
> Can answer love, and render bliss secure.

This struck home at once to the bosoms and businesses of men, and it helped forward the movement which has changed the whole conception of marriage. Nor did he only plead for the love-sick heart; he was even more insistent in his defence of the persecuted animal kingdom. He denounced the barbarity of blood sports, and exclaimed with fervour:

> Poor is the triumph o'er the timid Hare!
> Shook from the corn, and now to some lone seat
> Retir'd: the rushy fen; the ragged furze,
> Stretch'd o'er the stony heath; the stubble chapt;
> The thistly lawn; the thick, intangled broom;
> Of the same friendly hue, the wither'd fern;
> The fallow ground laid open to the sun,
> Concoctive; and the nodding sandy bank,

Hung o'er the mazes of the mountain-brook.
Vain is her best precaution; tho' she sits
By Nature rais'd to take th' horizon in;
And head couch'd close betwixt her hairy feet,
In act to spring away. The scented dew
Betrays her early labyrinth; and deep,
In scatter'd, sullen openings, far behind,
With every breeze she hears the coming storm.
But nearer, and more frequent, as it loads
The sighing gale, she springs amaz'd, and all
The savage soul of game is up at once:
The pack full-opening, various; the shrill horn,
Resounding from the hills; the neighing steed,
Wild for the chace; and the loud hunter's shout;
O'er a weak, harmless, flying creature, all
Mix'd in mad tumult, and discordant joy.

A number of Acts, passed in obedience to the public conscience, have mitigated the cruelty which was once a commonplace in English life, and Thomson's attitude now
appears to be that of any normal, civilized person; but
Thomson was far in advance of his time, and if we have
adopted his opinions it is the best tribute to the sincerity
and success of his missionary zeal. Had Shelley wished to
illustrate his dictum, that poets are the unacknowledged
legislators of mankind, he could not have chosen a better
example than Thomson's crusade against cruelty. His appeal
on behalf of the timid hare, expressed as it was in fine and
moving verse, was irresistible; his lonely voice was quickly
lost in a chorus which took up his strain.

Thomson was a man of feeling, a sentimentalist, long
before those terms were invented and generally adopted,
and it is hardly surprising that his most ardent readers were
first and last to be found among women. An early critic
recognized this, and, discussing the welcome afforded to
Winter and *Summer*, wrote: 'On this Occasion, I remarked,
with a particular Pleasure, that these Poems were very
favourably received by many of the *Fair Sex*. It is at
once an Instance of their right Discernment, and Relish for
Writings, which recommend and adorn Morality. But, to do

them Justice, they commonly discover a more exquisite Taste, and a finer Humanity, in their Judgments on polite Learning, than the Men do.'[1] A century later, James Northcote remarked sarcastically: 'For boarding-school girls Thomson's Seasons has an immense attraction, though I never could read it.' These two opinions clearly show the distance which English sensibility had travelled in a hundred years. If the early critic used the feminine interest as a reason to praise the poet, and Northcote used it to condemn him, that was because in the intervening time Thomson's originally fresh and urgent sentimentality had become, through long use by imitators and adapters, jaded and hackneyed.

The sentiments which have so far been reviewed affected the social behaviour of mankind, but there was in his work a deeper strain of emotion which invigorated and profoundly influenced English thought and sensibility. His theme was Nature, but he could not rest content to describe it objectively. Its beauty prompted his imagination to contemplate it philosophically and to appreciate it emotionally. It was not to him, as it was apparently to Rundle, 'merely inanimate'; it was a source of noble and holy emotions, and an illustration of divine power and goodness; and when he walked the autumn fields, his whole nature responded to what he saw:

> Mean-time, light-shadowing all, a sober calm
> Fleeces unbounded ether; whose least wave
> Stands tremulous, uncertain where to turn
> The gentle current: while illumin'd wide,
> The dewy-skirted clouds imbibe the sun,
> And thro' their lucid veil his temper'd force
> Shed o'er the peaceful world. Then is the time,
> For those whom Wisdom, and whom Nature charm,
> To steal themselves from the degenerate crowd,
> And soar above this little scene of things;
> To tread low-thoughted vice beneath their feet;
> To soothe the throbbing passions into peace;
> And woo lone *Quiet* in her silent walks.

[1] *Whitehall Evening-Post*, 17–19 March 1727/8.

This vein of feeling made a practical critic write of the poet's 'good heart', and Mrs. Rowe exclaim enthusiastically: 'In reading this a sort of Divine Contentment spreads on the Mind; I seem to want nothing but to be wiser and better.' The poet's contemporaries elevated reason above all other faculties but they also wished at times to escape from its rigid dictatorship. Thomson adapted Lord Shaftesbury's deistic and benevolent philosophy to the purposes of poetry and thereby began, under the guise of reason, an attack upon reason's dominance which led quickly to its over-throw and to the enthronement of the imagination. Thomson won over his contemporaries to his view and encouraged the attitude towards Nature which, widening and deepening, reached the full in Wordsworth's poetry. He moved the emphasis from reason to emotion, and when Keats cried, 'Oh! for a life of sensations rather than of thoughts', he was saying loudly what Thomson had whispered in the autumn fields.

The Seasons, however, is not confined in its scope to natural description and sentiment. Thomson's contemporaries expected the poet to instruct as well as to entertain them, and verse was used as commonly as prose for this purpose. Alexander Pope attempted in *An Essay on Man* to lay down a philosophy, and Soame Jenyns, in *The Art of Dancing*, to teach the latest steps; and both poems were received without surprise. Thomson followed this fashion and included in his poem some elementary lessons in physics and geography. A problem which puzzled his contemporaries was, how are the rivers continually supplied? The poet in *Autumn* turned into verse the answer given in the best text-books;[1] the sea-water is enticed by the sandy strata to the mountains' summits, and, purified on its upward passage, descends again to the sea:

> But sure 'tis no weak, variable cause,
> That keeps at once ten thousand thousand floods,
> Wide-wandering o'er the world, so fresh, and clear,

[1] See McKillop, *op. cit.*, pp. 77–88.

For ever flowing, and for ever full.
And thus some sages, deep-exploring, teach:
That, where the hoarse, innumerable wave,
Eternal, lashes the resounding shore;
Suck'd through the sandy *Stratum*, every way,
The waters with the sandy *Stratum* rise;
Amid whose angles infinitely strain'd,
They leave each saline particle behind,
And clear, and sweeten, as they soak along.
Nor stops the restless fluid, mounting still,
Tho' here and there in lowly plains it springs,
But to the mountain courted by the sand,
That leads it darkling on in faithful maze,
Far from the parent-main, it boils again
Fresh into day; and all the glittering hill
Is bright with spouting rills.

The geographical digressions in *Summer*, fruit of the time spent among the 'curious and compleat Apparatus for giving COURSES of GEOGRAPHY' at the Academy in Little Tower Street, were written in a similar vein. They could have been dull padding to fill out the poem, but the poet so infused them with his imagination that they rise above a recapitulation of facts to become evocative interpretations of foreign lands. He described the rigours of the African deserts and continued:

Nor stop the Terrors of these Regions here.
Commission'd Demons oft, Angels of Wrath,
Let loose the raging Elements. Breath'd hot,
From all the boundless Furnace of the Sky,
And the wide glittering Waste of burning Sand,
A suffocating Wind the Pilgrim smites
With instant Death. Patient of Thirst and Toil,
Son of the Desart! even the Camel feels,
Shot thro' his wither'd Heart, the fiery Blast.
Or from the black-red Ether, bursting broad,
Sallies the sudden Whirlwind. Strait the Sands,
Commov'd around, in gathering Eddies play:
Nearer and nearer still they darkening come;
Till with the general all-involving Storm
Swept up, the whole continuous Wilds arise;
And by their noonday Fount dejected thrown,

Or sunk at Night in sad disastrous Sleep,
Beneath descending Hills, the Caravan
Is buried deep. In *Cairo's* crouded Streets,
Th' impatient Merchant, wondering, waits in vain,
And *Mecca* saddens at the long Delay.

This skilful and convincing use of travel literature more than anticipates Coleridge's use of it in *The Ancient Mariner*; it pointed out to the later Romantic poets how the imagination could move at large beyond the narrow bounds of the familiar world.

Thomson's intellectual curiosity, which inspired these digressions, is to be seen even more clearly in his ready response to Newtonianism. His possible friendship with Sir Isaac Newton and the noble poem upon his death have already been discussed, but the scientist's influence was not confined to that particular work; it informed either obviously or subtly a great part of *The Seasons*. Although Newton himself drew no philosophic conclusions from his discoveries, his contemporaries seized upon them to illustrate the goodness and omnipotence of God, and it was inevitable that a poet who chose to write about Nature would study them closely. The influence of Newton upon Thomson's imagination was apparent to his contemporaries, and Thomas Rundle wrote: 'Nature and its explainer, and its author are his themes.'[1] The ordered immensity of the universe which Newton had disclosed widened Thomson's imaginative scope until it rose superior to this world as it strained to sing the Creator's praise:

Man marks *Thee* not, marks not the mighty hand,
That, ever-busy, wheels the silent spheres.

Newton's discoveries affected not only the scope and direction of his thought but the nature of his imagery. They made him, and his fellow poets, regard and describe Nature and, in particular, light, more nicely. Newton had shown in his *Opticks* that the white blaze of light

[1] *Letters of Rundle*, 1789, ii, 77.

was broken by the prism into the primary colours which
united to make its uniform body, and poets were quick
to see that this discovery could be used to heighten their
descriptions of light. Thomson was beforehand in his understanding of its possibilities, and many images which he
evolved from it are of remarkable complexity and beauty.
He imagined that the barren rock, acting like the prism,
broke the sunlight into its primary colours, which became
precious stones; and as these colours can be reunited to
make the original whiteness, he made the opal, a stone which
contains all the colours, duplicate within the rock the sun-
light without:

> Th' unfruitful rock itself impregn'd by thee,
> In dark retirement, forms the lucid stone;
> Collected light, compact; that polish'd bright,
> And all its native lustre let abroad,
> Shines proudly on the bosoms of the fair.
>
> At thee the ruby lights his deepening glow,
> A bleeding radiance, grateful to the view.
> From thee the saphire, solid aether, takes
> His hue cerulean; and, of evening tinct,
> The purple-streaming amethyst is thine.
> With thy own smile the yellow topaz burns.
> Nor deeper verdure dies the robe of Spring,
> When first she gives it to the southern gale,
> Than the green emerald shows. But, all combin'd,
> Thick thro' the whitening opal play thy beams;
> Or, flying several from its surface, form
> A trembling variance of revolving hues,
> As the site varies in the gazer's hand.

Thomson's influence on art was only less important than
on poetry. His imagination was primarily pictorial. His boyhood among the Borders had trained him to see Nature as
landscape, and whether the scenery in his poems was
English or foreign, known or imaginary, it was deliberately
arranged to conform to his early vision. His descriptions are
built up as formally as though they were intended to be
transferred on to canvas. His broad descriptions of land-

scape and his meticulous observation of all effects of light
and shade appealed to painters, and it would be a long task
to catalogue the pictures whose titles had appended to them
quotations from *The Seasons*. Two names, however, must be
mentioned. John Constable often used Thomson's verses to
describe his paintings, and his famous work *The Cornfield*
was accompanied in the Academy Catalogue of 1826 with
these lines from *Summer*:

> A fresher gale
> Begins to wave the woods and stir the stream,
> Sweeping with shadowy gusts the fields of corn.

J. M. W. Turner's great painting *Buttermere with a Rainbow*,
an early work of 1797–8, was also accompanied in the
Academy Catalogue with a quotation from *The Seasons*,
describing and explaining the appearance of a rainbow,
'which specifically anticipates the theories of impression-
ism'.[1]

The reason for the popularity of *The Seasons* is, indeed,
easily discovered. It held within its pages a multitude of
different subjects, each with their attendant sentiments,
which appealed to many different kinds of readers. A girl
could enjoy the mawkish story of Damon and Musidora, or
of Palemon and Lavinia; a sensitive woman, the refined
emotion raised by the contemplation of Nature and its
Creator; the curious man, the geographical and physical
digressions; the imaginative man, the philosophical dis-
quisitions; and all could delight in the fine poetry in which
these several themes were presented. *The Seasons* is as rich
and diversified as the Nature it describes.

Coleridge, after he had remarked, '*That* is true fame!',
continued to say that 'Thomson was a great poet, rather
than a good one; his style was as meretricious as his thoughts
were natural'. It has been customary to condemn Thomson's style; Wordsworth thought it 'vicious', and Tenny-
son 'hated it like poison'; and it is usually dismissed

---

[1] Kenneth Clark, *Landscape into Art*, 1949, p. 104.

as a crude pastiche of Milton's sonorous numbers. Dr. Johnson, however, saw long ago that he was not a mere imitator of the earlier poet: 'As a writer he is entitled to one praise of the highest kind,' he wrote; 'his mode of thinking and of expressing his thoughts is original. His blank verse is no more the blank verse of Milton or of any other poet than the rhymes of Prior are the rhymes of Cowley. His numbers, his pauses, his diction, are of his own growth, without transcription, without imitation. He thinks in a peculiar train, and he thinks always as a man of genius.'[1] It was, of course, impossible that there should be no likeness to Milton's blank verse in Thomson's; a great poet casts his shadow far forward, and those who live within it cannot be unaffected by it; but this likeness is superficial rather than real, and may be explained by reference to the state of literature in Scotland when Thomson began to write. Milton was not generally admired until Joseph Addison wrote his famous papers on him in *The Spectator*, which showed the majesty of his verse and the sublimity of his imagination: and because *The Spectator* was the favourite reading of those young Scotsmen who were attempting to write in English, Thomson must have been influenced by Addison's exposition. There was, moreover, another force at work which would make him admire and copy Milton. Thomson and his contemporaries spoke broad Scots, the foundation of their early education was Latin, and when they came to learn English, to them a foreign tongue, they would naturally be more at ease with the language when it most resembled Latin. The constructions and vocabulary of Milton's verse closely copy the classical poets, and Thomson would find Milton for this reason both easier to understand than the colloquial English poets, and, because he had been schooled to revere the ancients, more admirable. But even had he been unfamiliar with Milton, there would have been a resemblance between their verse, for he would have been prompted by his education to treat English, as Milton did, as though it were Latin.

[1] Johnson, *op. cit.*, iii, 298.

It is therefore surprising not that Thomson's blank verse should resemble Milton's, but that it should resemble it so little.

Thomson's adoption of blank verse is another proof of his originality. There had been little poetry written in blank verse after Milton's death; John Philips' two imitations of Milton, *Cyder* and *The Splendid Shilling*, are exceptions to this generalization; and rhyme was firmly established as the fashionable medium. But Thomson disregarded the fashion, and he was justified by the welcome which was accorded to his use of blank verse. The anonymous critic in the *Whitehall Evening-Post*, who prepared the public to expect *Spring*, praised him for venturing 'to lay aside the favourite Mode of writing in Rhyme'; and a later critic in the *London Journal* for 11 May 1728 made the same point: both Thomson and James Ralph—an imitator of Thomson's style—'seem to have been very happy in their Choice of *blank Verse*', he wrote; 'for the Mind is frequently and insensibly misled to a Pause by smooth and harmonious Couplets, whereby the Design of the Poet is interrupted, and the Connexion broke; but in this kind of Poetry we have all the Pleasures of Musick and Painting, and the Advantage of Prose in following the Thread of a Description uninterruptedly to the End of the Period'. His blank verse, however, was not admired by all his contemporaries, and James Bramston satirized in his poem *The Man of Taste*, published in 1733, those critics who openly decried it:

> Verse without rhyme, I never could endure,
> Uncouth in numbers, and in sense obscure.
> To him as Nature, when he ceas'd to see,
> Milton's a universal blank to me.
> Confirm'd and settled by the nation's voice,
> Rhyme is the poet's pride, and people's choice.
> Always upheld by national support,
> Of market, university, and court:
> Thomson, write blank; but know that for that reason,
> These lines shall live when thine are out of season.
> Rhyme binds and beautifies the poet's lays,
> As London ladies owe their shapes to stays.

I

Thomson's verse is, despite all the earlier criticism, always harmonious and sometimes sonorous, and distinguished by a peculiar quality of matured sweetness. It is 'of his own growth' and never to be mistaken for that of any other poet. But his diction cannot be so easily defended. When *The Seasons* was first written, he had not learnt to use English colloquially, and his education inclined him to choose those words which had a Latin root; there is consequently a cloudiness or uncertainty in his language which obscures the thought. While he described a natural scene, his diction was comparatively simple, appropriate, and unaffected, but when he attempted a higher strain it tended to degenerate into floridity and formlessness. This may be seen by comparing the two following quotations from *Spring*. He is describing in the first the welcome arrival of the expected showers:

> The North-east spends his rage, and now shut up
> Within his iron caves, th' effusive South
> Warms the wide air, and o'er the void of heaven
> Breaths the big clouds with vernal showers distent.
> At first a dusky wreath they seem to rise,
> Scarce staining ether; but by fast degrees,
> In heaps on heaps, the doubling vapour sails
> Along the loaded sky, and mingling thick
> Sits on th' horizon round a settled gloom.
> Not such as wintry storms on mortals shed,
> Oppressing life, but lovely, gentle, kind,
> And full of every hope, and every joy,
> The wish of nature. Gradual sinks the breeze
> Into a perfect calm; that not a breath
> Is heard to quiver thro' the closing woods,
> Or rustling turn the many-twinkling leaves
> Of aspin tall. Th' uncurling floods, diffus'd
> In glassy breadth, seem thro' delusive lapse
> Forgetful of their course. 'Tis silence all,
> And pleasing expectation.

In the second quotation he is praising the Divinity for commanding the annual revival of sap, and the foreign and involved diction make it a typical example of Thomson at his worst:

By THEE, the various vegetative tribes,
Wrapt in a filmy net, and clad with leaves,
Draw the live ether, and imbibe the dew.
By THEE dispos'd into congenial soils,
Stands each attractive plant, and sucks, and swells
The juicy tide; a twining mass of tubes.
At THY command, the vernal sun awakes
The torpid sap, detruded to the root
By wintry winds, that now, in fluent dance,
And lively fermentation, mounting, spreads
All this innumerous-colour'd scene of things.

Thomas Rundle laid his finger on the poet's most obvious fault when he wrote that his language was strong 'but inaccurate'. It was inaccurate because he was not writing in his mother tongue.

The Seasons, however, is vitiated as a poem by one fault inherent in the subject. Pope, talking about The Seasons, said that, 'It is a great fault, in descriptive poetry, to describe everything'.[1] Dr. Johnson also charged the poem with this fault but at the same time offered an excuse for it: 'The great defect of The Seasons is want of method; but for this I know not that there was any remedy. Of many appearances subsisting all at once, no rule can be given why one should be mentioned before another; yet the memory wants the help of order, and the curiosity is not excited by suspense and expectation.'[2] The Seasons is in fact a collection of many poems. It is a poetic repository into which Thomson tumbled at haphazard a host of subjects which were only slightly connected to each other by the style. The reader is consequently bewildered by their rapid and unordered succession, and his memory cannot retain any distinct impression of the whole poem. He is surfeited by its plenty, and at last chooses to read only those passages to which he is particularly attached. Thomson's remarkable sensibility was entirely ungoverned by his critical faculty; what he felt deeply, he had to describe, and what he described, he could not omit; and this defect is the source of the poem's primary weakness.

---

[1] Quoted Spence, *op. cit.*, p. 105.   [2] Johnson, *op. cit.*, iii, 299–300.

Despite the general and particular faults, *The Seasons* is a great if not a good poem, and it would be impossible to exaggerate its influence on English poetry. It is very difficult to imagine the impact of an original work upon a poet's contemporaries, but if we could hear as though for the first time these lines from *Autumn*, we should realize how profoundly original the poet was:

> The pale, descending year, yet pleasing still,
> A gentler mood inspires; for now the leaf
> Incessant rustles from the mournful grove,
> Oft startling such as, studious, walk below,
> And slowly circles thro' the waving air.
> But should a quicker breeze amid the boughs
> Sob, o'er the sky the leafy ruin streams;
> Till choak'd, and matt'd with the dreary shower,
> The forest-walks, at every rising gale,
> Roll wide the wither'd waste, and whistle bleak.
> Fled is the blasted verdure of the fields;
> And, shrunk into their beds, the flowery race
> Their sunny robes resign. Even what remain'd
> Of bolder fruits falls from the naked tree;
> And woods, fields, gardens, orchards, all around
> The desolated prospect thrills the soul.

CHAPTER VI

THE GRAND TOUR

The Muse gay roved the glad Hesperian round,
And drew th' inspiring breath of ancient arts.

BEFORE James Thomson left London in the first weeks of November 1730, to begin the Grand Tour of Europe as the companion to Charles Richard Talbot, he wrote a long letter to Bubb Dodington, in which he expressed his excitement at the prospect ahead. 'Travelling has been long my fondest wish', he wrote, 'for the very purpose you recommend. The storing one's imagination with ideas of all-beautiful, all-great, and all-perfect Nature: these are the pure *Materia Poetica*, the light and colours, with which fancy kindles up her whole creation, paints a sentiment, and even embodies an abstracted thought. I long to see the fields where Virgil gathered his immortal honey, and tread the same ground where men have thought and acted so greatly.'[1]

The motive which made so many Englishmen of the eighteenth century undertake the uncomfortable and often hazardous journey to Italy, was not a mere frivolous wish to seek abroad for pleasures which they could not know at home, but a desire to see the land whose scenery had been familiar to them from childhood through the classical authors, upon whose works their education had been founded, and to study the ruins of that city whose senators and emperors they had chosen as the standard by which to measure the abilities and achievements of their contemporaries. Satirists might sneer at the manners, or

---

[1] Letter of 24 October 1730; quoted William Seward, *Anecdotes*, 5th ed., 1804, ii, 344. Morel misdated this letter '1731', and thereby confused the chronology of Thomson's Grand Tour; see Morel, *op. cit.*, pp. 94 *et seq.*

quibble at the worth of the knowledge, or lash the perversity of the vices which these travellers were supposed to acquire abroad, but so long as the classical poets remained the staple of education, and youth was inspired to emulate Roman virtues and taught to admire Italian arts, the Grand Tour was a pilgrimage which everyone who could afford the expense thought it necessary to make. It was a voyage to come face to face with the reality of an ideal which had haunted their imaginations. Tobias Smollett wrote at the beginning of his journey: 'I felt an enthusiastic ardor to tread that very classical ground which had been the scene of so many great atchievements.'[1] He expressed in similar words the thought which was in Thomson's mind when he wrote to Dodington, and it was that thought which impelled on their way all their travelled contemporaries.

But Thomson was not only possessed by a pious longing to visit the places of antiquity; he was equally intent upon narrowly observing the country through which he would pass and thereby storing his imagination with new images, which would eventually find a place in some poem. Thomson, wrote Dr. Johnson, 'looks round on Nature and on Life with the eye which Nature bestows only on a poet',[2] and he certainly anticipated that his journey would provide him with the inspiration for some new work. If Thomson saw with a poet's eye, however, his vision was directed by a mind thoroughly infused with contemporary faults and virtues, which unfitted him in many ways from taking full advantage of the opportunities that foreign travel offered. The devotion to his country, which raised England during the eighteenth century to a height of unparalleled greatness, unfortunately prevented an Englishman from even tolerating the customs and behaviour of peoples whom he imagined to be backward in commercial progress or to threaten his own nation's supremacy. Even the most civilized travellers, Horace Walpole or Laurence Sterne,

---

[1] Smollett, *Travels through France and Italy*, 1766, ii, 2.
[2] Johnson, *op. cit.*, iii, 298.

admired reluctantly and were quick to condemn what they saw abroad. Thomson's passionate belief in British liberty, commercial genius, and naval power disposed him to suspect and denigrate France, England's nearest rival, and to scorn an enervate and impoverished Italy. He was prepared to dislike what he did not understand, to dismiss what was at variance with his own ideals, and to be pleased only with what seemed to constitute weaknesses in the character and government of the countries he intended to visit. The poet's vision was thus seriously narrowed by his nationalistic blinkers.

Unfortunately, we know little about this Continental tour, but we can roughly follow it in outline in the few letters which have survived, and in *Liberty*, the poem which embodied his experiences abroad. The travellers left London in the first weeks of November, and by the end of the following month had established themselves in Paris. Thomson grudgingly allowed himself to be impressed by what he observed, and like so many of his contemporaries who were loath to admit the appeal of that truly civilized capital, he thought he detected beneath its luxury and civility the seeds of dissolution. 'I have seen little of Paris yet,' he wrote to Bubb Dodington on 27 December, 'some streets and play-houses . . . You must, however, give me leave to observe, that admidst all that external and shewy magnificence which the French affect, one misses that solid magnificience of trade and sincere plenty.'[1] Horace Walpole made the same point some nine years later when he wrote: 'The French love show but there is a meanness reigns through it all.'[2] If Thomson and Talbot had really wished to become familiar with the French character and Parisian society, however, they hardly adopted a demeanour likely to conciliate their hosts; they appear to have been determined to let it be known that they were British and not to have deferred even momently to the social customs and requirements of the French. Thomas

---

[1] Quoted Seward, *op. cit.*, ii, 342.   [2] Walpole, *Letters*, ed. Toynbee, i, 26.

Rundle has succinctly described Charles Talbot's behaviour
in Paris, and it is certain that Thomson's would differ in no
way from that of his companion. Charles Talbot 'is at
Paris', wrote Rundle, 'and behaves as one would wish he
should behave. His rough *English* love for liberty, disdains
the embroidered slavery, that glitters in that trifling Court.
He hates chains, tho' made of gold; and contemns a nation,
who can be mean enough to be contented and in love with
wretchedness, because it hath a painted face. With a sort
of virtuous surliness, his good sense is so much offended at
their flattery of those that oppress them; in that chain of
mutual slaves and tyrants, that descends from the highest to
the lowest among them, that one almost fears he should,
instead of learning complaisance in that polite school of
dissimulation, run counter to the manners he hates, and be
in danger of growing in love with that plain dealing, which
is now no where fashionable, if his good sense and good-
nature did not secure him from it.'[1] Rundle must have
received this report from Thomson, who would clearly take
the opportunity to imply that his own behaviour was not
dissimilar to that of his companion. Such a truculent attitude, although it proved their patriotic spirit, would not
equip them to appreciate the French.

No matter how much they might affect to despise
their Continental neighbours, however, Englishmen could
not remain entirely oblivious to the attractions of Parisian
society, or resist affecting the manners elaborated by a
Court whose ceremonious and fastidious grace has never
been excelled. English society took advantage of each brief
interval of peace between the national conflicts which
distracted the eighteenth century to flock to Paris, where for
a time they could delight in a novel and intelligent world,
and acquire the latest fashions before an outbreak of hostili-
ties drove them all unwilling home again. Thomson sincerely disapproved of this social emigration, and when he
returned to Paris in 1732 he expressed himself strongly on

[1] Letter of 30 January 1730/1; *Letters of Rundle*, 1789, ii, 164-5.

PLATE I

JAMES THOMSON
by Stephen Slaughter

the question in a letter to Lady Hertford. 'It is hard that such a great nation as England', he wrote, 'cannot be decently proud enough, to have a standard of dress, exercises, and polite behaviour among themselves without thus always awkwardly imitating a people they never either can nor ought to be like. I wish we would also imitate them in one thing and that is being as indifferent about them as they are about us. There has been this season, and still are, such a crowd of all ages and sexes here as must give foreigners a strange opinion of England. Their common notion of us is I reckon, of a cold, dark, dull, dirty country where there is nothing but money.'[1] It is therefore obvious that the truculent attitude which the companions adopted was at least a sincere expression of their principles.

Every honest Englishman was forced to confess, however, that Parisian society was superior to that of London. The knowledge of the French in the polite arts put the English visitors to shame, and the standard of their conversation was much higher than that which passed for current in England. Lord Chesterfield, an exact and sensitive appraiser of the social virtues and graces, wrote to his son: 'It must be owned that the polite conversation of the men and women of fashion in Paris, though not always very deep, is much less futile and frivolous than ours here. It turns at least upon some subject, something of taste, some point of history, criticism, and even philosophy; which . . . is . . . better and more becoming rational beings than our frivolous dissertations upon the weather or upon whist.'[2] Thomson would have many opportunities of mixing with this society, and although he disapproved of its artificiality and its obsequious deference to rank, he too acknowledged that its liberal support of the arts was in marked contrast to the traditional neglect shown by the English. He would also be introduced to the French men of letters by Voltaire, whom he met when that great European visited England in 1726,

---

[1] Quoted Hughes, *op. cit.*; *Mod. Phil.*, xxv, 456.
[2] Quoted Lecky, *England in the Eighteenth Century*, 1878, i, 464 *n.* 2.

and he attended a performance of Voltaire's *Brutus* and was allowed to read the preface to that play, which was not published until some years later.[1] 'M. de Voltaire's Brutus', he wrote to Bubb Dodington, 'has been acted here seven or eight times with applause, and still continues to be acted. It is matter of amusement to me to imagine what ideas an old Roman Republican, declaiming on Liberty, must give the generality of a French audience. Voltaire, in his Preface, designs to have a stroke at criticism.'[2]

His experience of Parisian society and his introduction into the company of French men of letters partly reconciled the poet to France. His fervent love of liberty led him to despise their politics, and his patriotism compelled him to suspect a people who challenged his own country's naval and commercial supremacy, but he admitted that Britain could learn from her rival how to successfully encourage the arts. Thomson believed entirely in the dignity and necessity of the artist, and contrasted French patronage with English neglect. The Goddess of Liberty, in the last book of *Liberty*, strongly denounced the English attitude:

> To softer Prospect turn we now the View,
> To laurel's SCIENCE, ARTS, and PUBLIC WORKS,
> That lend MY FINISH'D FABRIC comely Pride,
> Grandeur and Grace. Of sullen Genius he!
> Curs'd by the *Muses*! by the Graces loath'd!
> Who deems beneath the Public's high Regard
> *These last enlivening Touches of* MY *Reign.*

After this denunciation, the Goddess continued to show that even the enslaved French assumed responsibility for the artist, and to praise Louis XIV for his patronage:

> These Laurels, LOUIS, by the Droppings rais'd
> Of thy Profusion, its Dishonour shade,
> And, green thro' future Times, shall bind thy Brow;
> While the vain Honours of Perfidious War
> Wither abhorr'd, or in Oblivion lost.

[1] See Morel, *op. cit.*, pp, 90–3.   [2] Quoted Seward, *op. cit.*, ii, 342.

After passing the winter at Paris, and reluctantly enjoying its diversions, they would begin in the spring, after the roads had recovered their condition, a leisurely journey down to Italy. They probably followed the route usually taken by contemporary travellers—from Paris to Sens, through Rouvry to Châlons, and so on down the Rhône to Lyons. At the last city, Thomson had the pleasure of renewing his acquaintance with Joseph Spence, the former Professor of Poetry at Oxford, who was travelling in the company of Charles, Earl of Middlesex, also a subscriber to *The Seasons*. They made one excursion from Lyons to see the famous fountain of Vaucluse, whose waters sound sadly in Petrarch's sonnets, and the poet intended to write a poem upon it and its associations. Lady Hertford wrote many years later to Lady Pomfret: 'I hope your route will lead you to the Fontaine de Vaucluse, which Petrarch has made so famous by his sonnets . . . Mr. Thomson told me he had seen this fountain; and he promised to give me the description of it in verse: but the promises of poets are not always to be depended upon.'[1] After this chance meeting with Spence, they continued on to Geneva, and the poet had nothing but praise for this republic, which he described as 'a small *State*, but a noble Example of the Blessings of Civil and Religious Liberty'. The Presbyterian Scot would immediately feel at home in the progressive, tolerant, and strictly puritan city, from which so many of his cherished ideals had stemmed. He held up Geneva as an example to England, which he believed was enslaved by Sir Robert Walpole's practice of government by parliamentary corruption: 'It is remarkable', he wrote, 'that since the founding of this *Republick*, not one Citizen has been so much as suspected to have been guilty of *Corruption* or *publick Rapine*. A *Virtue* this! meriting the Attention of every *Briton*.'[2] He praised the brave and industrious Swiss in verse as well, because

[1] *Correspondence between Countess of Hertford and Countess of Pomfret*, 1805, i, 104.
[2] *Liberty*, Book IV, 1736, note to l. 329.

> *equal Life,*
> Accorded gracious with *revolving Power*,
> Maintains them *free*; and in their happy Streets,
> Nor cruel Deed, nor Misery is known.
> For Valour, Faith, and Innocence of Life,
> Renown'd, a rough laborious People, There,
> Not only give the dreadful *Alps* to smile,
> And press their Culture on retiring Snows;
> But, to firm Order train'd and patient War,
> They likewise know, beyond the Nerve remiss
> Of *Mercenary Force*, how to defend
> The tasteful Little their hard Toil has earn'd.

He had, moreover, hoped to store his imagination with ideas of 'all-beautiful, all-great, and all-perfect Nature' during his travels, and he described in some noble lines the magnificence of the Alpine scenery around Lac Leman:

> The hollow-winding Stream; the Vale, fair-spread
> Amid an Amphitheatre of Hills;
> Whence, vapour-wing'd, the sudden Tempest springs:
> From Steep to Steep ascending, the gay Train
> Of Fogs, thick-roll'd into romantic Shapes:
> The flitting Cloud, against the Summit dash'd;
> And, by the sun illumin'd, pouring bright
> A gemmy Shower: hung o'er amazing Rocks,
> The Mountain-Ash, and solemn-sounding Pine:
> The snow-fed Torrent, in white Mazes tost,
> Down to the clear etherial Lake below:
> On Winter Winter shivering, and whose Top
> Licks from their cloudy Magazine the Snows.

This immediate response to the sublimities of Alpine scenery was exceptional at a time when poets usually dismissed mountains with the adjective, which Thomson used in the previous quotation, 'dreadful'; and it illustrates how far in advance Thomson was of contemporary sensibility.

They would cross the Alps from Switzerland into Italy by the route which ran over Mont Cenis, and the perils of this journey were later described by both Thomas Gray and Horace Walpole. The travellers, wrapped up in furs and 'seated upon a sort of matted chair without legs', would be borne

over the pass by teams of remarkably nimble mountaineers;
'they run with you down steeps and frozen precipices',
wrote Walpole, 'where no man, as men are now, could possibly walk'.[1] After the descent to Turin, the travellers made
their way down through Italy, pausing to admire the anti-
quities they passed, resting a day or a week at any town which
they thought was worth a more detailed study, until,
fatigued by the rough conditions and angered by the extor-
tionate inn-keepers, they at last arrived in Rome before the
end of November 1731.

Thomson was bitterly disappointed by the countryside
through which they journeyed, and almost every English
traveller to Italy shared his feeling. They had not allowed for
the operation of history, and instead of discovering the
people and country which the classical poets had described,
they met with misery and poverty where greatness had once
been, were introduced to a debauched and impoverished
aristocracy, and saw a landscape which was in harsh
contrast to their sedate and well-farmed England. As soon
as they set foot in Italy, they were prejudiced against it and
its people by the notorious squalor of the inns. Look into
'the Haunts of Men!' exclaimed Thomson,

> There buxom Plenty never turns her horn;
> The Grace and Virtue of exterior Life,
> No clean Convenience reigns; even Sleep itself,
> Least delicate of Powers, reluctant there
> Lays on the Bed impure his heavy head.

'I will venture to say', wrote Tobias Smollett, who shared
Thomson's disgust, 'that a common prisoner in the Marshal-
sea or King's-Bench is more cleanly and commodiously
lodged than we were in many places . . . The houses are
abominably nasty, and generally destitute of provision:
when eatables were found, we were almost poisoned by
their cookery: their beds were without curtains or bedstead,
and their windows without glass; and for this sort of entertainment we payed as much as if we had been genteelly

---

[1] Walpole, *Letters*, ed. Toynbee, i, 41.

lodged, and sumptuously treated.'[1] When Thomson turned from the nastiness of the inns to the neglected and infertile countryside, he anticipated in verse Smollett's comments upon the region around Rome. 'The view of this country', wrote Smollett, 'in its present situation, cannot but produce emotions of pity and indignation in the mind of every person who retains any idea of its antient cultivation and fertility. It is nothing but a naked withered down, desolate and dreary, almost without inclosure, cornfield, hedge, tree, shrub, house, hut, or habitation.'[2] 'Neglected round', wrote Thomson,

> Each Harvest pines; the livid, lean Produce
> Of heartless Labour: while thy hated Joys,
> Not proper Pleasure, lift the lazy Hand. . . .
> Hence drooping Art almost to Nature leaves
> The rude, unguided Year. Thin wave the Gifts
> Of yellow Ceres, thin the radiant Blush
> Of Orchard reddens in the warmest ray. . . .
> In vain, forlorn in wilds, the Citron blows,
> And flowering Plants perfume the desart gale.

Everywhere he turned Thomson met with something to distress him. The jumble of petty states, each governed by an arbitrary princeling, outraged his passionate belief in liberty and democracy. The cities which had degenerated from their ancient grandeur offended his admiration of commerce, and he could not help comparing their idle emptiness with London's bustling activity:

> See Streets whose Echoes never knew the voice
> Of chearful Hurry, Commerce many-tongu'd,
> And Art mechanic at his various task
> Fervent employ'd.

The Present so preoccupied his attention that he became incapable of appreciating the Past, whose greatness could be barely discovered beneath the covering of dirt and desolation; and the first letter he wrote to Dodington from Rome, dispatched, it would seem, soon after his arrival in that city,

---

[1] Smollett, *op. cit.*, ii, 165.   [2] *Ibid.*, ii, 80–1.

fully expressed his disillusionment: 'That enthusiasm which I had upon me with regard to travelling goes off, I find, very fast. One may imagine fine things in reading ancient authors; but to travel is to dissipate that vision: A great many antique statues (where several of the fair ideas of Greece are fixed for ever in marble) and the paintings of the first Masters, are indeed most enchanting objects. How little, however, of these suffices! How unessential are they to life! They are surely not of that importance as to set the whole world, man, woman, and child, a-gadding. I should be sorry to be Goth enough not to think them highly orna-mental in life, when one can have them at home without pay-ing for them an extravagant price. But for everyone who can support it to make a trade of running abroad only to stare at them, I cannot help thinking something worse than a public folly. Instead of travelling so furiously, it were wiser and more public-spirited, should they, with part of those sums of money spent that way, send persons of genius in Architec-ture, Painting, and Sculpture, to study those arts abroad, and import them into England. Did they but once take root here, how they might flourish in such a generous and wealthy country! The Nature, of the great Painter, Archi-tect, and Statuary, is the same she ever was; and is, no doubt, as profuse of beauty, proportion, lovely forms, and real genius, as formerly she was to the sunny realms of Greece, did we but study the one and exert the other. In England, if we cannot reach the gracefully superfluous, yet I hope we shall never lose the substantial necessary, and vital parts of life; such as depend on Labour, Liberty, and all-command-ing Trade. For my part, I (who have no taste for smelling of an old musty stone) look upon these countries with an eye to Poetry, in regard that the Sisters reflect light and images to one another. Now I mention Poetry, should you enquire after my Muse, all that I can answer is, that I believe she did not cross the Channel with me. I know not whether your gardener at Eastbury has heard anything of her amongst the woods there; she has not thought fit to visit me whilst I have been in this once poetic land; nor do I feel the least presage that she will.'[1]

He was in such a rage with all he saw that it is small wonder his Muse avoided his company, and while he continued in Rome little, except perhaps some better tended relics of antiquity, pleased him. He forcefully contrasted in *Liberty* the squalor of the proud, bankrupt aristocracy's palaces with their former magnificence:

> Mark how the Palace lifts a lying front,
> Concealing often, in magnific Jail,
> Proud Want, a deep unanimated Gloom!
> And often joining to the drear abode
> Of Misery, whose melancholy walls
> Seems its voracious Grandeur to reproach.

The Roman palaces made a similar impression upon Smollett—it is to be hoped that all Scotsmen were not as jaundiced as these two!—and he thus described them: they 'are so engaged among other mean houses, that their beauty and magnificence are in a great measure concealed . . . and their views are confined by dirty and disagreeable objects . . . the dullness of their small glass lozenges, the dusty brick floors, and the crimson hangings laced with gold, contribute to give a gloomy air to their apartments.'[2] The travellers made an excursion from Rome to Naples but once again the poet did not fail to compare the present to the past, and to point out the miseries devolving on the country from its despotic government:

> How chang'd, how vacant, VIRGIL, wide around,
> Would now your Naples seem? Disastered less
> By black *Vesuvius* thundering o'er the Coast,
> His midnight Earthquakes, and his mining Fires,
> Than by Despotic Rage.

'I long to see the fields where Virgil gathered his immortal honey', he had written before he set out on his travels, but the reality had not realized the dream, and he was glad to leave it behind.

---

[1] Quoted Seward, *op. cit.*, ii, 346–7.   [2] Smollett, *op. cit.*, ii, 103–4.

It is not known when they began their journey back to England. An earlier biographer suggested, on the evidence of a letter by Thomas Rundle, that they abruptly broke off their stay in Rome and returned in time to spend the Christmas of 1731 with the Talbot family at Ashdown Park.[1] Rundle's letter, which is dated in his collected correspondence, 'Ashdown-Park, Friday Morning, 1731', reads: 'This little solitary island, in the midst of a vast verdant ocean, secured from the intrusion of chance company, and the interruption of business, can afford no news to fill a letter. Every one that inhabits it, is gay and happy according to their various ranks and desires . . . All the nine Muses came hither with Mr. THOMSON.'[2] It is obvious from Rundle's phrase, 'in the midst of a vast verdant ocean', that the time of year was not winter but spring or early summer, and if the letter was written in 1731 it must have been written at the beginning of the year. It is very improbable that the travellers returned from France to England before continuing on to Italy, and Rundle's letter is manifestly misdated, like others in the same collection. It referred either to a house-party held at Ashdown Park before Thomson and Talbot set out on their Tour, or, more probably, to one given in the spring of 1733, when we know they had returned to England.

The travellers would make their way slowly from Rome to Paris in the spring of 1732, probably following a different route from their earlier one, and by October they were once again established in that capital. Thomson wrote to Lady Hertford from there on 10 October, and the letter summarized the impressions that Italy had made upon him. It is among the finest he wrote, and helps to refute the assertion that the poet was deficient in the art of letter-writing. The first sentence also proves conclusively that the travellers did not return to England for the Christmas festivities of 1731.

[1] See Morel, *op. cit.*, pp. 98–9.   [2] *Letters of Rundle*, 1789, ii, 180.

K

'Madam

'It was but yesterday that I received a letter you did me the honour to write April last, the Banker there not having known how to send it me—I mention this only to prevent my being judged altogether inexcusable and not by way of apology for having so long neglected to pay my respects where they are so justly due. To speak naturally, as one who longed mightily to hear of your Ladyships health, I resolved a thousand times to write, and continually reproached my self for neglecting it; but then a vain Imagination of writing in the character of a traveller still prevented me: and like one who finds himself quite unable to answer his engagements, I desperately turn'd Bankrupt. The letter however you have honoured me with has awakened me to such a lively remembrance of your goodness, as makes me flatter my Self that, upon this ingenuous confession you will absolve me from any rash promise I made while the fairy prospect lay before me—There are certainly several very fine natural Scenes to be seen abroad, but they are saddened by the misery of their Inhabitants, and Scenes of human misery ought never to please but in a tragedy. The bad Government in Italy, and particularly that of the Priests, has not only extirpated almost human arts and Industry but even disfigured Nature her self. Tho they might command all that can tend either to the convenience, pleasure, or magnificence of life, yet are they in some sort destitute of all. The gracious sun indeed still dispences to them his powerfull smiles, but him they are afraid of. It ought to be considered rather as the land of the dead than of the living. Suppose one who is perfectly master of the antient Poets and Historians suddenly transported there, without knowing what country it was; he would scarce I fancy find it out by their descriptions. After, 'tis true, having wandered through a vast desolate plain, where by degrees began to appear the tombs of Heroes, broken arches, and aqueducts, till at last thro' many majestic ruins he came to the palatine mount, the seat of the Imperial palace: here, would he say, astonished at the awful prospect, here must have stood Rome the mistress of the World—Behold an Empire dead! and those venerable ruins all around, these triumphal arches, pillars, remains of temples, Baths, aqueducts and Amphitheatres are but her wide spread monument—a monument, tho' made up of ruins, infinitely, infinitely more noble than all the other monuments of the world put together. Several pieces of Grecian sculpture that may be said to adorn this monument are divine. Was I writing to another than your Ladyship I might forget my self, and say, that they represent a finer nature than is to be found now-a-days. The famous Italian painters having taken their Ideas from them, no wonder that their works should be so vastly Superior to the painting of all other Nations, as they beyond comparison are. The language and musick of Italy are Inchanting. Being but an Infant in the language I ought not to pretend to judge of it, yet I cannot help thinking it not only very harmonious and expressive but even not at all incapable of manly Graces. As for their Music it is a sort of charming malady that quite dissolves them in Softness, and greatly heightens in them that Universal Indolence men naturally (I had almost said reasonably) fall into when they can receive little or no advantage from their Industry. They talk of the Tarantula in Italy for whose bite music is a cure. That Tarantula must, I fancy, mean the bad government, for whose oppression music if not a cure yet is at least some relief, by gently lulling them into a sweet forgetfullness of Misery. Now that I mention Music, one cannot, I believe, have a stronger instance of the power of custom with regard to taste than one meets with here in the french opera. While they themselves die away in raptures at what they call their beaux morceaux others whose taste is form'd to the Italian musick would rather hear the screech-owl than their screaming heroines. Their excessive vanity has led them into this difference of taste from others; for they will have a peculiar taste of their own, tho to have it they must forsake Nature.'[1]

[1] Quoted Hughes, *op. cit.*; *Mod. Phil.*, xxv, 455.

The poet, although he complained to Lady Hertford, that he was 'as much abandoned by the Muses as Spring in London', included in his letter a transcript of a poem he had written in memory of his friend William Aikman, who, after 'a tedious, lingering consumption', had died in June 1731.[1] William Aikman had quickly risen in his profession, and was fully employed. He had intended to visit his native country, Scotland, in 1728, but—as he wrote to Sir John Clerk on 10 October—'just as I was winding up the clue to make an excursion, My Lord Hubbard brought me an offer of 25 whole lengths which were to be gone through with all expedition as the Persons to be drawne could be gott in Towne; and sure you would have condemned me much to have slighted such an opportunity, I have begun and finished 5 of these pictures besides my other business in course since that time . . . Yesterday I begunn a whole length att my advanced price of 40 Guineas and am very hopefull it will not be any stop to the course of my business, if it should, these of my Lord Huppbard [sic], agreed for att the former prices will enable me to stand the first shock.'[2] But at the height of his success, he was stricken with consumption, and his sickness was aggravated by the knowledge that his favourite son, Jocky, was also affected. He was inordinately proud of this son, who he intended should follow his own profession, and he sent an interesting account of his progress to Sir John Clerk on 13 January 1729/30: 'Yow desire to know Dear Baron', he wrote, 'how Jocky goes on. I think I may safely say of him he is a very promising boy in his business, but what gives me most comfort in him [is] that he is a true hearted honest Boy and in spite of the folly and vice that he daily sees practis'd by the fashionable has them in great hatred and contempt: he has no pleasure but his business which he follows with great assiduity, he seems to have a pretty Genius for the Historical and beginns to draw from the Round and the Life both with

---

1 Quoted Whitley, *op. cit.*, i, 60.
2 *Clerk of Penicuik Papers*, Register House, Edinburgh.

a very good taste; he goes to a privat accademy every night and draws after the naked model which has improven him much, I allowe him to paint but very little as yet but he will be trying sometimes.'[1]

Aikman and his son made a journey to Edinburgh in 1730 in a vain attempt to recover their healths, and while they were in the north Mrs. Aikman wrote a letter to Sir John Clerk on 1 September, which provides an illuminating commentary on her husband's character: 'I am so glad that Mr Aikman has left of wine drinking for to tell you the truth it was that that brought on all his trouble on him for he is good naturd and every bodys body as the saying is: thatt if this dangerious Symtons had not cheekt him he had gon on every night it may be till his last night but I hop this will be a warning to him whith what good Advice no dout you have given him.'[2] Aikman did follow his wife's entreaties and Sir John's advice to leave off wine, and both he and Jocky returned to London slightly improved in health. But Jocky died at the beginning of 1731, and the shock caused his father to relapse at once. He wrote a pathetic letter to Sir John, on 16 March 1731, describing his condition: 'The Letter I receiv'd from yow this day putt me much out of countenance, for having been so long in your debt for severall kind and sympathyzing letters which came most seasonally to me, and was of great use to help me to struggle out of the chains of melancholly—but I have been so very weak of late, that is indeed even since I lost my son, that its a great burthen for me to undergoe the least fatigue of Soul or Body; yow enquire kindly about my health, my case is a constant hectick pulse that is about 40 beats to a natural one's 30, I am so emaciat I think I cannot loose much more before the end . . . I am so strongly advis'd to a journey to Naples that I have resolv'd to give up business and housekeeping about June next, mean time I endeavour to wind up my bottom here as well as I can; last week I was oblig'd to refuse the Lord Mayor and his family and this 3 whole

[1] *Ibid.*   [2] *Ibid.*

lengths of The Princess for Lady Ann Lumley who have
been waiting for me this half year.'[1] The journey to Naples
was prevented by his death.

Richard Savage spoke to Dr. Johnson, 'with the most
eager praise', of Thomson's 'warmth, and constancy of
friendship',[2] and his verses to the memory of William
Aikman are an illustration of the truth of Savage's observation. After praising his friend's genius and his character,
'modest, plain, sincere', he concluded with these noble
lines:

> As those we love decay, we die in part,
> String after string is sever'd from the heart;
> Till loosen'd life, at last but breathing clay,
> Without one pang is glad to fall away.
> Unhappy he who latest feels the blow,
> Whose eyes have wept o'er every friend laid low,
> Dragg'd lingering on from partial death to death;
> Till dying, all he can resign is breath.

These verses, the poet told Lady Hertford, 'are rather a
plain testimony of Friendship, than an attempt of poetry'.

Thomson ended his long letter to Lady Hertford with the
remark, 'I despair of the honour of seeing your Ladyship
till next Spring in London'; and early in the New Year,
after an absence of more than two years, the travellers
landed in England. The effect of his residence abroad upon
the poet was at once apparent to his friends. Lady Hertford,
whom he met in fulfilment of his promise, was very favourably impressed, and sent an account of him to Mrs. Rowe,
who replied, 'I am pleased to hear of any improvement
that so fine a Genius as Mr. Thomson's has gained by
his Travels'.[3] Perhaps the travellers' 'rough *English* love of
liberty', that 'sort of virtuous surliness', which Thomas
Rundle had so commended in Talbot, had been tempered by
familiarity with Parisian society. The poet's manners may
have acquired something of the polish which he had

---

[1] *Clerk of Penicuik Papers*, Register House, Edinburgh.
[2] Johnson, *op. cit.*, iii, 298.   [3] Quoted Hughes, *op. cit.*; *Mod. Phil.*, xxv, 459.

originally despised, and his imagination had certainly been quickened by what he had seen abroad. Upon his return, he resumed his friendships, arranged his affairs, and acquainted himself with the state of literature and politics, which were soon to preoccupy his attention.

The country was at this time torn by political dissensions. Sir Robert Walpole, the first Minister, who could only govern the irascible, amorous, and bellicose George II through his clever and ambitious Queen, Caroline, succeeded in upholding his administration by the dextrous employment of every political trick and device, from rhetorical finesse to outrageous bribery; but his foreign and domestic policies increasingly raised against him a clamorous and intelligent opposition, which, though continually baffled by defeat, was determined to destroy his power. Walpole's foreign policy was peace at any price, and his domestic, the consolidation of the Hanoverian dynasty and the comfortable enjoyment of the fruits of office. His personal character and methods of government made him peculiarly unpopular. His lavish and unscrupulous use of bribery, to ensure the passage of his measures through Parliament, was detested by those who upheld liberty and political honesty; his jealousy of power, which persuaded him to keep out of the administration every promising young politician, drove into opposition all ambitious men, who quickly learnt that they could rise only by his downfall; and his pacific policy angered the patriots, who wished Britain to resent even the least slight to her honour, and the commercial interests who were baulked in their attempt to seize oversea markets by force. Sir Robert, however, was not easily overturned, and he succeeded for many years in maintaining himself in power.

The pasteboard figure the opposition raised to confront Sir Robert was Frederick, Prince of Wales. The Prince inevitably became the centre round which there rallied every discontented politician, who, realizing that all hope of advancement was denied to him so long as Sir Robert had the Queen's support, cultivated an interest with the heir to the throne, who might be expected to reward fidelity upon his accession. Frederick needed little encouragement to embarrass his father and his minister. The relations between the Hanoverian kings and their heirs were traditionally bad, and George II and Caroline hated Frederick with hardly repressed fury, which he repaid with interest. Tedious and conceited, gifted with no real spark of decency or ability, Frederick was delighted to be courted by these able and discontented politicians, who used him for their own ends while they persuaded him that it was his example upon which they modelled their behaviour and his genius which inspired their machinations. During the long unrewarding years which it took to overthrow Sir Robert, the opposition moved constantly about the Prince, but its leaders, temporarily withdrawn by more immediate prospects of advancement or superseded by abler tacticians, frequently changed. Among those who were some time in the van were Lord Bolingbroke, the most gifted and unfortunate politician of his day, Lord Chesterfield, the brilliant wit, William Pulteney, who later committed political suicide by accepting the earldom of Bath, and Lord Cobham, who mustered from among his young relations George Lyttelton, Richard and George Grenville, and, an apprentice to greatness, William Pitt. Other prominent statesmen were occasionally allied to this party, and together they formed a distinguished and powerful force; that Sir Robert defended himself against their siege for so long is a testimony to his courage and management.

The opposition naturally engaged the support of literature. Sir Robert's neglect to patronize a single deserving man of letters was a slight upon them all, and they militated to defeat his bland indifference. The opposition were not slow to take advantage of Sir Robert's mistake, and they spared neither flattery nor patronage to win the support of those men of letters who were attracted to their cause from the first by conviction and necessity. James Thomson, upon his return to England, was at once numbered among their supporters. Thomson believed passionately in liberty, and Walpole's policy of corruption threatened to undermine parliamentary independence; he was a patriot, and Walpole's pacific attitude towards France and Spain appeared to encourage their pretensions at the expense of Britain's greatness; he had a peculiar delight in trade and its busy appearances, and the merchants' continual complaints convinced him that Walpole neglected it; he understood that it was a government's duty to encourage the arts and literature, and it was obvious that Walpole had no time for them; and he was temperamentally attracted to the erratic brilliance and fitful energy of the opposition rather than to the dull, mediocre competence of Walpole's administration. His interest coincided with his convictions, and he could engage in this political cause with a clear conscience.

Thomson had already had, before his return to England, a slight acquaintance with the Prince of Wales. Frederick, as we have seen, had attended two performances of *Sophonisba*, and the author's benefit on the sixth night had been 'By his Royal Highness's Command'. While he was abroad, Lady Hertford had taken the opportunity to further his interests by presenting to the Prince a copy of *The Seasons*, and the poet had gratefully acknowledged her kindness: 'Give me leave to return you my most humble acknowledgement for the honour you did me in presenting my Book to the Prince of Wales', he wrote; 'I wish it had been something more worthy of you to present, and of him to read. The approbation he was pleased to give a first imperfect essay does not so much flatter my vanity as my hopes, of seeing the fine arts flourish under a Prince of his so noble, equal, humane, and generous disposition; who knows how to unite the sovereignty of the Prince with liberty of the People, and to found his happiness and Glory on the publick good.'[1] Upon his return Thomson found, moreover, that Bubb Dodington had cleverly manœuvred himself into the

[1] Quoted Hughes, *op. cit.*; *Mod. Phil.*, p. 456.

position of 'first minister' to the Prince,[1] and he could expect that this friend would forward his interests. Thomson quickly ranged himself behind the Prince, and became one of his most active and effective propagandists.

The summer of 1733 would be spent visiting his friends. Dodington would welcome him at Eastbury, Lady Hertford may have invited him down to Marlborough Castle or to her more modest residence at St. Leonard's Hill in Windsor Forest, the Talbot family would expect him to spend some time with them at Ashdown Park, and the year passed on uneventfully until September, when it was interrupted by a great loss. Charles Talbot, the Solicitor-General, had either built or bought a town-house in Lincoln's Inn Fields, and he left his country-seat in Wales to take up residence there on 22 September. Charles Richard Talbot, the poet's companion, died in this house on the following Thursday. The newspapers carried this brief announcement: 'On Thursday morning died at his Father's House in Lincoln's-Inn-Fields, the eldest Son of the Right Hon. Charles Talbot, Esq; his Majesty's Solicitor-General: The young Gentleman was intended to have stood for Knight of the Shire for the County of Glamorgan at the next Election, from whence he came to Town about four or five days since.'[2] This was a sudden end to a friendship which, tested by the constant companionship of their journey, had meant much to Thomson, and he deeply mourned his loss. When Patrick Murdoch wished to console a friend upon Thomson's death, he could do no better than remind him of the poet's own fortitude upon this occasion: 'Think likewise on his own behaviour on the like occasions', he wrote. 'He lost Charles Talbot, as we have him; and tho' he retained to his latest hour a most devout veneration of that excellent person, yet he did not consume himself in unavailing grief. He remembered, and commemorated him, in that pious and affectionate manner, that we shall ever remember them both. At the

---

[1] Hervey, *Memoirs of the Reign of George II*, 1848, i, 211.
[2] *Universal Spectator*, 29 September 1733.

same time he acquiesced in the sovereign will of Providence; and bore his loss (the greatest, in all respects, that could possibly befall to him) with a manly fortitude.'[1] The poet commemorated his friend in the opening verses of *Liberty*:

> O my lamented Talbot! while with thee
> The *Muse* gay-rov'd the glad *Hesperian* Round,
> And drew th' inspiring Breath of Ancient Arts;
> Ah! little thought she her returning Verse
> Should sing our Darling Subject to thy *Shade*.
> And does the Mystic Veil, from mortal Beam,
> Involve those Eyes where every Virtue smil'd,
> And all the FATHER's candid Spirit shone?
> The Light of Reason, pure, without a Cloud;
> Full of the generous Heart, the mild Regard;
> Unblemish'd Honour, uncorrupted Faith;
> And limpid Truth, that looks the very Soul.

The death of Charles Talbot meant the end of the poet's hope that his young friend would have eventually provided for him, but it did not mean the end of the family's support and patronage. The father, a man of scrupulous conduct, would not lose any opportunity to reward Thomson's affection for his son, and he was soon able to show his appreciation. It was announced on 29 November 1733 that 'his Majesty was pleased to appoint the Hon. Charles Talbot, Esq; Solicitor-General, and Member of Parliament for the City of Durham, to be Lord High Chancellor of this Kingdom, and delivered the Seal accordingly into the Possession of the said Charles Talbot, Esq;'.[2] At the same time, he was raised to the peerage as Baron Talbot of Hensol. Everyone praised this choice, and agreed that Lord Talbot had 'as clear, separating, distinguishing, subtle, and fine parts as ever man had'.[3] The new Chancellor soon appointed Thomson to be his Secretary of the Briefs, at a salary of £300 a year, and it was 'a place of little attendance, suiting his retired indolent way of life, and equal to all his wants'.[4]

---

[1] *Culloden Papers*, 1815, p. 308. [2] *Daily Post-Boy*, 30 November 1733.
[3] Hervey, *op. cit.*, i, 280. [4] *Works of Thomson*, 1762, i, xi.

Thomson was now in a position of some affluence and influence, and an old friend reappeared to ask him a favour. Aaron Hill, who certainly deserved some return for his earlier services, requested him to read his translation of Voltaire's tragedy of *Zaire*, which Hill intended to produce, and to recommend it 'to such of your friends, as can promote its success, by their influence . . . And, if I might be particular, in tasking your indulgence, Mr. *Dodington* should be the first of the number.'[1] Thomson did not reply to Hill's letter for nearly a month, but his answer, written on 10 December, was a panegyric upon Hill's translation, which, he affirmed, was a more considerable work than the original, and he promised to do what he could to further its success and to engage Dodington's interest. *Zara* was not produced at Drury Lane Theatre until 1736, when it owed its success to the playing of the great tragic actress, Mrs. Cibber, rather than to the efforts, however strenuous, of the translator's friends.

Thomson excused his delay in replying to Hill's request by explaining that he had been 'rather hurry'd than employ'd in solliciting for the Benefit of old *Dennis*'.[2] John Dennis, the irascible critic and dramatist, had ended his furious warfare with life by falling into distress, and to relieve his necessitous old age his friends arranged that Vanburgh's and Cibber's comedy of *The Provoked Husband* should be performed for his benefit. The performance, which took place on 18 December at the New Theatre in the Haymarket, was a success. The newspapers announced that, 'There was an exceeding crowded Audience of Persons of Distinction last Tuesday Night at Mr. Dennis's Benefit, and his Royal Highness the Prince of Wales was pleased to send twenty Guineas as a present to that Gentleman'.[3] Alexander Pope wrote an ambiguous prologue for this performance, in which he contrasted with a certain relish his old enemy's miserable present with his happier past, and he may have

---

[1] Hill, *Works*, 1753, i, 182.   [2] Hill, *Collection of Letters*, 1751, p. 61.
[3] *General Evening Post*, 18–20 December 1733.

been prompted to this act of dubious charity by Thomson, who certainly was responsible for the Prince's generous subscription. That Thomson was the principal organizer of Dennis's benefit was immediately recognized by the appearance in the newspapers of some verses addressed to 'Mr. THOMSON, on occasion of the Part which that Gentleman took, in the concern for Mr. DENNIS's last Benefit':

> While I reflect thee o'er, methinks, I find
> Thy various SEASONS, in their Author's Mind!
> *Spring*, in thy flow'ry *Fancy*, spreads her Hues;
> And, like thy soft Compassion, sheds her Dews.
> *Summer*'s hot strength in thy *Expression* glows;
> And o'er thy Page a beamy Ripeness throws.
> *Autumn*'s rich Fruits th' instructed Reader gains,
> Who tastes the meaning *Purpose* of thy Strains.
> *Winter*—but *that* no 'Semblance takes from thee!
> That hoary Season's Type was drawn from ME—
> Shatter'd by Time's bleak Storms, I with'ring lay,
> Leafless, and whit'ning, in a cold Decay.
> Yet shall my propless *Ivy*,—pale and bent,
> Bless the short Sunshine, which thy Pity lent.

When these complimentary verses, which were signed with the initials 'J.D.', were shown to John Dennis, he is reported to have exclaimed, 'They could be no one but that fool Savage's'.[1] If Savage was the author, he would seem to have exaggerated Dennis's gratitude and to have expressed too convincingly the destitute critic's sense of humiliation. Dennis did not live long to enjoy the fruits of his benefit. He died at the beginning of the new year, and it was reported that 'On Thursday Night [10 January 1733/4] the Corpse of Mr. John Dennis, late Poet, was handsomely interred at St. Martin's in the Fields, being attended to the Grave by several of his Friends and Acquaintances in Mourning Coaches'.[2] Thomson would be among these mourners.

There was also confusion at this time about some other

---

[1] Isaac D'Israeli, *Calamities of Authors*, 1882, p. 55.
[2] *Whitehall Evening-Post*, 10–12 January 1733/4.

complimentary verses. A young Irish poet, James Dalacourt, published a poem entitled *The Prospect of Poetry*, and included in the volume some verses addressed to Thomson, which began:

> From sunless worlds, where Phoebus seldom smiles,
> But with his evening wheels hangs o'er our isles;
> A Western Muse to worth this tribute pays,
> From regions bordering on the Hebrides:
> For thee the Irish harp, new strung, once more
> Greets our rough rocks, and bleak Hibernian shore:
> Thou, Thomson, badest my fingers wake the strings,
> And with thy praise the wild wood hollow rings.

Thomson would probably acknowledge this compliment, which is a small indication of his contemporary fame, by letter, but there also appeared in the *London Magazine* for November 1733 a lengthy poem, addressed '*To Mr.* James Dalacourt *in* Ireland *upon his* Prospect of Poetry', which was signed 'J. Thomson'. The conclusion to the poem shows the style in which it was written:

> Thy country, tho' corrupted, brought thee forth
> And deems her greatest ornament; and now
> Regards thee as her brightest northern star.
> Long may you reign as such, and shou'd grim time
> With iron teeth deprive us of our *Pope*,
> Then we'll transplant thy blooming laurels fresh
> From your bleak shore to *Albion's* happier coast.

It must have appeared to Thomson's contemporaries that he had too handsomely repaid Dalacourt's praise. However, almost three years later, the real and anonymous author of the poem had the temerity to submit it to Edward Cave, the editor of the *Gentleman's Magazine*, for publication, and Cave cautiously asked Thomson whether he had indeed written it. Thomson immediately denied the authorship, and Cave printed his denial in the *Gentleman's Magazine* for August 1736: 'N.B. *The Poem in blank Verse, intitled to Mr* James Dalacourt *on his Prospect of Poetry, Sign'd* J. Thomson *is come to Hand, but we not only find it publish'd already in a Monthly*

Collection, for November 1734, *but are assur'd from Mr* Thomson, *that tho' it has some lines from his* Seasons, *he knew nothing of the Piece till he saw it in the* Daily Journal.' It is not known who played this trick upon Thomson but it cannot have harmed his reputation. Dalacourt, however, proudly printed the verses in front of later editions of *The Prospect of Poetry*, and his action is an illustration of his character. He entered the Church 'but neglected the duties and even the decencies of his profession, till habitual drunkenness produced derangement'.[1]

During the two years which followed his return to England, Thomson was engaged upon his political poem, *Liberty*. He had had such a poem in mind at the very beginning of his Grand Tour, and had set out the idea in his letter to Dodington of 27 December 1730 from Paris. 'Your observation I find every day juster and juster,' he had written, 'that one may profit more abroad by seeing than by hearing; and yet, there are scarce any travellers to be met with, who have given a landscape of the countries through which they have travelled; that have seen (as you express it) with the Muses' eye; though that is the first thing that strikes me, and what all readers and travellers in the first place demand. It seems to me, that such a poetical landscape of countries, mixed with moral observations on their governments and people, would not be an ill-judged undertaking. But then, the description of the different face of Nature, in different countries, must be particularly marked and characteristic, the Portrait-painting of Nature.' While he was abroad, however, he had had neither the will nor the time to continue with this idea, and he did not begin the poem until his return to England.

The plan he had thus briefly proposed to Dodington was altered in the execution. Instead of being a survey of contemporary Europe, in the manner of Goldsmith's *The Traveller*, the work became a history of the rise and progress of the ideal of civil and religious Liberty, and the portrait-

---

[1] Robert Southey, *Specimens of the later English Poets*, 1807, iii, 193.

painting of Nature became subservient to moral and political reflection. Through five long books, each published as a separate poem, the poet attended to the Goddess of Liberty as she meticulously related the vicissitudes of her reign. The first book, subtitled 'Antient and Modern Liberty Compared', opened with the poet wandering among the ruins of Rome:

> Ten thousand Wonders rowling in my thought,
> As the great Scene of death and deeds I tread,
> Tread the blest Ground by more than mortals trod,
> And see those Skies that breath'd the *Roman* Soul.
> Mean time wide-scatter'd round, awful, and hoar,
> Lies a vast Monument once glorious Rome,
> The Tomb of Empire!

His melancholy meditations, however, were interrupted by the appearance of the Goddess, who had assumed the 'port' of Britannia, and he saw

>   her bright Temples bound with *British* Oak,
> And naval Honours nodded on her Brow.
> Sublime her Port. Loose o'er her Shoulder flow'd
> Her sea-green Robe, with Constellations gay.
> An Island Goddess now; and her high care
> The Queen of Isles, the Mistress of the Main.

The Goddess directly inspired him to begin the work, and the first book closed with the poet invoking her assistance. This scene is a peculiar anticipation of Edward Gibbon's famous experience in the Capitol, and since he lived for a time with David Mallet, and would learn from him something about James Thomson, one might wonder if *Liberty* were not the germinal idea for *The Decline and Fall of the Roman Empire*.

The second book, subtitled 'Greece', traced the history of liberty from its remote beginnings down to its establishment in ancient Greece, and, after enumerating the great men and various arts it inspired, concluded with a description of its decline among the Greeks. The third book, subtitled 'Rome', was concerned with the transition of liberty from Greece to Rome, and there followed a commentary upon the Roman genius. The fourth book, subtitled 'Britain', the longest of the five, began with an account of the miraculous preservation of the ideal of liberty during the Dark Ages, and continued with a description of its arrival in Britain and an abstract of British history. The fifth book, subtitled 'The Prospect', showed the Goddess instructing the poet how liberty might be preserved in his country, and how it might be ornamented by the Arts and Sciences. The Goddess ended her dissertation by revealing to the poet in a vision the future greatness of his country. The moral informing the whole poem was that national glory depends upon liberty, and when it is denied by government the state declines.

The subject was too ambitious. It would have been beyond the power of any poet to rehearse in such detail the history of so many countries, to intersperse each catalogue of heroes and actions with appropriate reflections, and to praise the ideal of liberty with fervour through so many lines. The poem was inevitably a failure. It has, however, very real merits which have been consistently underrated. It is remarkable that the poet succeeded in handling such an intractable subject so well, and that he could maintain the interplay of reflection and description. The descriptive passages are naturally the best, and could have found an honourable place in *The Seasons*. The lines upon the Alps have been quoted earlier in this chapter, and there are some others upon a winter scene in Scythia of equal merit:

A sullen Land of Lakes, and Fens immense,
Of Rocks, resounding Torrents, gloomy Heaths,
And cruel Deserts black with sounding Pines;
Where Nature frowns; tho' sometimes into Smiles
She softens; and immediate, at the Touch
Of southern Gales, throws from the sudden Glebe
Luxuriant pasture, and a Waste of Flowers.
But cold-comprest, when the whole-loaded Heaven
Descends in Snow, lost in one white Abrupt,
Lies undistinguish'd Earth; and seiz'd by Frost,
Lakes, headlong Streams, and Floods, and Oceans sleep.

L

There are also many occasional lines and images which rise brightly above the uniformity of the verse:

> In ATTIC Bounds, hence Heroes, Sages, Wits,
> Shone thick as Stars, the Milky Way of Greece.

The poem's greatest fault, after the choice of subject, is the difficulty of the blank verse. Thomson summoned up all his abilities to do full justice to his theme but, like an athlete who has overtrained, his very effort hindered him from accomplishing his purpose. His language is nowhere else so conspicuously literary and modelled upon Milton; his periods are often so involved and difficult that the puzzled reader can only guess at their sense; and all those faults which were earlier apparent in *The Seasons* are even more evident and distracting. It is important, however, to emphasize that these faults do not entirely vitiate the verse, which is often harmonious, exact, and distinguished by Thomson's peculiar sweetness. Dr. Johnson concluded his criticism of Thomson's poetry with this remark: '*Liberty*, when it first appeared, I tried to read, and soon desisted. I have never tried again, and therefore will not hazard either praise or censure.'[1] Later critics have used this careless statement to sanction their own neglect of the poem, and they have consigned it to an oblivion which it does not deserve.

The first book of *Liberty*, published at the beginning of January 1735, was dedicated to Frederick, Prince of Wales. The Prince, who sedulously courted the people by posing as a patriot, was fulsomely celebrated as a lover of liberty: 'In you the Cause and Concerns of Liberty have so zealous a Patron', wrote the poet, 'as entitles whatever may have the least Tendency to promote them, to the Distinction of your Favour.' The Prince must have handsomely rewarded the poet for a work which is not only a history of liberty, but an attack upon Walpole and his administration. Thomson lost no opportunity which his subject offered to arraign those ministers who corrupt a people by bribery and

---

[1] Johnson, *op. cit.*, iii, 301.

prevent their greatness by pacific policies, and his gibes at
Walpole could not have been mistaken by even the most
stupid reader. The opposition must have been delighted by
lines such as these,

> *Corruption's Toils,*
> Foul Ministers, dark-working by the Force
> Of secret-sapping Gold.

Thomson's bookseller, Andrew Millar, clearly expected
that the poet's reputation and the contemporary significance
of many lines would ensure the poem's success, and he
printed no fewer than three thousand ordinary and two
hundred and fifty fine copies of the work.[1] Had the public
received *Liberty* as enthusiastically as did Aaron Hill,
Millar would have had little reason to complain. Hill wrote
to compliment Thomson on 17 January, and his studied
rhetorical praise, which may have been sincere, must have
flattered him. Hill claimed that he wrote 'with the sincerity
of a man, who loves, and who knows why he loves you;—
who has always been warm'd by your *genius*, and ambitious
of your *reputation*. I never saw more *energy* in poetry; never
imagery more glowing; never *sentiments* more elevated, than
in the pieces Mr. *Thompson* has published'. It is only fair to
Hill, who was in many respects an acute and sensitive critic,
to add that he called the poet's attention to his faulty style;
after censuring its 'transposition and obscurity', he continued to say that 'the glowing felicity of the thoughts' was
veiled in 'a kind of cloudiness', which is a sound criticism
admirably phrased. Other publishers besides Millar expected
the poem to succeed, and it was pirated by an Edinburgh
bookseller, W. Cheyne; but this rogue's initiative brought
him little fortune. 'We are assured from Edinburgh',
the newspapers announced, 'that by the Care and Diligence of the Worthy Magistrates of that City, a pirated
edition of Mr. Thompson's *Liberty* has been seized there,
and the Offender committed to Jail.'[2]

---

[1] *Notes & Queries*, I Ser., xii, 218.   [2] *Daily Post-Boy*, 24 February 1733/4.

The second and third books were published soon after
the first, and the fourth and fifth appeared in January 1736.
The plan was therefore successfully brought to a conclusion, but the records show that the poem failed to attract
readers. Three thousand ordinary and two hundred and fifty
fine copies of the first book were printed, two thousand
ordinary and two hundred and fifty fine copies of the second
and third, and only one thousand ordinary and two hundred
and fifty fine copies of the fourth and fifth books.[1] The poet
realized only too well that the poem was a failure, and, with
characteristic generosity, wished to reimburse Andrew
Millar for his loss. He wrote to Aaron Hill on 11 May 1736,
and after acknowledging 'the refin'd Pleasure, which your
generous Approbation of my late Performance gives me',
he continued: 'I will avow, that I am justly proud of,
charm'd with, and most agreeably rewarded by, your good
Opinion of my Poem. Allow me here, by the bye, to remark,
that tho' Poets have been long us'd to this truly-spiritual
and almost only Emolument arising from their Works; yet
I doubt much if Booksellers have any manner of Relish for
it; I think, therefore . . . of annulling the Bargain I made
with mine, who would else be a considerable Loser, by the
Paper, Printing, and Publication, of *Liberty*. As I shall, in
this Case be possess'd of the intire Property of it again, I
propose, in a Year or two hence, to give a new Edition of
it; and beg that you would, ere then, enrich me with some
Criticisms, which I hope I shall have the Grace to relish as
well as Praises.'[2] This proposed revised edition never
appeared, and Millar probably refused to allow the poet to
reimburse him for his loss.

It is very difficult to account for the contemporary neglect
of *Liberty*. It is a much greater achievement than many other
works which were enthusiastically acclaimed—than, for
example, Richard Glover's *Leonidas*, which appeared in 1737
—and the poet's reputation and the political significance of

---

[1] *N. & Q.*, I Ser., xii, 218.   [2] Hill, *Collection of Letters*, 1751, pp. 63–4.

many passages ought to have ensured it a sympathetic reception. But the public had come to consider Thomson as the
poet of Nature and sentiment, and when they opened
Liberty and found the poet writing about an unexpected
subject, they put it to one side unread. There are other
examples of popular authors who have failed when they
attempted a subject with which they were not associated in
the public's imagination. Whatever the reasons, the poem
failed, and Dr. Johnson's verdict cannot be improved upon:
'Upon this great poem two years were spent, and the author
congratulated himself upon it as his noblest work; but an
author and his reader are not always of a mind. *Liberty*
called in vain upon her votaries to read her praises and
reward her encomiast: her praises were condemned to har-
bour spiders, and to gather dust; none of Thomson's performances were so little regarded.'[1]

Thomson passed the summer of 1735 as the guest of Lady
Hertford at St. Leonard's Hill, and while he was there he
wrote some pleasant verses to his hostess on 13 June, which
she carefully copied into her commonplace book. Six of its
nine stanzas are particularly interesting because they illustrate one of Thomson's recurrent moods:

> Come, calm Retirement! Sylvan Power!
>   That on St. Leonard's lov'st to walk,
> To lead along the thoughtful Hour
>   And with the gentle Hartford talk. . . .
>
> Oh lead me to yon airy steep
>   With tufted Trees inviting Crown'd;
> Or plunge me in the Forrest deep,
>   A Sea of Wood that Waves around!
>
> There let me thrid the verdant maze,
>   In search of Scenes grotesque and new,
> Of Glades that draw the lengthen'd Gaze,
>   Of opening Lawns that chear the view.

[1] Johnson, *op. cit.*, iii, 289.

Hark! nought is heard but Nature's voice!
  The whispering Breeze, the tuneful Throat:
See! how her harmless sons rejoyce,
  Their wanton Tyrant man forgot.

Then is the time to calm the mind
  A trembling then uncertain Tide;
To bid the Heart's tempestuous wind
  Into a sighing gale subside.

And lo! where on Augusta's Shore,
  The Human Tempest roars amain;
What wretches there their fate deplore!
  Oh cover me ye woods again!

It is easy to understand how the gentle and melancholy tune which wanders through these lines would appeal to a society beginning to cultivate a sensibility for Nature and a taste for withdrawn, pastoral pleasures. The verses were written at the close of his visit to St. Leonard's Hill, and on 14 June Lord Hertford wrote to his wife: 'In the first place I must tell You that I got hither very well, but left Mr. Thomson at Hammersmith where he took boat as he said in order to go to Mr. Doddington, but I fancy he will go a little farther.'[1] Dodington had a villa, called 'Sans Souci', at Hammersmith, but it is impossible to tell whom Thomson intended to visit after he had paid his call at 'Sans Souci'.

The poet did not forget his impoverished family in the enjoyment of his own good fortune. His younger brother, John, joined him in England after his return from the Continent and acted for him as an amanuensis, but he was attacked by consumption in the summer of 1735 and advised to return to Scotland. Thomson wrote on this occasion to his old friend, Dr. William Cranstoun, and asked him to help his brother. 'The Bearer hereof, my Brother,' he wrote, 'was seized last spring with a severe cold, which seems to have fallen upon his Lungs, and has reduced him

[1] Quoted Hughes, *op. cit.*; *Mod. Phil.*, xxv, 462.

to such a low condition, that his Physician here has advised him to try what his native air can do, as the only remaining means of recovery. In his present melancholy circumstances it gives me no small satisfaction to think that he will have the benefit of your Directions: and for me to spend more words in recommending him to your care, were, I flatter myself, a superfluous formality. Your old acquaintance Anderson attends him, and besides the money necessary to defray the expenses of their journey, I have only given my Brother five guineas, chusing rather to remit him the money he will afterwards want, which shall be done upon the first notice.'[1] On his return to Scotland, John Thomson stayed at Chesters, the village near Southdean, with his Aunt Turnbull, whom the poet described as 'a very good tender-hearted Woman', but his disease was incurable and he died towards the end of September. Dr. Cranstoun immediately sent the news to the poet, who replied on 20 October 1735 to thank him for all his kindness and to arrange for the disposal of his brother's few effects. 'Being but lately returned from Mr Dodington's Seat in Dorsetshire,' he began, 'I only received your's of Sept. the 23rd a few Days ago. The account it brought me of my Brother's Death I was pretty much prepared against, considering the almost hopeless Condition he had for some time been in. What you mention is the true Point of View, wherein to place the Death of Relations and Friends. They then are past our Regret: the Living are to be lamented, and not the Dead. And this is so true, and natural, that people when they grieve for the Death of those they love, from a Principle of Compassion for the Departed without a Return upon themselves, they envisage them in the Article of Death, and under the Pains, both real and imagined, thereof; that is to say, they grieve for them whilst they were alive. Death is a Limit which Human Passions ought not, but with great Caution and Reverence, to pass. Nor indeed can they easily pass that Limit; since beyond it things are not clearly and distinctly

[1] *Forster Coll.*, 48 E.4.; V. & A.

enough perceived formally to excite them. This, I think, we may be sure of, that a future State must be better than this; and so on thro' the never-ceasing Succession of future States; every one rising upon the last, an everlasting new Display of infinite Goodness! But hereby hangs a System, not calculated perhaps for the Meridian where you live tho' for that of your own Mind, and too long to be explained in a Letter.'[1]

He was no less solicitous for the welfare of the sisters he had left in Edinburgh, and he wrote to his friend George Ross on 6 November 1736 requesting him to act on his behalf in their interest. 'My sisters have been advised by their friends', he wrote, 'to set up at Edinburgh a little milliner's shop; and if you can conveniently advance to them twelve pounds, on my account, it will be a particular favour. That will set them a-going, and I design from time to time to send them goods from hence. My whole account I will pay you when you come up here, not in poetical paper credit, but in the solid money of this dirty world. I will not draw upon you, in case you be not prepared to defend yourself; but if your purse be valiant, please to inquire for Jean or Elizabeth Thomson, at the Reverend Mr. Gusthart's; and if this letter be not sufficient testimony of the debt, I will send you whatever you shall desire.'[2] The poet could of course afford to help his sisters, although his office of Secretary of the Briefs was not quite as secure as he would have wished. Apparently one of the occasional but usually ineffectual attempts at reform which troubled the peace of eighteenth-century sinecurists, had threatened to reduce Thomson's emoluments; and in a letter of 7 August 1735, to Cranstoun, he wrote: 'Should you enquire into my circumstances—they have blossomed pretty well of late, the Chancellor having given me the office of Secretary of the Briefs under him; but the blight of an idle enquiry into the fees and offices of the courts of Justice which arose of late, seems to threaten its destruction.—In that case, I am made to hope amends; to be reduced, however, from enjoyment

[1] Quoted McKillop, *op. cit.*, p. 178.   [2] Quoted *Works of Thomson*, ed. Nicolas, i, lxx.

to Hope, is but an awkward affair: awkward or not, Hope and I, (I hope) shall never part.—Hope is the breath in the Nostrils of Happiness, when that goes this dies. But then, one ought at the same time to distinguish between the fair star of Hope, and that Meteor, Court-expectation: with regard to this, I subscribe to a new Beatitude of Pope's, or Swift's I think it is—Blessed is he who expecteth nothing, for he shall never be disappointed.'[1]

The 'idle enquiry' was apparently a 'Commission of the Great Officers of State for enquiring into public offices', and Thomson, summoned before them, 'made a speech explaining the duty, &c., of his place in terms that, though very concise, were so perspicuous and elegant, that Lord Chancellor Talbot publicly said he preferred that single speech to the best of his poetical compositions'.[2] He must have explained the duties too exactly and honestly because, it was reported, the 'income of the place was reduced from about £300 to £100 a year'.[3]

His sisters seem to have failed in their business, and in 1738 he had to make another arrangement for their support. He wrote to his friend Gavin Hamilton on 18 February 1737/8: 'I lately heard from my sisters at Edinburgh, that you were so good as to promise to advance to them, on my account, a trifle of money, which I proposed to allow them yearly. The sum is sixteen pounds stirling, and which I would have paid them eight pounds stirling at Martinmas, and the other eight pounds at Whitsuntide, the payment to begin from last Martinmas. So that the first year will be completed at Whitsunday next. Your doing this I shall look upon as a particular favour, and the money shall be paid here at your order as you please to direct.'[4] Thomson had lost his sinecure by this time, and that he should still attempt to forward an allowance to his sisters from his own scanty and inadequate means is a further proof of his affectionate disposition and his unimpeachable loyalty.

---

[1] *Forster Coll.*, 48 E.4.; V. & A.   [2] *Critical Review*, xix (1765), 141.   [3] *Ibid.*
[4] Quoted *Works of Thomson*, ed. Nicolas, i, lxxii.

CHAPTER VII

PLAYWRIGHT AND POLITICIAN

In this rank Age,
Much is the Patriot's weeding Hand required.

WHILE James Thomson lived in London he had lodgings in Lancaster Court in the Strand. He had occupied lodgings in this Court as early as 1726, according to his friend James Robertson, who lived opposite him;[1] and he had asked William Cranstoun, in his letter of 7 August 1735, to direct his reply to him 'at the Lancaster Coffee House, Lancaster Court, in the Strand', which shows that he still lived in either the same or neighbouring lodgings. He asked Aaron Hill, however, in his letter of 11 May 1736, to address his reply to him 'in *Kew-Lane, Richmond, Surrey*; and order your Letter to be put into the General Post'.[2] Hill understood from this direction that the poet was only on a visit to Richmond, and in his letter of 20 May he asked: 'Pray how long do you stay in *Kew-Lane?*—I have no other reason for asking, but because I have long been resolving a visit to *Richmond*, and, while you are so near it, my inducement will be doubled.'[3] Thomson had in fact made Richmond his home.

The retreat from London into the neighbouring countryside was a marked feature of eighteenth-century social behaviour. Along the reaches of the Thames, or on the pastoral heights rising about the city, those who wished could withdraw from the world into a rural solitude to cultivate their gardens and contemplate Nature, and yet be near enough to London to enjoy the amenities of civiliza-

---

[1] Hone, *op. cit.*, ii, 108.   [2] Hill, *Collection of Letters*, 1751, p. 65.
[3] Hill, *Works*, 1753, i, 238.

tion and continue an uninterrupted intercourse with their friends. It was the beginning of both suburban development and the great revolt against civic complexity in favour of rustic simplicity. The poets who were, as always, in the van of contemporary taste, led the way, and throughout the eighteenth century they continued to emigrate from the coffee-houses, among whose bustle they had flourished during the previous century, until hardly a stream or hill in the home counties was without one to celebrate its beauties. This movement, deepening and quickening like a flood, pressed on inexorably until by the close of the century it had reached as far outward as the Lake District, which found its ultimate and greatest poet in William Wordsworth.

Alexander Pope was among the first to move out of London, and in 1718 he took his famous house at Twickenham, where he 'twisted and twirled, and rhymed and harmonized' his five acres of garden 'till it appeared two or three sweet little lawns opening and opening beyond one another, and the whole surrounded with thick impenetrable woods'.[1] Thomson had early expressed his desire to withdraw into a similar seclusion. He exclaimed in a letter of 1728, 'I too am far from that divine freedom, that independent life which the Muses love; but it shall not be long thus, and soon will I hang up my harp upon the willows'.[2] Later, in his letter to Lady Hertford from Paris, he wrote: 'How I long to get a little out of the storms of the city, where all the fiercer passions blow; and to pursue again the friendly calm of the country, agitated alone by the gentler ones'. He also gave absolute expression to this ideal of rural retirement in four lines of verse:

> An elegant Sufficiency, Content,
> Retirement, rural Quiet, Friendship, Books,
> Ease and alternate Labour, useful Life,
> Progressive Virtue, and approving Heaven.

He could not have chosen a lovelier place than Richmond, which was still, in the first half of the eighteenth

---

[1] Walpole, *Letters*, ed. Toynbee, iv, 397.   [2] Cunningham, *op. cit.*, p. 34.

century, a small unspoilt village. It was already, however, becoming a favourite place of residence, and the new villas which sprang up yearly, and a small theatre which had opened at the beginning of the century, testified to its popularity. It also had some reputation as a health resort, and visitors were attracted to its Wells both by the medicinal waters and by its amusements. There were as early as 1724 'balls at Richmond Wells every Monday and Thursday Evening during the summer season', and the company who frequented these entertainments has been vividly described: 'Here are men of all professions and all religions—Jews and Gentiles, Papists and Dissenters—so that be one's inclination what it may, you will find one's own stamp to converse with. If you love books, every gentleman hath a library ready at your service; if you make love, a stranger is every where welcome. At play, they will indeed be a great deal too cunning for you; even the ladies think it no crime to pawn handsomely; and for drinking, you may be matched from night to morning. Field exercise, also, as much as anywhere. In short, for a man of no business, whose time hangs on his hand, recommend me to Richmond.'[1] Who could have resisted such a catholic appeal? John Armstrong, a friend of Thomson's, also referred to Richmond's popularity in some verses of his poem on *The Art of Preserving Health*:

> To us there wants not many a happy seat;
> Look round the smiling land, such numbers rise
> We hardly fix, bewilder'd, in our choice.
> See where enthron'd in adamantine state,
> Proud of her bards, imperial Windsor sits;
> There chuse thy seat, in some aspiring grove
> Fast by the slowly-winding Thames; or where
> Broader she laves fair Richmond's green retreats,
> (Richmond that sees an hundred villas rise
> Rural or gay.)

An examination of the Richmond Rates Books shows that Thomson occupied two cottages in Kew Foot Lane. He

[1] *Journey thro' England in 1724*, quoted Richard Crisp, *Richmond and its Inhabitants*, 1866, p. 358.

lived in the first only until 1739 when he removed to the
second and larger of the two, which was built on the ground
now covered by the Royal Hospital. The grounds of this
cottage were 'by Estimation in front thirty two feet from
North to South and one hundred and five feet in depth from
East to West abutting West on Kew Lane'.[1] The catalogue
of his effects, which were sold by auction in 1749, proves
that this second cottage was commodious and well furnished. There appear to have been seven rooms and a kitchen,
and the style in which they were fitted out may be gathered
from the inventory made of the contents of two of the principal rooms. The 'Right-hand Parlour' was furnished with
'A compass stove compleat brass fender; six mahogany
elbow chairs, green worsted damask seats; two pair of green
damask window curtains; a Sconce in a gilt frame, with brass
arms: a large mahogany dining table; a mahogany pillar and
claw tea table; a mahogany card table, lined with green cloth:
five bottle dishes, one small waiter, two tea boards, a reading desk and knife tray; a backgammon table compleat,
with chess men; and a scotch carpet'. A bedroom, up 'One
Pair of Stairs', had among other furnishings 'a four post
wainscoat bedstead, foot post mahogony, with green morine
furniture; a mahogony bottle cistern, brass hoops and
handles; a wallnut-tree inlaid dressing table, and dressing
glass in a wallnut-tree frame; four wallnut-tree chairs, black
leather seats; and six Pieces of Paper Hangings, and bordering to ditto'. There were many engravings after famous
painters, and the names of Raphael, Carlo Maratti, Guido
Reni, Nicholas Poussin, and Veronese often recur in the
catalogue. The library was not very extensive—only two
hundred and sixty lots were listed in the catalogue, and
these usually consisted of only one work, although lot No.
226, for example, was made up of 'fifty two Quarto Pamphlets, mostly Poetry'—but it was remarkably catholic in its
scope. There were classical, Italian, and French texts, contemporary poetry, handbooks on husbandry and medicine,

[1] *Court Rolls of the Manor of Richmond 1746-67.*

and, of particular interest, a collection of travel literature. Although the poet cannot be said to have lived in luxury, he certainly had an 'elegant sufficiency', and if the inventory of his goods is compared with that of his mother's, it may be said that his cottage was luxurious.

He was attended by a housekeeper, a Mrs. Hobart,[1] and by two nephews, Thomas and Gilbert Thomson, whom he employed as gardeners. When James Robertson was asked if these nephews lived with Thomson, he retorted, 'Rather lived on him, you mean',[2] and it would appear that only the poet's charitable and loyal disposition made him tolerate their company. One died in obscurity, and one ended by tumbling out of a tree,[3] but their deaths did not occur until many years after the poet's own.

When Thomson took up his residence in Kew Foot Lane he was thirty-six, and his appearance and character had greatly altered during the ten years since the publication of *Winter*. The eighteenth-century gentleman ran to fat; few had the will of Horace Walpole to rigorously control their habits; and the unresisted attractions of rich food and wines quickly bred those porcine countenances which stare out in their portraits from beneath the thatching of vast wigs. James Thomson was for once at one with his time in this matter. His face broadened and coarsened with the years, and the quick, sensitive features, which were depicted by William Aikman in the early sketch of his friend, soon subsided under corpulence. As he grew older, his originally athletic physique became heavy and unwieldy, and a pronounced stoop exaggerated the untidiness of his dress, which 'was clean, and yet slovenly'.[4] His appearance was certainly unprepossessing to the casual observer who saw him 'walking alone, in a thoughtful mood', but when a friend accosted him and entered into conversation, his face would immediately brighten and his eyes would dart their 'peculiar animated fire'. 'The case was much alike in company; where, if it was mixed, or very numerous, he made but an

---

[1] See Hone, *op. cit.*, ii, 589.   [2] *Ibid.*   [3] *Ibid.*   [4] *Ibid.*, ii, 588.

indifferent figure: but with a few select friends, he was open, sprightly, and entertaining. His wit flowed freely, but pertinently, and at due intervals, leaving room for everyone to contribute his share. Such was his extreme sensibility, so perfect the harmony of his organs with the sentiments of his mind, that his looks always announced, and half expressed, what he was about to say; and his voice corresponded exactly to the manner and degree in which he was affected. This sensibility had one inconvenience attending it, that it rendered him the very worst reader of good poetry: a *sonnet*, or a copy of tame verses, he could manage pretty well; or even improve them in the reading: but a passage of *Virgil*, *Milton*, or *Shakespeare*, would sometimes quite oppress him, that you could hear little else than some ill-articulated sounds, rising as from the bottom of his breast.'[1] The later portraits of the poet confirm Patrick Murdoch's delightful impression of his friend. Despite the corpulence and the heavy, unanimated lower face, there is the suggestion that his countenance could be fired into activity and expression, and that a latent sensibility was ready to seize command and dispel the lethargy. His senses were responsible for this obesity. He could not resist the temptations of the table or the bottle, and his sensual reaction to the thought of tropical fruits is an admirable illustration of this weakness. He exclaimed ecstatically in *Summer*:

> O stretch'd amid these Orchards of the Sun,
> Give me to drain the Cocoa's milky Bowl,
> And from the Palm to draw its freshening Wine!
> More bounteous far than all the frantic Juice
> Which *Bacchus* pours. Nor, on its slender Twigs
> Low-bending, be the full Pomegranate scorn'd;
> Nor, creeping thro' the Woods, the gelid Race
> Of Berries. Oft in humble Station dwells
> Unboastful Worth, above fastidious Pomp.
> Witness, thou best Anana, thou the pride
> Of vegetable Life, beyond whate'er
> The Poets imag'd in the golden Age:

[1] *Works of Thomson*, 1762, i, xvi–xvii.

Quick, let me strip thee of thy tufty Coat,
Spread thy ambrosial Stores, and feast with *Jove*!

His poetry is a more eloquent witness to his extreme sensibility than either portraits or friends. Impressions came crowding in upon his imagination so quickly that he was unable to choose between them, but ran them all indiscriminately into verse. He was at the mercy of his sensibility, and should it break away from his loose government, it would inevitably destroy him.

His indolence was notorious. It is said that he was once seen to eat the sun-streaked side of some peaches as they hung on the tree without even troubling to take his hands out of his pockets. This may be an exaggeration, but his usual hour of rising was certainly noon. His laziness has been emphasized too often however; *The Seasons* and *Liberty* are both very long poems, and in addition he wrote five tragedies and many minor pieces; an idle man could never have accomplished so much. But if by his indolence nothing more is meant than that the poet delighted in the passive enjoyment of his senses, then he carried this trait to a fault.

His habits of life at Kew Foot Lane are fairly well known. His friend, James Robertson, when asked, 'I hear he kept very late hours?' laconically replied, 'No, sir, very early; he was always up at sunrise, but then he had never been in bed'.[1] Patrick Murdoch also witnessed that 'the deep silence of the night' was the time he commonly chose for composition, 'so that he would often be heard walking in his library, till near morning, humming over in his way, what he was to correct and write out next day'.[2] Another observer of his habits said that 'he had an arbour at the end' of his garden, 'where he used to write in summer time. I have known him lie along by himself upon the grass near it, and talk away as though three or four people were along with him'.[3] He preferred autumn to the other seasons, and said, 'I think

---

[1] Hone, *op. cit.*, ii, 109.   [2] *Works of Thomson*, 1762, i, xvii–xviii.
[3] Hone, *op. cit.*, ii, 589.

that season of the year the most pleasing and the most
poetical. The spirits are not then dissipated with the gaiety
of Spring, and the glaring light of Summer, but composed
into a serious and tempered joy.'[1] His delight in autumn is
linked to the sentiment uttered by him which Joseph Spence
recorded: 'A serene melancholy, the most noble and most
agreeable situation of the mind'.[2] His pleasure in night,
music, and sober melancholy made him particularly attentive to the nightingales' song, and he 'would sometimes
listen a full hour at his window to the nightingales in *Richmond* gardens'.[3] He himself admirably described their
singing:

> Where all abandon'd to Despair, she sings
> Her Sorrows thro' the Night; and, on the Bough
> Sole-sitting, still at every dying Fall
> Takes up again her lamentable Strain
> Of winding Woe; till wide around the Woods
> Sigh to her Song, and with her Wail resound.

He attempted again in other memorable lines to describe the
bird:

> while in our Shades,
> Thro' the soft Silence of the listening Night,
> The sober-suited Songstress trills her lay.

Among the many friends who often visited the poet at
his cottage perhaps the most interesting was Alexander
Pope, who could easily make the short journey from
Twickenham. The friendship between the two poets had
been close ever since their first meeting. Thomson, as we
have seen, praised Pope in *Winter*, and Pope, according
to Dr. Johnson, addressed an epistle to Thomson while he
was travelling on the Continent.[4] These lines were supposed
to have been included in Pope's *Epistle to Arbuthnot*, but
they have never been identified. Upon his return from
abroad, Thomson was quickly intimate with Pope again,

---

[1] Letter to Lyttelton, 14 July 1743; quoted *Works of Thomson*, ed. Nicolas, i,
lxxxvii.   [2] Spence, *op. cit.*, p. 248.
[3] *Works of Thomson*, 1762, i, xviii.   [4] See Johnson, *op. cit.*, iii, 291.

M

and he wrote to Aaron Hill on 18 December 1733: 'Soon I
propose to fix in Town for the Winter, during which Time,
I hope to pass several happy Evenings in your Company:
Mr. *Pope* earnestly wishes the same.'[1] Once Thomson was
established in his cottage, they must have seen each other
more often, and James Robertson, answering the question,
'Pope, as I have heard, used often to visit Thomson?'
replied: 'Yes, frequently. Pope has sometimes said, Thomson, I'll walk to the end of your garden, and then set off to
the bottom of Kew-foot-lane and back. Pope, sir, courted
Thomson, and Thomson was always admitted to Pope
whether he had company or not; but Pope had a jealousy of
every eminent writer; he was a viper that gnawed the file.'[2]
Thomson's loquacious barber, William Taylor, also remembered Pope's frequent visits, and added that Pope 'used
to wear a light-coloured great coat, and commonly kept it
on in the house; he was a strange, ill-formed, little figure of
a man'.[3] Pope's meagre body and fine features must have
made a strange contrast to Thomson's corpulence, but their
conversations were so entrancing that the barber could 'have
listened to them for ever'.

Naturally enough, Scotsmen predominated among the
friends who frequented Thomson's cottage. Patrick Murdoch—who was later to write the poet's biography—a
mathematician of some reputation and a man of affable
manners, was among his closest friends. After acting as a
tutor, Murdoch decided to seek the security of the Church
of England, and Thomson wrote on 12 January 1738 to
give the news to their mutual friends in Edinburgh: 'I have
not yet seen the round Man of God, to be', he wrote face-
tiously; 'he is to be Parsonifyed a few days hence. How a
Gown and Cassock will become him! and with what a holy
Leer he will edify the devout Females! There is no doubt of
his having a Call, for he is immediately to enter upon a
tolerable Living—God grant him more, and as fat as him-

---

[1] Hill, *Collection of Letters*, 1751, p. 61.   [2] Hone, *op. cit.*, ii, 109–10.
[3] *Ibid.*, ii, 589.

self.'[1] Murdoch duly entered into the living of Stradishall, Suffolk, and could write that he was 'very well content' with the stipend of a hundred pounds. Another and more brilliant Scottish friend was Dr. John Armstrong, who, when he was little more than sixteen, wrote a poem upon winter 'in imitation of Shakespeare'. This poem was finished at the time when Thomson's own poem of *Winter* appeared, and Thomson, 'soon hearing of it, had the curiosity to procure a copy by the means of a common acquaintance. He shewed it to his poetical friends, Mr. Mallet, Mr. Aaron Hill, and Dr. Young, who, it seems, did great honour to it.'[2] The poem suggested to Thomson some of the additions which he later made to *Winter*, and when Armstrong, after qualifying in medicine at Edinburgh, moved to London, Thomson sought his acquaintance. Armstrong was a saturnine, satirical fellow who became embittered by his failure in his profession. His poetry contributed something to this failure. He published in 1736 a coarse and humourless performance entitled *The Economy of Love*, and an apothecary, who knew the doctor well, remarked, 'He ruined himself by that foolish performance of his . . . How, in the name of heaven, could he ever expect that a woman would let him enter her house again, after that?'[3] He later redeemed this error by publishing in 1744 his didactic poem—perhaps the finest of its kind in the language—*The Art of Preserving Health*, in which he introduced between his dissertations upon the necessary rules for health delightful descriptive passages in the manner of Thomson.

Since his return from the Continent, Thomson had been too preoccupied by *Liberty* and social engagements to turn his attention again to the theatre. Before he had set out on his travels, however, he had been considering a suitable subject for a second play, and had written in his letter of

---

[1] MS. 3278, ff. 40–1; Nat. Library of Scotland.
[2] John Armstrong, *Miscellanies*, 1770, i, 145.
[3] Charles Bucke, *Life, Writings, and Genius of Akenside*, 1832, pp. 29–30.

24 October 1730 to Dodington: 'At my times of leisure abroad, I think of attempting another Tragedy, and a story more addressed to common passions than "Sophonisba". The Sophonisba people now-a-days must have something like themselves, and a public-spirited monster can never interest them.' His leisure abroad, however, had been otherwise employed, and the tragedy was still unwritten when he returned. His friends and admirers were not slow to encourage him to a further attempt, and Thomas Rundle's correspondent, Mrs. Barbara Sandys, even suggested to him a proper subject, which, Rundle assured her, the poet had 'drawn out into acts and scenes';[1] but he may have given this assurance only to hide from her that the poet intended to disregard her suggestion. Thomson had, meanwhile, made his own choice of subject, and he had already made some progress in the work by the end of 1736. He wrote in a letter of 6 November, 'I am whipping and spurring to finish a tragedy for you this winter, but am still at some distance from the goal, which makes me fear of being distanced'.[2] The subject he had chosen was that of the death of Agamemnon on his return home from the siege of Troy, and Rundle gave his frank opinion on both the merits and defects which he believed would be apparent in the work. 'My friend, THOMPSON, the *Poet*,' he wrote, 'is bringing another untoward Heroine on the stage . . . His present story is the death of AGAMEMNON. An adultress, who murthers her husband, is but an odd example to be presented before, and admonish the beauties of *Great Britain*. However if he will be advised, it shall not be a shocking, though it cannot be a noble story. He will enrich it with a profusion of worthy sentiments, and high poetry, but it will be written in a rough, harsh stile, and in numbers great, but careless. He wants that neatness and simplicity of diction, which is so natural in dialogue. He cannot throw the light of an elegant ease on his thoughts, which will

[1] *Letters of Rundle*, 1789, ii, 195.
[2] Quoted *Works of Thomson*, ed. Nicolas, i, lxx.

make the sublimest turns of art appear the genuine unpre-
meditated dictates of the heart of the speaker. But with all
his faults, he will have a thousand masterly strokes of a great
genius seen in all he writes. And he will be applauded by
those, who most censure him.'[1] The poet, however, did not
whip and spur enough, and the tragedy was not finished in
time to be produced during the season of 1736/7.

The security and even tenor of his life were, moreover,
suddenly threatened by the death of Lord Talbot on 14
February 1737. The Lord Chancellor was only fifty-four,
and Thomson must have expected a long continuance of
his patronage. Few contemporary statesmen commanded
as sincere a respect as Talbot, and his death was held to be a
national calamity. 'He rose, by Merit, to the *Head of his
Profession*,' wrote *The Craftsman*, 'and not only supported
himself in it with Dignity, but adorn'd it, and acquired
every Day new Praise and Esteem.' Newspaper obituaries
are, however, always to be suspected, and it is as well to
quote from a letter which Thomas Rundle wrote after the
death of his patron and companion: 'All parties unite to
call him the best and greatest man that ever lived. The
whole town, from the Court to the city, are under the deepest
astonishment . . . Great as he was allowed to be in his
public character, you know he was more amiable, more
delightful in his domestic behaviour. Was there ever any so
reasonably beloved as himself, by all, from the highest to
the lowest, in his family? Did his children ever enjoy more
ease, more sprightly innocence, and entertaining instructive unbendings to mirth, than in his conversation and
laughter?'[2] Thomson was not behind in paying his tribute
to the memory of so good a man and staunch a friend, and
he published in the following June, his *Poem to the Memory
of the Right Honourable the Lord Talbot*. He confessed in
the opening verses that he found it almost impossible

---

[1] *Letters of Rundle*, 1789, ii, 195. This letter is dated in the collection '1730', but
since it refers to the delay in George II's return from Hanover, it clearly belongs to
either December 1736 or January 1736/7.   [2] *Ibid.*, ii, 201.

to 'sing his matchless Virtues', and used a fine image to
describe his difficulty; he likened Talbot's 'matchless
Virtue' to a diamond, and asked,

> How from the Diamond single out each Ray,
> That, tho' they tremble with ten thousand Hues,
> Effuse one poignant undivided Light?

He continued, after the manner of Rundle in his letter, to
praise him for the just and punctilious performance of his
public duties, and then passed to a consideration of the kind
and witty character he revealed in private life. The poem
suffers, like most elegies, from the poet's attempt to pitch
his commendations too high, and the man who is remembered appears to be improbably good. There were, however,
many good lines and striking thoughts, and the poet's transparent sincerity of grief saved it from failure. Lord Talbot's
and Thomson's friend, Thomas Rundle, was not forgotten,
and he was pictured in the poem straying sadly, 'with
Memory conversing', along 'the pebbled Shore' where
'Derry's Mountains a bleak Crescent form'.

The first serious effect of the Lord Chancellor's death was
that Thomson lost his position as Secretary of the Briefs.
The sinecure had earlier been threatened by 'the blight of
an idle inquiry', and the emoluments had been reduced from
three hundred to one hundred pounds a year, but even this
reduced sum must have contributed something towards the
poet's comfort.[1] Patrick Murdoch—whose evidence is
always to be respected—said that the poet would have
retained the office had he troubled to solicit Lord Hardwicke, Talbot's successor as Lord Chancellor, to continue
him in it: 'This place fell with his patron,' wrote Murdoch,
'and although the noble Lord, who succeeded to Lord *Talbot*
in office, kept it vacant for some time, probably till Mr.
Thomson should apply for it, he was so dispirited, and so list-
less to every concern of that kind, that he never took one
step in the affair: a neglect which his best friends greatly

---

[1] See Johnson, *op. cit.*, iii, 290 *n.* 5.

blamed in him.'[1] A writer in the *Critical Review*, however, categorically stated that he had the poet's 'own authority for saying that it was not optional to him whether he should remain in the place after his patron's death'.[2] It may have been indolence that prevented Thomson from making the necessary and customary application to be continued in office, but it is much more probable, as the writer in the *Critical Review* would seem to imply, that Lord Hardwicke, who was closely concerned in Walpole's administration, never intended that Thomson, a known supporter of the opposition, should continue to fill an office which could be more usefully bestowed elsewhere. Even if he kept it open for some time in expectation of the poet's application, Thomson was too principled to desert the opposition for a bribe of a hundred pounds.

Murdoch said that this loss made little difference to his economy—and if the suggestion is true, although Murdoch had no knowledge of it, that he had never drawn the salary after it was reduced to a hundred pounds,[3] that is understandable. 'He resumed, with time, his usual chearfulness, and never abated one article in his way of living; which, though simple, was genial and elegant.'[4] He had the profits arising from his works, which 'were not inconsiderable', and Andrew Millar, his publisher, 'was always at hand to answer, or even to prevent, his demands; and he had a friend or two besides, whose hearts, he knew, were not contracted by the ample fortunes they had acquired; who would, of themselves, interpose, if they saw any occasion for it'.[5] It is most improbable that his loss of office reduced Thomson to want. He certainly lived throughout his life from hand to mouth, but this was the consequence of his notorious carelessness in money matters, which is well illustrated by an anecdote told by Thomas Parke, the poet: 'Mr. Collins, the brewer, has told me, that he (Thomson) was so heedless in his money concerns, that in paying him a bill

---

[1] *Works of Thomson*, 1762, i, xi.   [2] Quoted Johnson, *op. cit.*, iii, 290 *n.* 5.
[3] *Ibid.*   [4] *Works of Thomson*, 1762, i, xi-xii.   [5] *Ibid.*

for beer, he gave him two bank notes rolled together instead of one. Collins did not perceive the mistake until he got home, and when he returned the note Thomson appeared perfectly indifferent about the matter, and said he had enough to go on without it.' James Robertson, when he was told this anecdote, said, 'it was like him', and capped it with another: 'I remember', he said, 'his being stopped once between London and Richmond, and robbed of his watch, and when I expressed my regret for his loss, "Pshaw, damn it," said he, "I am glad they took it from me, 'twas never good for any thing".'[1] Even if he had been temporarily distressed, he had many friends, as Murdoch affirmed, who would have been only too ready to relieve him.

There is, however, one curious anecdote connected with this time. It is said that Thomson was arrested for a debt of almost seventy pounds and confined in a sponging-house, from which he was rescued through the generosity of James Quin, the actor; who, visiting him in his confine-ment, announced after the dinner which he had ordered to be sent up had been eaten, that he had come to settle his account with the poet; that he judged the pleasure which his works had given him to be worth at least a hundred pounds, and laying a bank bill for that amount upon the table, left the room.[2] This story is not referred to by any of the earlier biographers, and it is probably only an exaggerated account of the manner in which Quin made the poet a loan. It seems to have been so generally known, however, that it must have had some foundation in fact, and Christopher Anstey referred to it in his satirical poem of *The New Bath Guide*, in which Quin's shade is thus greeted by Thomson's upon its arrival in Elysium:

> There Thomson, poor Thomson, ingenuous bard,
> Shall equal thy friendship, thy kindness reward,
> Thy praise in mellifluous numbers prolong,
> Who cherish'd his Muse, and gave life to his song.

[1] Hone, *op. cit.*, ii, 108–9.   [2] See Morel, *op. cit.*, pp. 120–1.

Thomson had probably struck up a friendship with Quin long before 1737, but whenever they were introduced, they became close friends. Quin was the last great actor of the old school, and maintained his supremacy until displaced by Garrick. There were those, however, who preferred his playing of many parts to that of his young rival, and as a man, he was certainly a much greater and more lovable character. He was famous also as a gourmand, a heavy but imperturbable drinker, and a wit whose *bons mots* have not yet lost their humour. He was brusque in manner with strangers but no one could show greater amiability with chosen friends. He was a frequent visitor at Kew Foot Lane, and Mrs. Hobart, Thomson's housekeeper, dreaded his arrival because he persuaded her master to drink too much. The barber, William Taylor, said, 'I have seen him and Quin coming from the Castle together at four o'clock in a morning, and not over sober you may be sure'.[1] Taylor also undertook to shave Quin as well as Thomson, and that was apparently no easy task. 'I have often taken Quin by the nose too,' he said, 'which required some courage, let me tell you. One day he asked particularly if the razor was in good order; and protested he had as many barbers' ears in his parlour at home, as any boy had of birds' eggs on a string; and swore, if I did not shave him smoothly, he would add mine to the number. "Ah," said Thomson, "Wull shaves very well, I assure you".'[2]

The poet was not long without a patron. Frederick, Prince of Wales, had taken an interest in Thomson ever since he had attended the performances of *Sophonisba*; Lady Hertford had presented a copy of *The Seasons* to him; Bubb Dodington, while he was his most untrustworthy and ineffectual 'first minister', must have often spoken about Thomson in his presence; and he had been pleased to accept the dedication of *Liberty*. Thomson was also a very useful propagandist to win over to the opposition, and there was

[1] Hone, *op. cit.*, ii, 589.   [2] *Ibid.*, ii, 590.

thus every reason why the Prince should reward his past and prospective services by conferring on him a pension. Patrick Murdoch was very definite that this pension was not conferred until George Lyttelton—who became secretary to the Prince in 1737—had made representations on his behalf. Lyttelton's recommendation, Murdoch continued, 'came altogether unsollicited, and long before Mr. *Thomson* was personally known to him'.[1] It is difficult to accept this statement. It is most improbable that Thomson had not met Lyttelton, either at the houses of some of the opposition or at Alexander Pope's, who was a close friend and admirer of Lyttelton, long before 1737. It may be, however, that their intimacy only dated from this year. According to one account, Thomson, after 'being gaily interrogated' by the Prince 'about the state of his affairs, said, "that they were in a more poetical posture than formerly", and had a pension allowed him of one hundred pounds a year'.[2]

Although Thomson, like so many of his contemporaries, was beguiled by the Prince's patriotic and liberal pronouncements into admiring his character, he cannot have relished accepting even his patronage. Any contemporary man of letters who did not enjoy a private income had to seek out, secure, and flatter some patron if he wished to live. Alexander Pope was the only poet whose writings provided an independency. Thomson was forced to behave like any other impoverished poet of the time, but he behaved so unwillingly. He wrote to Aaron Hill in 1736: 'With regard to Arts and Learning, one may venture to say, that they might yet stand their Ground, were they but merely protected. In lieu of all Patrons that have been, are, or will be, in *England*, I wish we had one good Act of Parliament for securing to Authors the Property of their own Works . . . And can it be, that those who impress Paper with what constitutes the best and everlasting Riches of all civiliz'd Nations, and of all Ages, should have less Property in the

---

[1] *Works of Thomson*, 1762, i, xii.   [2] Johnson, *op. cit.*, iii, 291.

Paper, so enrich'd, than those who deal in the Rags which make that Paper?'[1] The 'one good Act of Parliament' was not passed until long after Thomson's death, and in the meantime poets had to live on flattery or in poverty. Thomson had liberally praised his chosen patrons, but Tobias Smollett, who knew him well, affirmed that he had intended, had he lived longer, to have retracted these praises. Smollett wrote in the Dedication to his novel, *Ferdinand, Count Fathom*: 'Sometimes too, dazzled by the tinsel of a character which he [any contemporary author] has no opportunity to investigate, he pours forth the homage of his admiration, upon some false Mæcenas, whose future conduct, gives the lie to his eulogium, and involves him in shame and confusion of face. Such was the fate of a late ingenious author [Thomson], who was so often put to the blush for the undeserved incense he had offered, in the heat of an enthusiastic disposition, misled by popular applause, that he had resolved to retract, in his last will, all the encomiums which he had thus prematurely bestowed, and stigmatize the unworthy by name: A laudable scheme of poetical justice, the execution of which was fatally prevented by untimely death.'

However much Thomson may have secretly disliked his dependence upon the Prince, he quickly became a frequenter of his Court, and an amusing story was told which proves the intimate terms on which he lived with the Prince. When William Shenstone, the poet, was on his way to London, he 'had taken a tailor of Hales Owen to carry his portmanteau. The trusty squire, having walked out to view the Thames at Maidenhead, returned saying, "Lord, Sir, what do you think? I have seen the Prince of Wales and all his nobles walking by the river's side". The nobles were Thomson and Mallet.'[2] Mallet had been rewarded for his loyalty at the same time as Thomson received his pension, being appointed under-secretary to the Prince at a salary of two

---

[1] Hill, *Collection of Letters*, 1751, pp. 64–5.
[2] Quoted Johnson, *op. cit.*, iii, 291 *n.* 2.

hundred pounds a year. An announcement which appeared in the *Daily Gazetteer* for 13 September 1737, introduces some old and new acquaintances, and also shows how closely Thomson was concerned with the Prince's Court. 'On Friday Evening last', it was announced, 'at Old Man's Coffee-house, Charing-Cross, the Hon. William Hawley, Esq; Gentleman Usher to the Prince of Wales, James Thomson, Esq; Author of the Seasons, Dr. Armstrong, Author of the Synopsis of the Venereal Disease (abridg'd from Astruc) and of several beautiful Poems, Mr. Paterson, of Three Kings Court, Lombard Street, Author of a Tragedy not yet published, and Mr. Sargent, Linen Draper near Mercer's Chapel, were admitted Free and Accepted Masons. Richard Savage, Esq; Son of the late Earl Rivers, associated as Master, and Mr. Charine and Dr. Schomberg, Jun. as Wardens; after which the new-made Brethren gave an elegant Entertainment.' William Paterson and his unpublished tragedy were to cause some slight trouble a year later; John Sargent was a friend and correspondent of Thomson, and probably intended to help him to stock his sisters' millinery shop in Edinburgh; and Isaac Schomberg was to become both famous and notorious as a medical practitioner, and the friend and consultant of many eighteenth-century poets, actors, and artists.

Thomson, however, earned his pension by the support he gave to the Prince of Wales in the feud which he was at this time conducting against his father, the King. Frederick had married in 1736 the Princess Augusta of Saxe-Gotha, and when it was known that she was pregnant, he determined, in order to insult his parents and flaunt his independence publicly, that the child should be born in London, in direct contradiction to the King's command that it should be born at Hampton Court. When she was unexpectedly taken in labour at Hampton Court on the evening of 31 July 1737, he secretly dragged her with incredible brutality from the palace to take her to St. James's. She begged 'for God's sake, that the Prince would let her stay in quiet where she was, for that her pains were so great she could not set one foot before the other, and was upon the rack when they moved her. But the Prince, with an obstinacy equal to his folly, and a folly equal to his barbarity, insisted on her going, crying *"Courage! Courage! ah quelle sottise!"* and telling her, with the encouragement of a toothdrawer, or the consolatory tenderness of an executioner, that it would be over in a minute.'[1] The child was safely born at St. James's. The Prince, to persuade the people that he had been wronged by the King and Queen, circulated many excuses to explain away his incredible conduct; and when the Queen visited the child a few days after its birth, he escorted her down to her coach, and, 'to make the mob believe he was never wanting in any respect, he kneeled down in the dirty street, and kissed her hand'.[2] The result of these repeated insults was that the King and Queen, who were not loath to punish a son whom they hated, expelled the Prince from St. James's and denied their Court to his followers. The Prince now assiduously courted the people, and posed before them as a patriot and a lover of liberty in contrast to the King, who was believed, with some reason, to be more anxious for the interests of Hanover than for those of Britain.

Thomson shortly after these events addressed an ode to the Prince, which he entrusted to Andrew Millar to place with the newspapers. The verses, which appeared in the *Whitehall Evening-Post* for 13–15 September and the *St. James's Evening-Post* for the same date, prophesied the glories which would devolve on Britain from the Prince's progeny, and pointed out the French and Spanish threats to British commerce, which the corrupt, pacific administration of Sir Robert Walpole was doing little to avert. It was only an occasional poem, but it usefully illustrates the politicial ideals which Thomson tenaciously held and continually announced.

[1] Hervey, *op. cit.*, ii, 364.   [2] *Ibid.*, ii, 409.

I

While *secret-leaguing* Nations frown around,
  Ready to pour the long-expected Storm;
While SHE, who wont the restless *Gaul* to bound,
  BRITANNIA, drooping, grows an empty Form;
While on our Vitals selfish-Parties prey,
And deep *Corruption* eats our Soul away:

II

Yet in the GODDESS OF THE MAIN appears
  A Gleam of Joy, gay-flushing every Grace,
As she the cordial Voice of Millions hears,
  Rejoycing, zealous, o'er THY RISING RACE;
Strait her rekindling Eyes resume their Fire,
The *Virtues* smile, the *Muses* tune the Lyre.

III

But more enchanting than the Muses Song,
  United BRITONS thy dear OFFSPRING hail:
The City Triumphs thro' her glowing Throng;
  The Shepherd tells his Transport to the Dale:
The Sons of roughest Toil forget their Pain,
And the glad Sailor chears the midnight Main.

IV

Can ought from fair AUGUSTA's gentle Blood,
  And Thine, THOU FRIEND OF LIBERTY! be born;
Can ought, save what is lovely, gen'rous, good;
  What will, at once, defend us, and adorn?
From thence prophetic Joy new EDWARDS Eyes,
New HENRYS, ANNAS, and ELIZAS rise.

V

My Fate my fond devoted Days extend,
  To sing the promis'd Glories of THY REIGN!
What tho', by Years depress'd, my *Muse* might bend,
  My Heart will teach her still a nobler Strain:
How, with *recover'd* BRITAIN, will she soar,
When *Fr---e* INSULTS, and *Sp--n* shall ROB, no more!

Thomson was not altogether pleased with the poem as it was printed in the newspapers. 'I thank you for getting my ode printed', he wrote to Millar on 18 September. 'In the meantime, who was so very cautious as to advise France & Spain being printed with a dash? You, I dare say, it was not —you have a superior Spirit to That.'[1] The *Ode* must have contributed something to raise the Prince's popularity, because a vicious attack was made on both it and its author in the ministerial paper, the *Daily Gazetteer*, on 6 October. The anonymous traducer began his article by pretending to be unfamiliar with Thomson's name: 'Who this Mr. *Thomson* is', he wrote, 'that has thought fit to address his *Royal Highness* in this extraordinary manner, I don't know.' After some further sparring, he really settled down to his attack: 'We must therefore look upon the Author of this *Ode*, as it is call'd, to be some ignorant, insignificant, officious, little Fellow, utterly destitute both of good Breeding and common Discretion, who is below Notice, and by Consequence not worth Reproof, or else we may be assured that both himself and his Verses would be treated with that Resentment which they deserve.' To prove that the verses were not worthy even of reproof, the traducer spent several hundred words in a commentary upon them. Lack of space confined his remarks to the first stanza only, but he concluded with the promise that if 'my present Observations should meet with so favourable a Reception, as to give me any Encouragement for it, I will proceed in my Remarks at another Opportunity'. He was not welcomed as he would have wished, and lapsed once more into silence and obscurity.

Thomson's letter of 18 September to Millar introduces another of his friends. 'Send me', he wrote, 'one of the large Edition of the Seasons, which I must give to Stephen Duck, he having made me a Present of his Poems.'[2] Stephen Duck was a remarkable character. He had begun life as an agricultural labourer but had taught himself to write verses good enough to attract the attention of the Wiltshire gentry, and when his first collection was published in 1730, it was immediately popular. Queen Caroline patronized him and gave him a small house in Richmond

---

[1] Quoted McKillop, *op. cit.*, p. 180.   [2] *Ibid.*

Park. Swift wrote some unnecessarily cruel verses upon his success, which began,

> The Thresher *Duck*, could o'er the Queen prevail.
> The Proverb says; *No Fence against a Flayl*.
> From *threshing* Corn, he turns to *thresh* his Brains;
> For which Her Majesty allows him Grains.

Duck was also patronized by Lady Hertford, to whom he addressed some verses, which contained praise of Thomson, printed in his *Poems on Several Occasions*. It was this volume, published in 1736, which he probably presented to Thomson. Duck was, however, a dangerous man to be intimate with; his Court patronage had not softened his muscles; and it was reported on 12 September 1737 that 'Last Saturday Evening a sad Accident happened at Hampton-Court to Mr. Griffith, First Clerk to his Grace the Lord Chamberlain of his Majesty's Household; who playing at the Game, Fives, a Welch Diversion, along with Stephen Duck, the Poet and others, Duck struck a Ball with such violence into Mr. Griffith's Face, that it put out one of his Eyes, and much endangered the other'.[1] Thomson's indolence, however, would insure him against suffering a fate similar to Griffith's, and his friendship with Duck was founded upon their mutual delight in Nature.

During the first months of 1738 Thomson published two further pieces in support of the opposition. Sir Robert Walpole, at the close of the session, in July 1737, had hurried through Parliament a Bill to restrain the licentiousness of the stage, which was designed to prevent the theatre from being used as an instrument to attack him and his administration. The Bill authorized the Lord Chamberlain to prohibit any dramatic piece which he thought was unsuitable for representation, and provided that 'no new play or addition to an old play could be acted if he had not first inspected it'.[2] The opposition understood this Bill to be the first step towards the licensing of the Press, and Lord

---

[1] *Caledonian Mercury*, 12 September 1737.   [2] Lecky, *op. cit.*, i, 542.

Chesterfield, in a brilliant speech on the Bill in the House of Lords, remarked, that 'altho' it *seems designed* only as a *Restraint* on the Licentiousness of the *Stage*, I fear, it looks farther and tends a Restraint on the *Liberty* of the *Press*, a Restraint even on *Liberty itself*'.[1] Andrew Millar printed the following advertisement in the *London Evening-Post* for 14–17 January: '*This Day is Published, Price* 1s. AREOPA-GITICA: A Speech of Mr. JOHN MILTON, for the *Liberty* of UNLICENS'D PRINTING, to the Parliament of England. First publish'd in the Year 1644. With a Preface, by another Hand.' It was inevitable that the opposition would reprint the greatest defence of the freedom of the Press that has ever been written, and it was fitting that the preface to this reprint should have been written by Thomson. It is an able performance, and it briefly announces the argument, which was greatly developed in the pamphlet which followed, that without liberty of the Press there can be no real liberty. 'Take away the liberty of the Press', Thomson affirmed, 'and we are all at once stript of the use of our noblest faculties: our souls themselves are imprisoned in a dark dungeon: we may breathe, but we cannot be said to live.'[2]

Two months later, another of Milton's political tracts was reprinted in support of the opposition's popular agitation for a war against Spain in order to prevent her interference with British trade to the Spanish colonies in America. Millar was again the publisher, and he advertised in the *London Evening-Post* for 14–16 March, that '*This Day is Published, Price* 6d. A Manifesto of the Lord Protector of the Commonwealth of England, Scotland, Ireland, &c. publish'd by Consent and Advice of his Council; wherein is shewn the Reasonableness of the Cause of this Republick against the Depredations of the Spaniards. Written in Latin by *John Milton*, and first printed in 1655: Now translated

---

[1] *London Mag.*, 1737, p. 378.
[2] *New Foundling Hospital for Wit*, 1786, iv, 199–200, where the Preface is re-printed under Thomson's name.

N

into English . . . To which is added, *Britannia*, a Poem. By Mr. Thomson. First publish'd in 1727.' There can be little doubt that Thomson was responsible for the republication of this tract, and the sentiments expressed in *Britannia* were in harmony with it. It is of course inaccurately stated in the advertisement that the poem was first printed in 1727; it had not been published until two years later. The popular outcry forced Walpole to demand compensation from Spain for the illegal capture of English ships, and eventually to declare war on her in 1739, an action which brought about his own downfall. Thomson, in so far as he succeeded in inflaming the people against Walpole's domestic and foreign policies, rendered the opposition good service by the republication of these two Miltonic tracts.

Meanwhile, Thomson had been able to finish his tragedy of *Agamemnon*, which he had originally intended to produce the previous season. He wrote to his friend George Ross in Edinburgh on 12 January 1737/8: 'Having been intirely in the Country of late, finishing my Play, I did not receive Your's till some days ago. It was kind in you not to draw rashly upon me, which, at present, had put me into Danger: but very soon (that is to say about two Months hence) I shall have a golden Buckler, and you may draw boldly—My Play is received in Drury-Lane Play-House, and will be put in to my Lord Chamberlain's, or his Deputy's Hands to-morrow—May we hope to see you this Winter, and to have the Assistance of your Hands, in Case it is acted?'[1] The Licensing Act had made this formality necessary, but it is most surprising that the Lord Chamberlain allowed *Agamemnon* to be performed—he must have been either a careless reader, or a lenient administrator—the tragedy was a flagrant attack upon Queen Caroline and Sir Robert Walpole. The story was taken from the play by Aeschylus, and,

[1] This letter is simply dated 'London, Jan. the 12th 1737', and earlier biographers have overlooked that Thomson is using the Old Style calendar. The contents make it plain that the date is 1737/8: he refers to Murdoch as 'about to enter upon a tolerable living', which he did not do until 1738, and he mentions that *Agamemnon* is in the hands of the Lord Chamberlain, which was unnecessary before the Licensing Act of 1737.

in the light of Joseph Warton's remark that 'Thomson was well acquainted with the Greek tragedies, on which I heard him talk learnedly',[1] it is plain that the poet had an intimate knowledge of his original; but the plot was entirely distorted to provide a commentary upon contemporary politics.

The play opens with the guilty Clytemnestra awaiting the heralded return of the victorious Agamemnon from the Trojan war. She has been seduced during his absence by the crafty and unscrupulous Aegisthus, whom Agamemnon left with her to be a joint-regent of his kingdom. Aegisthus has determined to overthrow Agamemnon, and upon his return he persuades Clytemnestra to agree to his murder, which is successfully carried out in spite of the prophesies of Cassandra. The play closes with the guilty pair being warned by the escape of Agamemnon's son, Orestes, to expect in the future retribution at his hands for their crime. Contemporary critics were quick to point out one of the more obvious weaknesses in the play; they 'very justly observed, that he had not entirely preserved antient manners and characters; Clytemnestra did not ressemble the portrait drawn of her by Aeschylus, which is more consistent and agreeable to history'.[2] The weak, timorous, and despondent Clytemnestra whom Thomson drew certainly had little resemblance to the Aeschylean portrait, but—apart from the impossibility of transferring such a character from the Attic to the eighteenth-century stage—there were particular reasons why she should be so portrayed. Aaron Hill, with his usual acuteness, drew Thomson's attention to an even greater fault in the play's construction. Agamemnon, who first appears in Act II, 'supports but a *second* or *third* part, in his own Tragedy', wrote Hill, when 'he ought to have animated, and stood obvious in every part of it'. The tragedy, continued Hill, also 'falls off on a sudden, and leaves the fourth and fifth acts, in particular, much too cold for their place, and their purpose'.[3] The weakness of the

---

[1] Quoted Johnson, *op. cit.*, iii, 282 *n.* 2.   [2] Davies, *Life of Garrick*, 1780, ii, 33.
[3] Hill, *Works*, 1753, i, 309.

two characters, Agamemnon and Clytemnestra, and the failure of the last two acts derive entirely from Thomson's attempt to make his play a political commentary.

Thomson was 'whipping and spurring to finish a tragedy' at the end of 1736, and Thomas Rundle, who may have seen the first acts in manuscript, knew the chosen plot by January of the following year. George II had set out on 22 May 1736 to make one of his visits to Hanover, and had left Queen Caroline in England as the Regent. He did not return until 15 January 1737. While he spent his time at Hanover with his new mistress, Madame Walmoden, the two most hated figures in England, Walpole and Queen Caroline, who could not be anathematized enough to please the populace, ruled the country. Thomson wrote the first two acts of *Agamemnon* during the King's absence, and it is plain that he intended Clytemnestra to represent Queen Caroline, and the wicked and debased Aegisthus, Sir Robert Walpole. The faults of construction and characterization to which Aaron Hill and other contemporary critics objected are thus simply explained. Thomson did not dare to make his condemnation of Queen Caroline too obvious but he did not scruple to make his portrait of Walpole as odious as possible. Clytemnestra, therefore, could not be actively evil; she could not be the Aeschylean queen; she had to be a weak, misguided woman whom Aegisthus unscrupulously imposed upon to further his own ambitions. Agamemnon was relegated to a second or third part in his own tragedy because the whole interest of the play turned entirely upon the characters and machinations of Aegisthus and Clytemnestra. The play inevitably fell off in the last two acts when the fable ceased to correspond with the contemporary political situation. George II was not murdered upon his return to England but welcomed by the Queen, whose lust for power could be more easily satisfied by his continued existence than by his death, which would have placed her hated son, the Prince of Wales, upon the throne. Thomson could only retreat therefore from reality into fiction, and wind up as best he could.

He probably found it very difficult to elaborate a convincing conclusion, and this difficulty may have prevented him from finishing it in time for it to be produced during the season of 1737. He did manage to complete it by the beginning of 1738, but by then the death of Queen Caroline in the previous November had robbed it of much of its sting; and apart from the character of Aegisthus, who would be popularly and correctly judged to represent Sir Robert, the fable had been rendered harmless.

Thomson wrote to his friend, Gavin Hamilton, in Edinburgh, on 18 February 1737/8, to tell him that at last *Agamemnon* was about to be produced. 'I have a tragedy, entitled Agamemnon, to be represented here about three weeks hence', he wrote. 'Please to let me know how many copies I shall send to you, and you shall have them in full time. I have some thoughts of printing it for myself, but if I do not, I will take care you shall have what copies of it you demand[1].' There is an amusing anecdote told about Thomson's behaviour at a rehearsal of his play. 'Thomson, in reading his play of Agamemnon to the actors, in the green-room, pronounced every line with such a broad Scotch accent, that they could not restrain themselves from a loud laugh. Upon this, the author good-naturedly said to the manager, "Do you, Sir, take my play, and go on with it; for, though I can write a tragedy, I find I cannot read one".'[2]

The parts were brilliantly cast. Quin appeared as Agamemnon, and his personal dignity and sonorous declamation would be enough to give life even to that ill-conceived character; Milward played the villain, Aegisthus, and his 'singular fault', 'the love of ranting',[3] may not have been out of place on this occasion; Mary Porter, one of the great actresses of the time, took Clytemnestra; and Susannah Maria Cibber had the difficult task of representing Cassandra. Mrs. Cibber, the sister of Thomas Arne, the com-

---

[1] This letter is dated '18th Feb. 1737' (William Goodhugh, *English Gentleman's Manual*, 1827, pp. 269–70), but it is clear from the definite manner in which Thomson speaks of the performance of *Agamemnon* that the date is 1737/8.
[2] Davies, *Dramatic Miscellanies*, 1785, iii, 498 *n.*   [3] *Ibid.*, iii, 117.

poser, and the unhappy wife of the rascally Theophilus Cibber, had been discovered and coached by Aaron Hill. Quin pronounced the opinion on her that '*that woman has a heart, and can do any thing where passion is required*',[1] and she was to become the finest of tragic actresses, to whom David Garrick was deeply indebted for his successes. Although the play was badly constructed, it contained some excellent verse which provided the actors with many chances to show all their skill. Thomson's dramatic blank verse is generally much more fluent and harmonious than that of his poems, and the actors must have relished declaiming it. Clytemnestra pronounces in the first scene this admirable reflection upon reason and passion, and Mrs. Porter would know how to make the most of it:

> Oh, Nature! wherefore, Nature, are we form'd
> One Contradiction? the continual Sport
> Of fighting Powers? Oh! wherefore hast thou sown
> Such War within us, such unequal Conflict,
> Between slow Reason and impetuous Passion?
> Passion resistless hurries us away,
> Ere lingering Reason to our Aid can come,
> And to upbraid us then it only serves.

It has never been sufficiently emphasized what admirable poetry Thomson's plays contain, and what a remarkable strain of romanticism runs through them all. An example from *Agamemnon* is a speech by Melisander, who explains how he was seized by ruffians, hired by Aegisthus, and carried off to a desert island:

> Next Night—a dreary Night!
> Cast on the wildest of the *Cyclade Isles*,
> Where never human Foot had mark'd the Shore,
> These Ruffians left me—Yet, believe me, *Arcas*,
> Such is the rooted Love we bear Mankind,
> All Ruffians as they were, I never heard
> A Sound so dismal as their parting Oars—
> Then Horrid Silence follow'd, broke alone
> By the low Murmurs of the restless Deep,

---

[1] Davies, *Dramatic Miscellanies*, i, 36–7.

Mixt with the doubtful Breeze, that now and then
Sigh'd thro' the mournful Woods.

These lines are reminiscent of those upon a shipwrecked mariner which Thomson had earlier included in *Summer*.

The tragedy was first performed on 6 April 1738, and the advertisement in the *London Daily-Post* read: 'DRURY-LANE. *Never Acted before. By His Majesty's Company of Comedians*, At the Theatre-Royal in Drury Lane, this day, April the 6th, will be presented a New Tragedy, call'd AGAMEMNON. The principal Parts to be perform'd by Mr. Quin, Mr. Milward, Mr. Cibber, Mr. Wright, Mr. Hill. Mrs. Porter, Mrs. Cibber, and Miss Brett. Boxes 5s. Pit 3s. First Gallery 2s. Upper Gallery 1s. BY HIS MAJESTY'S COMMAND, No Persons to be admitted behind the Scenes, nor any Money to be return'd after the Curtain is drawn up. Places to be taken at Mr. Moor's, Box Book-Keeper, in the Play-house Passage. To begin exactly at Six o'Clock.' Alexander Pope, who had written two letters to the managers of Drury Lane Theatre in favour of *Agamemnon*, attended the first night, and as 'he had not been for some time at a play, this was considered as a very great instance of esteem'.[1] The play was introduced by an admirable Prologue, written by David Mallet and spoken by Quin, in which the audience was begged to indulge the author's pride,

that bids him own,
He aims to please, by noble Means, alone:
By what may win the Judgment, wake the Heart,
Inspiring Nature, and directing Art:
By Scenes, so wrought, so rais'd, as may command
Applause, more from the Head, than from the Hand.

Once again, as in *Sophonisba*, Thomson owed his success to the singular ability of a leading actress. 'Mrs. Porter gave a striking proof of her great power in expressing the passions. —Her action and deportment, through the part of Clytemnestra, marked the consummate actress. In the second act,

[1] Cibber, *op. cit.*, v, 210.

when, in the distress of her mind from conscious guilt, she is torn with conflicting passions at the approach of her injured husband, the force of her action and expression, when she said to her attendant—

Bring me my children hither, they may perhaps relieve me—

struck the audience with astonishment, who expressed the highest approbation by loud and reiterated applauses.'[1] The political allusions were no less popular, and they too were 'greatly applauded'.[2] The first performance, however, did not end as happily as it had begun. Thomson had written a light, mocking Epilogue to be spoken by Mrs. Cibber, but the audience, with an uncommon show of good taste, shouted her down, and the poet had to rewrite the Epilogue for the second performance. It began:

> Our Bard, to Modern Epilogue a Foe,
> Thinks such mean Mirth but deadens generous Woe;
> Dispels in idle Air the Moral Sigh,
> And wipes the tender Tear from Pity's Eye:
> No more with social Warmth the Bosom burns;
> But all th' unfeeling, selfish Man returns.

The audience approved the Epilogue up to this point but the lines which followed offended them, and Mrs. Cibber continued in the revised version to say:

> Thus he began:—And you approv'd the Strain;
> 'Till the next Couplet sunk to light and vain.
> You check'd him there.—To You, to Reason just,
> He owns he triumph'd in your kind Disgust.
> Charm'd by your Frown, by your Displeasure grac'd,
> He hails the rising Virtue of your Taste.

Thomson, who never enjoyed the first nights of his plays, was naturally upset by this unfavourable reaction to his Epilogue. Thomas Davies told a story to illustrate the effect of the audience's criticism upon him, but he undoubtedly exaggerated in the telling the hostility shown to *Agamemnon*, which was probably confined entirely to the unfortunate

[1] Davies, *op. cit.*, iii, 499.   [2] See Davies, *Life of Garrick*, 1780, ii, 32.

Epilogue. 'The displeasure of the audience shewn to certain scenes produced a whimsical effect upon the author; he had promised to meet some friends at a tavern as soon as the play was ended, but he was obliged to defer his attending them to a very late hour. When he came, they asked him the reason of his stay; he told them, that the critics had sweated him so terribly by their severe treatment of certain parts of his tragedy, that the perspiration was so violent, as to render his wig unfit to wear; and that he had spent a great deal of time amongst the peruke-makers in procuring a proper cover for his head.'[1] Andrew Mitchell, a close friend of the poet, told James Boswell that 'Thomson used to sweat so much the first nights of his Plays, that when he came and met his freinds at a tavern in the Piazza, his wig was as if it had been dip'd in an Oil-pot'.[2] Thomson, however, must have expected to spoil a wig on such occasions, and his barber, William Taylor, thought he was very extravagant with them: 'I have seen a dozen at a time', said Taylor, 'hanging up in my master's shop, and all of them so big that nobody else could wear them. I suppose his sweating to such a degree made him have so many; for I have known him spoil a new one only in walking [to Richmond] from London.'[3]

Despite statements to the contrary, and particularly one by Dr. Johnson, who wrote that *Agamemnon* 'was only endured, but not favoured',[4] the tragedy was a success. It was played nine times—the usual run of an ordinarily successful play—and on the sixth night, the 18th April, it was performed for the benefit of the author 'By Command of their Royal Highnesses the Prince and Princess of Wales'.[5] Frederick certainly supported his pensioner, and both he and the Princess attended the performance on the seventh night, which was also commanded by him. The audiences, on the occasions of these Royal Command performances, probably cheered the Prince to the echo, and Thomson's

---

[1] *Ibid.*, ii, 33.   [2] Boswell, *Private Papers*, iii, 37.   [3] Hone, *op. cit.*, ii, 588.
[4] Johnson, *op. cit.*, iii, 291.   [5] *London Daily Post*, 18 April 1738.

allusions to contemporary politics would allow them many
chances to show their admiration for Frederick and their
contempt for the King and Sir Robert's administration. The
ninth and last performance, which was also played for the
Benefit of the author, was given on 25 April, and that the
play had not yet lost its popularity is shown by an announcement in the *Daily Post* for that date: 'The Season
being so far advanced, and Benefits [for the actors] intervening, we hear that the Tragedy of Agamemnon, which is
to be acted this Day for the Benefit of the Author, will be
acted no more till next Winter.' The general interest which
the tragedy aroused is also proved by the fact that Andrew
Millar printed three thousand ordinary and one hundred fine
royal copies of the play, and three days after these were
printed he found it necessary to issue a second edition of
one thousand five hundred copies.[1] The published play was
dedicated to the Prince of Wales, and the manliness and
brevity of the dedication are a marked contrast to the poet's
earlier effusions on his patrons' merits.

Although *Agamemnon* must have yielded a good sum and
allowed the poet to pay off some of his debts, he began
almost immediately after its production to write another
play; that he was able to finish it in time for it to be performed in 1739 is a further proof that his indolence has been
exaggerated. He cannot, however, have spent much of either
the summer or autumn upon its composition, because Pope
wrote to Aaron Hill on 8 December to say that he had been
confirmed 'by Mr. Thomson as to the retardment of his
play, of which he has written but two acts'; and he added
in a letter to Hill of 12 February 1739 that he had 'yet seen
but three acts'.[2] Meanwhile, David Mallet had also been
writing a play, and his tragedy of *Mustapha*, with Quin
playing the title role, was first performed at Drury Lane
Theatre on 13 February 1739. 'On the first night of its
exhibition were assembled all the chiefs in opposition to the

---

[1] *N. & Q.*, I Ser., xii, 218.
[2] *Works of Pope*, ed. Elwin and Courthope, 1886, x, 72, 75.

court; and many speeches were applied by the audience to the supposed grievances of the times and to persons and characters.'¹ *Mustapha* was a great success, running for fourteen nights, and it will be gathered from the account of the audience's behaviour on the first night that Mallet had loyally supported his master, the Prince of Wales. The fable told how the heroic Mustapha, heir to Solyman the Magnificent, was traduced by an evil councillor, Rustan, and eventually and mistakenly killed for disloyalty to his father. The audiences quickly discerned that Mustapha, Solyman, and Rustan were intended to represent Frederick, George II, and Sir Robert Walpole, and the Lord Chamberlain must have been asleep when he gave the play his licence. The success of *Mustapha*, however, abruptly awakened him to his duties, and when the next play written with similar political intentions, Henry Brooke's tragedy of *Gustavus Vasa*, was submitted to him for his licence, it was prohibited. The 'Piece was about five Weeks in Rehearsal, the Day was appointed for Acting', and the author 'had disposed of many hundred Tickets',² when authority interposed to prevent its performance. Among those who came forward to defend Brooke against this arbitrary treatment was Samuel Johnson, a young and little-known journalist, who indicted the Lord Chamberlain in an ironical pamphlet. Brooke determined, however, to recoup his loss by printing his tragedy by subscription, and, since to subscribe was to protest against the Government, he met with remarkable success. The names of the subscribers to the edition filled six close pages, and among them were all the members of the opposition.

Thomson had at last hurriedly finished his own play, which was to be entitled *Edward and Eleonora*, only to meet with another obstacle to its performance. The manager of Drury Lane Theatre, either disliking the play's political implications or having already committed himself to the production of another play, refused to accept it, and Thom-

---

¹ Davies, *op. cit.*, ii, 34.   ² Brooke, *Gustavus Vasa*, 1739, p. v.

son was forced to submit it to Covent Garden Theatre. 'Mr. Thomson,' wrote Pope on 12 February, 'after many shameful tricks from the manager, is determined to act his play at the other Theatre, where the advantage lies to the women, and the success of *his* will depend upon them.'[1] The manager of Covent Garden Theatre, John Rich, the famous panto- mimist, was willing to produce it, and it was duly cast and put into rehearsal. The news of the play was welcomed, and an anonymous pamphlet, entitled *The History of the Life and Reign of the valiant Prince Edward*, told the fable upon which the plot was founded. The pamphleteer concluded by praising Thomson and his forthcoming play: 'The whole, if good Judges may be depended upon, shews his Noble Genius in Poetry, his Energy of Stile, his exuberant Fancy, and his noble Sentiments; and that farther, his dramatic Management of this Story, will be equal to any thing exhibited on the Theatre: But I am only saying 'tis broad Day at Noon.' But suddenly the Lord Chamberlain, still smarting from the success of *Mustapha*, intervened to prohibit the play's performance. 'During the Rehearsal of a new Tragedy, written by Mr. *Thomson*, call'd *Edward* and *Eleonora*, (which was to have been acted this Day),' announced the *London Evening-Post* for 27–29 March, 'he receiv'd, to his great Suprize, a message from the Lord Chamberlain, absolutely forbidding the acting of the said Play. No objec- tion having been made to the Whole or any Part of it, we must conclude it was consider'd as *immoral* or *seditious*. If the Author is concious of not having writ with any such Inten- tion, it is hoped that, for his own Justification, he will print this Play, and so *submit* it to the *Judgment* of his *Country*.' The poet was not slow to accept this invitation, and he decided to follow Brooke's example and print his play by subscription. His proposals were issued in the *London Even- ing News* for 12–14 April, and after announcing that the play was to be printed on 'a superfine Royal Paper' and to be priced at five shillings, they continued: '*The Representation of*

1 *Works of Pope*, 1886, x, 75.

this Tragedy on the Stage has been prohibited by AUTHORITY; *for what Reason the Author knows not. He is conscious that he had no other Intention but to paint Virtue and Vice in their proper Colours; and, he hopes, there is neither Sentiment nor Reflection introduced that does not flow naturally from the Subject. The Characters in the Play cannot offend those whom they may be thought to ressemble; they are virtuous. If they displease, they cannot displease those alone to whom they never were intended to be apply'd. And how moral Reflections and Sentiments of Liberty should offend, in a free Nation, he will not enquire. He is only sollicitous to approve himself, to all who judge impartially, an honest Man and a Lover of his Country. For his Success, he trusts to that Candour and Indulgence which he has already met with from the Publick on other Occasions.'* Subscriptions were to be taken in by Andrew Millar and by six other booksellers, 'And at the following Coffee-Houses, viz. the Sword-Blade in Birchin-Lane; Tom's in Devereux-Court near the Temple; the Rainbow in Lancaster-Court in the Strand; the British near Charing Cross; the Smyrna in Pall-Mall; Depuis's in Conduit-Street; and the Parliament Coffee-House in the Court of Requests'. The success of this subscription may be gathered from the number of copies it was found necessary to print; three thousand and five hundred ordinary and one thousand fine royal copies were printed. It became a gesture of allegiance to the opposition either to join the subscription or to buy an ordinary copy, and Thomson must have been amply compensated for what he had lost by the Lord Chamberlain's prohibition of the play's representation.

Thomson's naïve and provocative disclaimer that the play had political significance was of course untrue. The play was based upon the apocryphal story that while Edward, Prince of Wales, afterwards Edward I, was on a crusade in the Holy Land, he was stabbed with a poisoned dagger, which would have killed him if his wife, Eleanor of Castille, had not sucked the poison from the wound at the risk of her own life. Edward was intended to be the prototype of Frederick, who was thus lavishly and indirectly praised. Gloster, in the first scene, urged Prince Edward to withdraw from Jaffa and return home to free his aged father from the counsels of evil ministers, and his speech was designed to remind a contemporary audience of Sir Robert Walpole's supposed wickedness and his exclusion of Frederick and his supporters from all offices of government. '*Edward*, return,' exclaimed Gloster,

> Lose not a day, an hour,
> Before this city. Tho' your cause be holy,
> Believe me, 'tis a much more pious office,
> To save your father's old and broken years,
> His mild and easy temper, from the snares
> Of low corrupt insinuating traitors:
> A nobler office far! on the firm base
> Of well-proportion'd liberty, to build
> The common quiet, happiness and glory,
> Of king and people, *England's* rising grandeur.
> To you, my prince, this task, of right, belongs.
> Has not the royal heir a juster claim
> To share his father's inmost heart and counsels,
> Than aliens to his int'rest, those, who make
> A property, a market of his honour?

The administration clearly could not tolerate such sentiments, even if they did '*flow naturally from the Subject*', but there are few passages in this strain, and had they been excised the play would have been rendered inoffensive. *Agamemnon* had been a complete and direct commentary upon the political situation, but *Edward and Eleonora* reflected only incidentally upon the administration. Thomson was more concerned in the second to write a good play than a political tract, and his management of the plot showed a considerable advance on his earlier dramatic work. Pope, in his letter of 12 February to Aaron Hill, said: 'I have yet seen but three acts of Mr. Thomson's [play], but I am told, and believe by what I have seen, that it excels in the pathetic.' The pathetic was to be simply attained. For the first half of the play, the nobility of the poisoned Edward and the lamentations of Eleonora are dwelt upon at length;

and in the second, the feminine heroism of Eleonora, who
had poisoned herself in her attempt to save her husband,
and the masculine lamentations of Edward are drawn in
equal detail. The play is, however, spoilt by two faults.
First, the fable is improbable; no audience could believe
that two people, alternately waiting for death, could resist
a fierce poison for so long, and declaim so admirably and
collectedly. Second, the characters are too virtuous, and
as they move on effortlessly from heights of nobility to
peaks of sensibility, they pass beyond our imagination and
attention. But Thomson handled the action with considerable skill, and in both construction and choice of subject, a
welcome change from the classical courts in which the poet
had so far moved, the play is superior to his earlier work.
Despite the evidence of the sales, the play was not popular—
at least among those readers who cared for the drama rather
than for politics—and Lady Hertford wrote in a letter of 14
June 1739: 'I have read Mr. Thomson's Edward and
Eleonora. I hear it is the fashion to decry it extremely; but',
she added with an understanding of the dramatic advance
which it showed, 'I am ungenteel enough to prefer it
infinitely to Agamemnon.'[1]

One anecdote has been told about the effect of the Lord
Chamberlain's prohibition of *Edward and Eleonora*. William
Paterson, who had been admitted a Free and Accepted
Mason at the same time as Thomson, acted for a period as
the poet's amanuensis, and the copy of *Edward and Eleonora*
which was submitted to the Lord Chamberlain was in his
hand. When Paterson submitted his own tragedy of
Arminius to the Lord Chamberlain, his handwriting was
recognized and the play was immediately refused a licence
without its having been read.[2] It was a wise decision, however, because *Arminius* was much more provocative than
Edward and Eleonora.

Thomson had performed some signal services for the

[1] *Correspondence between Countess of Hertford and Countess of Pomfret*, 1805, i, 100
[2] *Works of Thomson*, 1762, i, xiii.

Prince of Wales in the two years since he had received his pension, and he served him again in 1740. The Prince had taken in 1737, as his country residence, Cliveden House, on the Thames near Maidenhead, and he decided to celebrate in its grounds the birthday, on 1 August, of his eldest child, the Princess Augusta. He commissioned Thomson and Mallet to write a masque for this occasion, and they chose as their subject an incident from the life of King Alfred. After he has been defeated by the Danish invaders, Alfred retires to the security of the Isle of Athelney where he is joined by his wife, Eltruda. He is comforted in his distress by a hermit, who raises a spectral procession of kings and queens whom fate intends will rule England greatly. The hermit's comforting prophecies and the masque are ended by the news that a British victory has restored Alfred to his throne. The slight piece had a few pretty songs, some resounding declamatory verse, and many complimentary references to the Prince and his family, and was eminently suited to the occasion. It was decided to produce it as lavishly as possible, and many players were engaged from the London theatres; James Quin took the part of the hermit, and his speeches were made as long as possible to allow him the fullest opportunity to show his powers; Milward, the Aegisthus of *Agamemnon*, played Alfred; Mrs. Horton, a fine tragic actress, took the part of Queen Eltruda; and Kitty Clive, the most sprightly of all comic actresses, was cast as the peasant lass, Emma. The music was composed by Thomas Arne.

There were also other secondary entertainments, and on a brilliant evening the celebrations were held in the open air, by the riverside, and under the heavy, motionless trees. The account in the *London Daily-Post* is prosaic but the reader may infer from it the graciousness, civility, colours, lilting voices, and delight of the vanished scene. 'On Friday last was perform'd at Cliefden (by Comedians from both Theatres) before their Royal Highnesses the Prince and Princess of Wales, and a great Number of Nobility, and others, a Dramatic Masque call'd *Alfred*, written by Mr. Thomson; in which was introduc'd Variety of Dancing, very much to the Satisfaction of their Royal Highnesses, and the rest of the Spectators, especially the Performance of Signora Barbarini (lately arriv'd from Paris) whose Grace, Beauty, and suprising Agility, exceeded their Expectations. Also was perform'd a Musical Masque call'd *The Contending Deities* . . . and the humorous Pantomimical Scene of The Skeleton taken from the Entertainment of Merlin's Cave, by Mr. Rich and Mr. Lalauze. The whole was exhibited upon a Theatre in the Garden compos'd of Vegetables, and decorated with Festoons of Flowers, at the End of which was erected a Pavilion for their Royal Highnesses the Prince and Princess of Wales, Prince George, and Princess Augusta. The whole concluded with Fireworks made by Dr. Desaguliers, which were equal in their kind to the rest of the Performance. Their Royal Highnesses were so well pleas'd with the whole Entertainment, that they commanded the same to be perform'd on Saturday last, with the Addition of some favourite Pantomime Scenes from Mr. Rich's Entertainments, which was accordingly began, but the Rain falling very heavy, oblig'd them to break off before it was half over; upon which his Royal Highness commanded them to finish the Masque of *Alfred* in the House.' The stage may have been admirably contrived but the arrangements for the actors were so poor that their pleasure in the performance was spoilt. 'The accomodations for the company, I was told,' wrote Thomas Davies long after the event, 'were but scanty, and ill-managed; and the players were not treated as persons ought to be who are employed by a prince. Quin, I believe, was admitted among those of the higher order; and Mrs. Clive might be safely trusted to take care of herself any where.'[1]

The greatest moment in the masque and the whole evening's entertainment—and it is to be hoped that the audience were not so eagerly awaiting the Skeleton's Dance that

[1] Davies, *op. cit.*, ii, 36.

O

they did not attend to it—was in the last scene, when a blind and venerable bard advanced forward on the flower-festooned stage to sing the ode, *Rule, Britannia*. This was the first time that these verses, which, wrote Robert Southey, 'will be the political hymn of this country as long as she maintains her political power', were heard. It has been disputed whether Thomson or Mallet was the author of this ode but only Thomson could have written in such a spirit of lyrical patriotism. Mallet could imitate his friend's blank verse well enough but such a noble flight was quite beyond his power. He never claimed to be its author, and it was published under Thomson's name in *The Charmer* only a year after Thomson's death. It is impossible to separate with any certainty the individual contributions which the two poets made to the masque; but *Rule, Britannia* can be safely ascribed to Thomson.

CHAPTER VIII

LOVE AND ELIZABETH YOUNG

Alas! how frail the state of human bliss!
When even our honest passions oft destroy it.

ALTHOUGH James Thomson was preoccupied during
these years with his dramatic work and his attendance
upon the Prince of Wales, he did not forget the earlier
friends who had helped him at the outset of his career.
Among the 'ladies of high rank and distinction' who became his 'declared patronesses',[1] after the publication of
Winter, was Mrs. Sarah Stanley, the daughter of Sir Hans
Sloane. Sir Hans was President of the Royal Society for
many years, and his great scientific collection became the
nucleus of the British Museum's collections. If Patrick
Murdoch was right in his statement that Mrs. Stanley was
one of Thomson's original London friends, their friendship
must have remained constant throughout the succeeding
years, although only one letter of their correspondence
appears to have survived. Mrs. Stanley's daughter, Elizabeth, died at the age of eighteen, after a year's serious illness,
in December 1738, and there ended, if the impression her
beauty and intelligence made upon the poet was a true
image of the reality, a life of remarkable promise. Her
mother requested Thomson to write the epitaph for the
memorial she intended to raise to her daughter's memory
in Holyrood Church, Southampton, and he at once complied
with her wishes. The epitaph was delayed by the performance of *The Masque of Alfred* but he was able to write
to Mrs. Stanley on 25 August 1740: 'My late Task, with
some toher avocations since, have prevented me from carry-

---

[1] *Works of Thomson*, 1762, i, viii.

ing you the Inscription; whose Merit, if it has any, is, I wrote it from the Heart, and had a strong and affecting Idea of Excellence to draw. But some day this Week I will have the Pleasure of waiting on you, with a Copy thereof.'[1] The epitaph began:

E. S.
Once a lively image of human nature,
Such as God made it
When he pronounced every work of his to be good,

and continued with the celebration of her virtue, intelligence, knowledge, and fortitude in suffering. It can only have delighted the mother who must have discerned that its rather diffuse language was dictated by sincerity. Thomson also commemorated Elizabeth Stanley in a passage added to the revised edition of *The Seasons*. He imagined that as he stood alone on a summer evening, he suddenly saw a host of spirits 'glide athwart the Dusk', and he asked,

And art thou, STANLEY, of that sacred Band?
Alas, for us too soon!—Tho' rais'd above
The Reach of human Pain, above the Flight
Of human Joy; yet, with a mingled Ray
Of sadly-pleas'd Remembrance, must thou feel
A Mother's Love, a Mother's tender Woe:
Who seeks Thee still, in many a former Scene;
Seeks thy fair Form, thy lovely-beaming Eyes,
Thy pleasing Converse, by gay lively Sense
Inspir'd: where moral Wisdom mildly shone,
Without the Toil of Art; and Virtue glow'd,
In all her Smiles, without forbidding Pride.

This typical incident illustrates once again the poet's loyalty to his friends, and his eagerness to pay homage to their memory.

The epitaph was the last achievement of a long period of creative effort, and for the next year or two the poet would seem to have been mastered by his indolence and his love of

---

[1] C.28 e.17; British Museum.

conviviality. It can be inferred from a remark in one of Lady Hertford's letters that the nights when Quin and Thomson staggered from the Castle Inn to the cottage in Kew Foot Lane had become very frequent. Lady Hertford, in a letter of 7 September 1742, wrote: 'I have not seen Thomson almost these three Years, he keeps Company with scarce any Body but Mallet & one or two of the Players, & indeed hardly any body else will keep Company with him. He turns Day into Night, & Night into Day & is (as I am told) never awake till after Midnight & I doubt has quite drown'd his Genius.'[1] Lady Hertford, piqued by the poet's neglect of her society, may have exaggerated the rumours that had reached her, but although he had certainly not drowned his genius, he was, on the evidence of his later letters, in a fair way of doing so.

This dissolute life cannot have lasted long after Lady Hertford reported the rumours which she had heard. At about this time, Thomson renewed his acquaintance with a Scottish surgeon, James Robertson, whom he had known as long ago as 1726, when they had lived opposite to each other in Lancaster Court in the Strand. Robertson had sailed soon after 1726 for the East Indies, but upon his return they had renewed a friendship which was to last until Thomson's death. Unfortunately, when Robertson was questioned about his intimacy with the poet, he was an old man, and his answers are tantalizing in their brevity. 'I became acquainted with him', he said, 'in the year 1726, when he published his poem of *Winter* . . . I went to the East Indies soon after, which caused a chasm in our acquaintance; but, on my return, our intimacy was strengthened . . . I do not know any man, living or dead, I ever esteemed more highly, and he was attached to me.'[2] Robertson did not say in what year he returned to England but certainly by the end of 1742 Thomson was intimate in his household. The society which gathered at the Robertsons' house was principally Scottish, and some were earlier friends of the poet—David Mallet

---

[1] Quoted Hughes, *op. cit.*; *Mod. Phil.*, xxv, 464.   [2] Hone, *op. cit.*, ii, 108.

and William Paterson, the author of *Arminius*—but others
were relations of the Robertsons, and these the poet would
meet for the first time.

Mrs. Robertson was also a Scot, the daughter of a Captain
Gilbert Young of Gulyhill, in Dumfriesshire, who had died
before her marriage. She had been ill throughout 1742, and
was advised by her doctors in November of that year to
spend the winter at Bath. She was attended during her visit
to Bath by her sister, Elizabeth Young, and another friend,
Miss Berry, and they were escorted on their way by her
husband, William Paterson, and some other friends on
horseback. Thomson did not make one of this escort, probably because, as his barber said, 'he was too fearful to ride'.[1]
As soon, however, as Mrs. Robertson and her attendants
were settled at Bath, he sent her a long and cheerful letter
to amuse her, but he also used the letter to inveigh against
Bath and its society. 'I hope the ladies have at last got
their clothes', he began; 'To be at Bath, yet debarred
from the rooms, must be a cruel situation to such as
knew less how to converse with, and enjoy themselves.—
the very situation of Tantalus! up to the lip in diversions,
without being able to catch a drop of them.—And yet,
notwithstanding all the diversions, I do, from my soul,
most sincerely pity you, to be so long doomed to a place
so delightfully tiresome. Delightfully, did I say? No; it
is merely a scene of waking dreams, where nothing but the
phantoms of pleasure fly about, without any substance or
reality. What a round of silly amusements, what a giddy
circle of *nothing* do these children of a larger size run every
day! Nor does it only give a gay vertigo to the head, it has
equally a bad influence on the heart. When the head is full
of nothing but dress, and scandal, and dice, and cards, and
rowly powly, can the heart be sensible to those fine emotions,
those tender, humane, generous passions that form the soul
of all virtue and happiness! Ah! then, ye lovers, never think
to make any impression on the hearts of the dissipated fair.

---

[1] Hone, *op, cit.*, ii, 589.

So could I proceed in my tedious homily; but I ask pardon for railing at a place you are obliged to be at, and which I hope will restore you to perfect health.'[1]

Thomson was deeply sincere in his detestation of Bath and its sophisticated society but it was odd, to say the least, that he should have expressed his opinions so forcibly to a sick woman, whom necessity and not choice had driven there. The tirade must have had as its origin some fear other than that morality and fine emotions were threatened by Bath's social duplicity and artificiality. He knew that his letter would not be read by Mrs. Robertson alone. He wrote to her again on Christmas Day 1742, to say that he had seen her baby, which he imagined was thinking of its mother's recovery, and he was led by this theme into a panegyric on marriage, illustrating his remarks by quoting Milton's sonorous passage,

> Hail, wedded love! Mysterious law, true source
> Of human offspring.

'Now that I have been transcribing some lines of poetry,' he continued, 'I think I once engaged myself while walking in Kew-lane to write two or three songs. The following is one of them, which I have stolen from the Song of Solomon; from that beautiful expression of Love, "Turn away thine eyes from me, for they have overcome me".'

I

O THOU, whose tender serious eyes
Expressive speak the mind I love;
The gentle azure of the skies,
The pensive shadows of the grove:

II

O mix their beauteous beams with mine,
And let us interchange our hearts;
Let all their sweetness on me shine,
Pour'd thro' my soul be all their darts.

[1] Quoted Buchan, *Essay on the Life of Thomson*, 1792, pp. 264-5.

III

Ah! 'tis too much! I cannot bear
At once so soft, so keen, a ray;
In pity, then, my lovely fair,
O turn these killing eyes away!

IV

But what avails it to conceal
One charm, where nought but charms we see?
Their lustre then again reveal,
And let me, Myra, die of thee.[1]

It may have been Mrs. Robertson who asked him, while they were once walking together near his cottage, to write some songs, but it is clear that the verses he included in this letter were not intended for her; nor would it be easy, had we only the evidence of these two letters, to guess who Thomson wished should read and understand their implicit declaration of love. Miss Young and Miss Berry, Mrs. Robertson's attendants, were mentioned quite casually in both letters, and he concluded the second with the brief salute, 'My best respects attend Miss Young and Miss Berry, who I hope are heartily tired of Bath, and will leave it without the least regret'. There is little to show that he was in love with Elizabeth Young, but so much in these letters was clearly intended for her alone that neither she nor her sister can have been unaware of his intention. He also made a slight attempt in the last line of the song to disguise the identity of the person to whom it was addressed by calling her 'Myra'. He called her either by the diminutive of her Christian name, Eliza, or by the fictitious name, Amanda, in the other poems which he wrote for her.

It is difficult to discover when Thomson met and fell in love with Elizabeth Young. Among the songs he transcribed for her, and which she kept with his letters, was one which began, 'Come, gentle God of soft desire', and ended, 'Put on Eliza's winning form'. This song had been printed, however, as early as 1736 in the *Gentleman's Magazine*, and in that text the last line had read, 'Put on *Amanda*'s winning

---

[1] Quoted Buchan, *Essay on the Life of Thomson*, 1792, pp. 276–8.

form'. This might suggest that he was writing songs to her as early as 1736. He had also used the name, Amanda, in an even earlier song, 'Forever, *Fortune*, wilt thou prove', which was printed in the fourth volume of *The Hive*, published in 1732, and this evidence makes it plain that he had always chosen to address his songs to an 'Amanda', who possibly changed her identity very often. He probably met and fell in love with Miss Young shortly before she accompanied her sister to Bath, and until that time he had declared his passion only by such indirect, if transparent, hints as he had used in the two letters to her sister. He was already, however, disturbed by jealousy, and the affected facetiousness of the appeal, 'Ah! then, ye lovers, never think to make any impression on the hearts of the dissipated fair', was intended to recall him to her mind.

Thomson kept his forty-second birthday in 1742. He had achieved fame both as a poet and a dramatist, but he was poor; he lived upon what fortune threw in his way, and if that was small, he borrowed until his luck turned. His figure was corpulent, his movements ungainly, and his expression sullen, although these defects were forgotten when his character was known. He had lived until now a life of complete freedom. He could turn his day into night when he wished, go where he pleased and stay as long as he liked, and had become confirmed in all his habits. A young woman could hardly consider him as a suitable husband. Nor would it appear likely that he would have wanted to marry and radically change the whole routine of his life. His indolence and his habits, however, were little more than a crust to protect his extreme sensibility. Each mood and movement in Nature, and every sentiment of pity and affection, deeply impressed his imagination, and as they were recorded in verses, they became that extraordinary work, *The Seasons*, which is not only a Nature poem but a sentimental autobiography of the poet. He had earlier described to David Mallet, in his letter of 20 September 1729, how susceptible he was to feminine beauty: 'What is my heart made of?' he had asked. 'A soft system of love-nerves, too sensible for my quiet, capable of being very happy or very unhappy; I am afraid the last will prevail . . . To have always some secret darling idea, to which one can still have recourse amidst the noise and nonsense of the world, and which never fails to touch us in the most exquisite manner, is an Art of Happiness that Fortune cannot deprive us of.' He had lost his heart, no doubt, in the intervening years since 1729 to a succession of 'darling ideas', who shadowily moved in to take possession of his dreams and waking fantasies; but none of these affairs, it would appear, had been very serious, because if his emotions tried to betray him into excess, an antipathetical power was always ready to rescue him in time. Thomson, like all his contemporaries, worshipped the ideal of harmony. He sought to discover in Nature the harmonious operation of a divine power; he attempted to establish within himself a correspondence between thought and feeling as balanced as that which exists between the moon and the tides; and he suspected and avoided excess, which was the destroyer of harmony. This ideal informed all his thought and poetry. Marriage, he believed, of course should reflect the peaceable, equable, and fruitful relationship that could be distinguished between God and His creation, and he had fully defined in the conclusion to *Spring*, as that poem stood in 1730, the ideal marital condition. After condemning arranged marriages and those whose original motive was lust, he described the ideal:

> While those whom love cements, in holy faith,
> And equal transports, free as nature, live,
> Disdaining fear; for what's the world to them,
> Its pomp, its pleasure, and its nonsense all!
> Who in each other clasp whatever fair
> High fancy forms, and lavish hearts can wish.
> Something than beauty dearer, should they look
> Or on the mind, or mind-illumin'd face,
> Truth, goodness, honour, harmony, and love,
> The richest bounty of indulgent HEAVEN.

PLATE II

JAMES THOMSON
by J. Patoun

This ideal marriage admitted of no excess. It was beset by two contending forces, apathy and passion, and between them, as if through a channel, it had to be steered carefully into content. It demanded satisfaction but not satiety, tenderness but not infatuaticn, quietness but not loneliness, and so on down a neatly arranged list of juxtaposed virtues and vices. This was the ideal, and Thomson feared as early as 1729 that he was temperamentally incapable of its attainment; it seemed to him then that he would be either 'very happy, or very unhappy'; excess threatened him and he dreaded its power. This fear, in addition to his poverty, may have prevented him from marrying earlier in life, and he chose instead to brood imaginatively upon a 'darling idea'. The cause of this threatened unhappiness was, of course, infatuated passion and its cruel attendant, jealousy, and he had described the condition of the man who strayed into this excess; that man, he wrote,

> leads a life
> Of feaver'd rapture, or of cruel care;
> His brightest aims, extinguish'd all, and all
> His lively moments running down to waste.

These lines were a curiously accurate prophecy of his own fate.

It is improbable that Thomson had proposed to Miss Young before she had set out for Bath with her sister, but she must have been aware of his affection and expected a proposal. It was not long delayed. He wrote his first letter to her on 10 March 1743, and without hesitation in either hand or expression, and mastered by his passion, he unrestrainedly poured out his love. The letter is numbered in a contemporary hand, 'No. 1', and this evidence suggests that it was the first letter Miss Young received from him. This is corroborated by the formality of addressing her as 'Madam', a formality which ceased with this letter.

'Madam,
    'As I have not an Opportunity of speaking, I can no

longer forbear writing to you. And now that I am sit [*sic*] down to write, my Heart is so full and Words so weak to express it, I am at a Loss where to begin and what to say. What shall I say but that I love you, love you with the utmost Ardor, the most perfect Esteem and inexpressible Tenderness. Imagination, Reason and the Heart, all conspire to love you. I may venture to say, without Extravagance, I love you better than my own Soul. My Happiness is only a secondary Consideration to yours, can alone consist in making you happy: there is no Happiness for me but in passing my Life with you, in devoting it to please you. Never had one Being a stronger Propensity to seek the Good of another than I to seek yours: to gain that dearest Purpose all Fortune if in my Power would seem Dross, Toil Ease, and Pain Pleasure. I shall be thought romantic, and yet the most passionate Expressions upon this Occasion are poor to what I feel. My Heart labours, is oppressed, with unutterable Fondness.

'But the Design of this Letter is not to tell you what one Look, one Sigh, one faultering Word could better speak. My Purpose in it is to address myself to the lowest Degree of your Regard, to your Compassion. And can you refuse to pity one whom you have made unhappy, who is unhappy from his loving you? If you knew but a small Part of what I feel, of those various Emotions that, by Turns, charm, distress, delight and torture me: if you saw me anxious, musing, absent; lost to all Regards of Interest, Study, Society and Friendship: you would you must do more than pity me. For what avails Pity without Relief? Such Pity only heightens the Woes it pretends to compassionate, is a Kind of disguised Triumph. I can no longer remain in this cruel State of Anxiety and Doubt. It is miserable to love as I do, thus deprived of Opportunities of declaring my Passion, and learning it's Fate from your own charming Lips. Oh let me conjure you by all that is humane and tender, to give me an Opportunity of speaking to you. Be what your own good Sense gives you a Right to be, above the Vanity and

Triumphs of your Sex. Or if you do triumph triumph more
divinely in filling my Heart with Joy with Transport inexpressible, or at least in softening my Pain: either bless me
with some Ray of Hope, or bid me despair. The first will
awaken me to the Pursuit of whatever can be agreeable to
you, of whatever can recommend to your Esteem and
Friendship—I would fain also add, Love and Tenderness.
And what is there, in the whole Compass of Honour and
Virtue, to which that would not excite the Heart? The last
will plunge me in a gloomy careless Indolence. It may perhaps take off a little from the Keeness of what I suffer in
this State of tormenting Uncertainty; but it will render Life
a dead Circle of hopeless, joyless, worthless Days: I shall
grow regardless of it and all its Duties, disgusted at it and
all it's Enjoyments. Not even Friendship and the Study of
Nature will be able to maintain any Charms for me. I care
not where I am if I am not with you: I care not what I am if
I live not for you—But why should I teaze you with a Subject about which I have Reason to suspect you are quite
indifferent, my Hopes and Fears, what will make me happy
or unhappy? Tho' I could dy for you, there is little, I am
afraid, you would do for me: not even take the least un-
formal Step to deliver me from this miserable Anxiety, this
unsupportable Fear of losing all that is dear and excellent
to me in the World, the Life of Life, the Soul of Happiness.
What signifies my languishing here in this tiresome Town,
where I seldom see you, and which is utterly disagreeable to
me in every Respect but that you are in it? Let me hide
myself again in the Country, more distressfully in Love than
ever. There I shall better enjoy my Sufferings; there, without
Interruption, indulge the melancholy Pleasure of continually
musing on those Charms that have undone me. You cannot
deprive me of That; and if I am to be unhappy it will give
a Sort of Relish to my Misfortunes that I am unhappy by
the Means of you—But I will not yield to so dispirited a
Thought. Surely Nature is too just and benevolent to suffer
a Passion like mine to be in vain, or to Purposes of Ruin:

and such it must be, if by a mutual Return you make it not
the Source of Virtue and Happiness. I shall have Cause either
to bless the Time I was acquainted with you, those delightful Moments when I first began to gaze upon your lovely
Eyes with more than Pleasure; or else to reckon that the
greatest Misfortune of my Life.

> Ah wise too late! from Beauty's Bondage free,
> Why did I trust my Liberty with thee?
> And thou, why didst thou with inhuman Art,
> If not resolv'd to take, seduce my Heart?
> Yes, yes, you saw (for Lovers' Eyes speak true)
> You must have seen how fast my Passion grew;
> And when your Glances chanc'd on me to shine,
> How my fond Soul extatic sprung to thine.
> But mark me, fair-one. What I now declare
> Thy deep Attention claims, and serious Care.
> It is no common Passion fires my Breast;
> I must be wretched, or I must be blest:
> My Woes all other Remedy deny;
> Or pitying give me Hope, or bid me dy.

'Pardon me if I only add. Whatever Reception you give
to this, you can never be so sincerely, so ardently, so
tenderly beloved, as by him who is with unalterable Truth,
and the most cordial Friendship and Affection yours James
Thomson.'
'March 10th, 1743.'

This letter shows how completely the ideal harmony had
been destroyed. A seventeenth-century sensibility might
have accepted this passionate disturbance, and, by subtly
exploring its extent and weighing its power, attempted to
master it; but Thomson had never recognized it, and was
swiftly overpowered by its sudden and unexpected on-
slaught. He had nourished, like all his cultured contemporaries, the gentler emotions. Friendship, affection,
restrained joy, contentment, and serene melancholy were
what he had always hoped and expected to experience, and
this furious love in a moment threatened to make them its
prey. He was unable to understand its appearance, and

was both frightened and ashamed at its irrational operation; 'I shall be thought romantic', he wrote, and he meant that he would be deemed crazy, deluded, possessed. Because his passion was so incomprehensible, he was confused and almost sickened by it, and alternately praised and blamed Miss Young for raising such an alien power within him. His letter is in many ways childish. The attempt to blackmail her into returning his affection by holding up to her view a picture of what he would become should she refuse to love him, is a childish gesture, and the fluent whine of self-pity which wavers through the letter sounds like the insistent sobbing of a hurt child. But he only behaved in this fashion because the careful harmony, which had governed until this time his adult responses to life, had been destroyed at a blow. Any severe shock, whether it is hatred or love, has a similar effect upon an adult in any society, but the eighteenth century's sensibility was peculiarly susceptible to derangement, because its insistence upon rationality and its refusal to recognize the passions left it at their mercy when they did strike from the backward, unexplored hinterland of the mind. Thomson's case was not unique; parallels may be found in the personal histories of many eighteenth-century poets; and the names of Jonathan Swift and Thomas Gray will at once spring to mind.

Unfortunately, there is little to be discovered about Elizabeth Young. James Robertson, her brother-in-law, merely said, 'She was a fine sensible woman, and poor Thomson was desperately in love with her'.[1] Another of her intimate friends added a little to this information: 'she was not a striking beauty, but a gentle-mannered, elegant-minded woman, worthy of the love of a man of taste and virtue.'[2] The poet's own description of her is in accordance with these opinions:

> And thou, AMANDA, come, Pride of my Song!
> Form'd by the Graces, Loveliness itself!
> Come with those downcast Eyes, sedate and sweet,

[1] Hone, *op. cit.*, ii, 108.   [2] Ramsay, *op. cit.*, i, 23 *n*.

Those Looks demure, that deeply pierce the Soul;
Where with the Light of thoughtful Reason mix'd,
Shines lively Fancy and the feeling Heart:
Oh come! and while the rosy-footed May
Steals blushing on, together let us tread
The Morning-Dews, and gather in their Prime
Fresh-blooming Flowers, to grace thy braided Hair,
And thy lov'd Bosom that improves their Sweets.

This is little enough but it allows us to picture her appearance and to imagine her quality. She was sensitive but sensible, modest but self-assured, demure but humorous, and, above all, eminently practicable and self-controlled. Had her letters survived, her portrait might have been made more particular, but they seem to have been destroyed. She never wrote, of course, to Thomson; she was too wise to be inveigled, no matter how hard he tried, into such an impossible correspondence.

After writing this letter of 10 March, Thomson contrived to meet her alone on 18 April, and when he returned to his cottage he wrote a long letter to her on the following day, the 19 April, which tells us something of what had passed between them at their meeting. 'Miss Young, my Love, my Soul!' he began in the hurry of his emotion, 'it is impossible to speak the Agitation of my Heart ever since I parted from you. All that an absent Lover can feel I feel in it's most exquisite and charming Distress. I would not wish you had a better and more affecting Picture of my Love than to have been Conscious to what passed in my mind as I returned. Then you could never doubt it more; never tell me again that it will be transitory, and that there is no such thing as undecaying Love in the World. Mine will not only last but grow forever.' This was the prelude to a rapturous outburst in her praise; and he then continued with a passage which shows that she had been indirectly reflecting upon his habits and the irregular life he had been leading in the company of David Mallet and James Quin. 'Were not those Hints,' he asked, 'with Regard to Regularity and Temperance, which you now and then so prettily insinuated, meant for me?

Yes, I will interpret them so; for it most exquisitely flatters my Heart to think that you would wish all Objections removed that may ly betwixt us. And shall such low, such vile, such false Pleasures ever stand in the least Competition with that Happiness, that darling Happiness, I shall enjoy with you? with you, whose every Look gives infinitely more Delight than Ages of these can give?' She would not have been so unkind as to hint that his lack of fortune might also prevent his marriage but, realizing this, he dismissed the objection and held up the ideal of harmony, which is strangely out of place in such a passionate context. 'As to Objections from unkind Fortune, which you are too generous to make, and I too much concerned for your Happiness not to give them their full Force; they may, they shall be removed. It is saying nothing to say, that the largest Fortune, if in my Power, would seem poor to what my Heart wishes to lay at your Feet . . . I feel for you the Kindness of creating Nature. But Heaven has constituted Things so graciously, that Happiness does not consist in Fortune, or those external Advantages that are out of our own Power. Competency with Contentment, a virtuous improved well-ordered Mind, right Affections, Friendship and Love, these give the truest Happiness, and these we may command. Encouragement from you will inform me with a new Soul, will inspirit me to the Pursuit of all that can be agreeable to you, and that can promote your dearest Welfare. Yet, o Miss Young! (for I love to repeat your Name) I cannot recover any tolerable Degree of Peace without still more Encouragement, more Assurance from you. The Hope you permitted me to indulge is not enough. There are Remains of Doubt and Anxiety that still distract my Mind, that render me incapable of performing what I have promised my Friends, the Public, and above all my own Heart upon your Account. If you have any Regard, any Tenderness, or even any Pity for me, bless me with a Line.' He concluded by appealing to her again to write to him and say that she loved him.

P

She did not reply, and it is apparent from his letter that the hope she had permitted him to indulge at their meeting had been but slight. It would rather seem that she had done as much as she could to tell him that she could not marry him. James Robertson thought that she would not marry him because he was so impecunious: 'Thomson, indeed,' he said, 'was never wealthy enough to marry.'[1] Another friend, however, believed that it was her mother who interposed the objection of Thomson's lack of fortune. Mrs. Young, 'a coarse, vulgar woman', certainly seems to have been avaricious, shallow, and humourless. When her daughter married James Robertson, 'which was but a few days after the death of the father, the females of her family laid aside mourning. Next morning, at breakfast, Mrs. Young, casting an angry look at her married daughter, said, "Betty, what is the meaning of that dress? How long has your father been dead?" Mrs. Robertson answered, "I thought it pardonable on this occasion; besides, madam, you are in colours likewise". "And what of that?" retorted the mother; "he was your father, but not a drop of blood to me!"'[2] She apparently designed a better marriage for her daughter than one with a poor poet. 'She constantly opposed the poet's pretensions to Amanda, saying to her one day, "What! would you marry Thomson? He will make ballads and you will sing them".'[3] At a time when parental authority was absolute, and when women were prevented by both convention and education from deciding upon their own conduct, particularly in so important an article as marriage, Mrs. Young's objection to Thomson must have greatly influenced her daughter's decision. But Elizabeth Young herself must have seen many objections to Thomson in his age, habits, impecuniosity, and perhaps in his manner of courtship; his letters, and probably his conversation, were too self-pitying, hesitant, and gauche to win a woman's heart, and their passion was too often inspired by fear rather than by love.

[1] Hone, op. cit., ii, 108.   [2] Ramsay, op. cit., i, 23 n.   [3] Ibid.

Ten days passed without either another interview or an answering letter, and he wrote to her again on 28 April to tell her how miserably happy he was in his doubt. 'Yet I will hope;' he continued, 'you gave me Leave so to do. Your Words, your dear Words, the most charming I ever heard in my Life—I know not what Time may produce—are engraved on my Heart. How critically I consider these Words! I examine them in all Manner of favourable Lights; I draw all possible pleasing Consequences from them, with the utmost Subtilty of refining Love.' His love must have been subtle indeed to refine comfort from so non-committal an answer, and even he found it was inadequate for the purpose: 'Without further Encouragement and Assurances', he added, 'I must still fluctuate in miserable Uncertainty'. He was at this time, however, in spite of alternating hope and despair, exhilaration and lassitude, continuing with his revision of *The Seasons*, and making those additions which, for clarity of style and vision, are a remarkable advance on his earlier work. This revision might never have been carried through if love had not stimulated his imagination and cleared from his senses and reason the incumbrance of apathy and indolence. 'I am going, if I can,' he wrote, 'to put a finishing Hand to the Description of a Season now in high Song and Beauty, but to which I am dead. You alone I hear, you alone I see: all Harmony and Beauty are comprized in you. Those Parts, however, will be obliged to you which attempt a Picture of virtuous happy Love. O Miss Young! thou loveliest of thy Sex, and the most beloved! as you have taught me the Virtue, so teach me the Happiness of this best Passion! O let the Picture be ours!' The picture is one of the ideal of harmony. The poet saw through the spume of his fretful passion the quiet withdrawn bay where he longed to walk in peace. The passage on 'virtuous happy Love' had appeared in the earlier editions of *Spring* but he now added some more lines, and the whole is the best illustration of the ideal that haunted him:

But happy they! the happiest of their Kind!
Whom gentler Stars unite, and in one Fate
Their Hearts, their Fortunes, and their Beings blend.
'Tis not the coarser Tie of human Laws,
Unnatural oft, and foreign to the Mind,
That binds their Peace, but Harmony itself,
Attuning all their Passions into Love;
Where Friendship full-exerts her softest Power,
Perfect Esteem enliven'd by Desire
Ineffable, and Sympathy of Soul;
Thought meeting Thought, and Will preventing Will,
With boundless Confidence: for nought but Love
Can answer Love, and render Bliss secure . . .
                    What is the World to them,
Its Pomp, its Pleasure, and its Nonsense all!
Who in each other clasp whatever fair
High Fancy forms, and lavish Hearts can wish:
Something than Beauty dearer, should they look
Or on the Mind, or mind-illumin'd Face,
Truth, Goodness, Honour, Harmony, and Love,
The richest Bounty of indulgent HEAVEN.
Mean-time a smiling Offspring rises round,
And mingles both their Graces. By degrees,
The human Blossom blows; and every Day,
Soft as it rolls along, shews some new Charm,
The Father's Lustre, and the Mother's Bloom.
Then infant·Reason grows apace, and calls
For the kind Hand of an assiduous Care.
Delightful Task! to rear the tender Thought,
To teach the young Idea how to shoot,
To pour the fresh Instruction o'er the Mind,
To breathe th' enlivening Spirit, and to fix
The generous Purpose in the glowing Breast.
Oh speak the Joy! ye, whom the sudden Tear
Suprizes often, while you look around,
And nothing strikes your Eye but Sights of Bliss,
All various Nature pressing on the Heart:
An elegant Sufficiency, Content,
Retirement, rural Quiet, Friendship, Books,
Ease and alternate Labour, useful Life,
Progressive Virtue, and approving HEAVEN.
These are the matchless Joys of virtuous Love;
And thus their Moments fly. The Seasons thus,
As ceaseless round a jarring World they roll,

Still find them happy; and consenting SPRING
Sheds her own rosy Garland on their Heads:
'Till Evening comes at last, serene and mild;
When after the long vernal Day of Life,
Enamour'd more, as more Remembrance swells
With many a Proof of recollected Love,
Together down they sink in social Sleep;
Together freed, their gentle Spirits fly
To Scenes where Love and Bliss immortal reign.

He was able to meet Miss Young a few days after he had written this letter of 28 April, and passed some time with her alone, but again she was prudent and neither yielding nor unkind. He wrote to her on 14 May after he had arrived back at his cottage:

'My dearest Miss Young! let me pour forth my Soul in Gratitude to you, for the Peace and Harmony of Mind you have at last given me. Yes, I will now exert myself, and perform the Promises I have made my own Heart; I will keep your enlivening Image ever in my View, and endeavour to render myself worthy not only of your Esteem but of your Love and Tenderness. Virtue was always my determined Choice; I always loved it with my warmest Approbation, and resolved upon a more attentive and regular Practice of it: but now I love it doubly, it is doubly beautiful, as proceeding from you. Should my Name live, and I be mentioned hereafter, I shall be ambitious to have it said of me, that when seduced by that most fatal Syren Indolence and false Pleasure, to the very Brink of Ruin, the Angel of Love came in your form and saved me.

'I cannot enough admire, upon cool Reflection, your Behaviour, during those happy miserable Days I last saw you. What Grace, what Decency, what Dignity, what amiable Prudence it displayed. It has charmed me to such a Degree, that my Reason is as much enamoured of you as my Heart, and my Friendship for you ventures even to rival my Love. What an invaluable Treasure is such a lovely Friend, who while by gentle Insinuations she teaches

Wisdom makes it at the same Time charming! The pompous
Lessons of Philosophers, of all your proud Moralists, are
insipid, and void of Power, compared to the slightest Hints
from the Lips of those we love.'

This happy and confident mood was suddenly interrupted, however, by the recollection of an incident that had
happened while he had been in her company. They had been
turning over some prints together, and he had asked her to
explain the subject of one. Her answer had been unexpected:
'I remember your Words', he wrote, '—Sir, it is a serious
View of an ill-concerted Marriage—And the Manner with
which you spoke them made them keener still . . . Afterwards you made a malicious Comparison betwixt Painters
and Writers, in which you could not be in earnest: you have
too good Taste and Judgment for That.' This recollection
at once brushed aside his transitory happiness and unleashed
his despair. 'I am afraid I deceive myself', he agonized, '—I
feel this Moment a sweet Anguish stirring in my Breast,
which tells me my Peace is far from being secure—Remembrance bleeds afresh. Alas! you are too sparing of the Balm
of kind Words and healing Hopes—A thousand things
crowd upon me, and pierce me in every Thought—did ever
Love triumph so much in any Bosom as mine? But I must
conclude here, or I shall undo all again.'

James Robertson was Physician to the Court at Kew, and
Elizabeth Young, who was still looking after her sick sister,
moved with his family as he found it necessary to live either
in London, where he had lodgings in Lancaster Court, or in
Kew. When she was at Kew, Thomson tried as often as possible to arrange walks with her in the countryside, and he
celebrated these excursions in some lines written at this
time which he included in the new edition of *The Seasons*.
The time is a summer evening, and

> Now from the World,
> Sacred to sweet Retirement, Lovers steal,
> And pour their Souls in Transport, which the SIRE
> Of Love approving hears, and *calls it good*.

Which Way, AMANDA, shall we bend our Course?
The Choice perplexes. Wherefore should we chuse?
All is the same with Thee. Say, shall we wind
Along the Streams? or walk the smiling Mead?
Or court the Forest-Glades? or wander wild
Among the waving Harvests? or ascend,
While radiant Summer opens all its Pride,
Thy Hill, delightful *Shene*?

He found, however, that these walks were often difficult to arrange. While she was at Kew, he sent her a note by hand on 26 May requesting an opportunity to walk with her. 'The Bearer of this tells me', he wrote, 'that you have been for sometime proposing to take a Walk to Chealsey. If it does not interfere with the Party to Richmond, you will make me truly happy by doing this on Saturday or Sunday next; and he will let me know when and where I shall find you—for it would be Madness in me to think you will write yourself. I might as well hope to hold a Correspondence with superior Beings. Do you know, Madam, that I shall begin to put a vain Interpretation on your obstinately refusing to write? "You think it improper to write kindly, and your Heart will not permit you to write indifferently." Thus will I turn your very Silence into a Love-Letter. I remember you threatened me with a Letter, which, you said, perhaps I would not like, and I rashly dared you to it. Upon second Thoughts my Courage fails me. No, dont write unless the Spirit of the Letter be kind . . . o take care of hurting me. I am infinitely tender, and the least Shadow of a real Unkindness would kill me, would make me more miserable than I have ever yet been, for I hope more.'

He went to Chelsea on the Sunday only to learn that she was walking at that very time in Kew Lane. She may have been tired by his company, or commanded by her mother not to encourage his suit, or determined to punish him for his importunity. After he had learnt of her deception, he sent her a letter of passionate upbraiding on the following Monday. 'Unkind, yet ever dearest Miss Young!' he began, 'did you but know what I suffered yesterday, and still suffer, you must pity me even from common Humanity. Indifference itself would pity me . . . could you not have contrived how to prevent my miserable Walk? Was there no Method to give me a Hint of your Intention to walk in Kew-Lane, that I might have had the Pleasure of walking with you—any Way? The only Opportunities almost I have of conversing with you are during the little Time you are here, and these too are lost! I begin to fear I am utterly undone . . . let me tell you in plain Words, and with the strictest Truth, if you do not give me an Opportunity of talking with you before you go to Town, if you will not settle my Mind into some Peace and Harmony, I am the most miserable Man alive, as the most in Love. I shall see I shall converse with no Body, I shall do nothing—but break my Heart. This very Moment it labours under a terrible Oppression, it bursts from my Breast in Sighs, it flows from my Eyes in Tears, and I must hasten to conclude before David [Mallet?] comes down and finds me in this Disorder. If you will not take Compassion on me, then conclude me lost, undone; I shall not be able to support it, I shall dy with excessive Love.'

At this moment, opportunely enough, George Lyttelton invited Thomson down to stay with him at Hagley, his father's country-seat in Worcestershire. Lyttelton was a man greatly ridiculed by his wittier contemporaries. His very appearance made him their butt, and Lord Hervey, with the smooth venom he reserved for his political enemies, thus described him: 'Mr. Lyttelton, was, in his figure, extremely tall and thin; his face was so ugly, his person so ill made, and his carriage so awkward that every feature was a blemish, every limb an encumbrance, and every motion a disgrace; but, as disagreeable as his figure was, his voice was still more so, and his address more disagreeable than either. He had a great flow of words that were always uttered in a lulling monotony.'[1] He also wrote competent, uninspired verses, 'which cannot much tire because they are short',[2] and was anxious to appear as a patron of letters. But if his

---

[1] Hervey, *op. cit.*, i, 433-4.   [2] Johnson, *op. cit.*, iii, 457.

voice was monotonous, opinions trite, and abilities few, he was at least a sincere and honest politician, and his numerous speeches in Parliament made an effective contribution towards Sir Robert Walpole's downfall. Pope complimented him in these lines upon his political activity:

> Sometimes a patriot, active in debate,
> Mix with the world, and battle for the state,
> Free as young Lyttelton her cause pursue,
> Still true to virtue, and as warm as true.

He was as eager in religion as he was in politics, and although his Methodism was laughed at by his worldly compeers, his evangelical zeal testified to a good heart.

Hagley Park itself, even without Lyttelton's company, would have been enough to persuade Thomson to accept an invitation to stay there. It was one of the most beautiful parks in the country, and a magnificent example of that great English art, landscape gardening. Horace Walpole, a connoisseur in such matters, praised it ecstatically: 'You might draw, but I can't describe, the enchanting scenes of the park: it is a hill of three miles, but broke into all manner of beauty; such lawns, such wood, rills, cascades, and a thickness of verdure quite to the summit of the hill, and commanding such a vale of towns, and meadows, and woods extending quite to the Black Mountain in Wales, that I quite forgot my favourite Thames . . . There is extreme taste in the parks: the seats are not the best, but there is not one absurdity. There is a ruined castle, built by Miller, that would get him his freedom even of Strawberry: it has the true rust of the Barons' Wars. Then there is a scene of a small lake, with cascades falling down such a Parnassus! with a circular temple on the distant eminence; and there is such a fairy dale, with more cascades gushing out of rocks!'[1] And on Walpole ran through a list of beauties, which, if they could so excite him, must have been extraordinarily impressive to a less fastidious taste.

[1] Walpole, *Letters*, ed. Toynbee, iii, 186.

Thomson accepted Lyttelton's invitation on 14 July, and there was nothing in his letter to show his distressed state of mind. 'Hagley is the place in England I most desire to see', he wrote; 'I imagine it to be greatly delightful in itself, and I know it to be so to the highest degree by the company it is animated with. Some reasons prevent me from waiting upon you immediately, but, if you will be so good as to let me know how long you design to stay in the country, nothing shall hinder me from passing three weeks or a month with you before you leave it. As this will fall in Autumn I shall like it the better, for I think that season of the year the most pleasing and the most poetical. The spirits are not then dissipated with the gaiety of Spring, and the glaring light of Summer, but composed into a serious and tempered joy. The year is perfect. In the mean time I will go on with correcting "The Seasons", and hope to carry down more than one of them with me. The Muses, whom you obligingly say I shall bring along with me, I shall find with you—the muses of the great simple country, not the little, fine-lady muses of Richmond Hill.'[1]

The reason that prevented him from travelling at once to Hagley was, of course, Miss Young, whom he was still fruitlessly endeavouring to persuade to marry him. He had at last made, however, all the arrangements for his journey by the middle of August when another trivial act of unkindness upset him so much that he almost deferred his visit. He wrote to her on 17 August: 'It is, besides, a cruel Time you take to exercise the Tyranny of your Power over me: for by that Means you will disappoint me in the most essential Views and Purposes of my Life. Have you a Mind intirely to ruin me? I am at present utterly unfit to go any where, or to execute any Scheme I may have formed. Let me once more conjure you either to treat me with frank open generous Kindness, or to dismiss me for ever. In this last Case, it is true, I shall be undone and miserable, but then I shall be more calmly so, and I will retire to enjoy my Mis-

[1] Quoted *Works of Thomson*, ed. Nicolas, i, lxxxvi–vii.

fortunes out of the Eye of the World. O say, my dearest Miss Young! where and when shall I have a Meeting with you, here or in Town? I have taken a Place in the Worcester Stage-Coach, that sets out on Friday Morning early; but if you do not restore my Mind to Peace, I lay aside the Thoughts of That, and of every thing else. If you stay here to-day, I beg to have a Walk with you in Twitnam-Park Meadows before Dinner: if you go to Town, give me Leave to wait upon you to-morrow Evening in Lancaster Court.'

She must have granted him his meeting and set his mind to peace because on Friday, 19 August, he took his place on the Worcester stage coach. Ten days later, he wrote to her from Hagley to describe the company and the grounds, and this letter is among the best he ever wrote.

'Hagley, August 29, 1743.

'After a disagreeable Stage-Coach Journey, disagreeable in itself, and infinitely so as it carryed me from you, I am come to the most agreeable Place and Company in the World. The Park, where we pass a great Part of our Time, is thoroughly delightful, quite enchanting. It consists of several little Hills, finely tufted with Wood and rising softly one above another; from which are seen a great Variety of at once beautiful and grand extensive Prospects: but I am most charmed with it's sweet embowered Retirements, and particularly with a winding Dale that runs thro' the Middle of it. This Dale is overhung with deep Woods, and enlivened by a Stream, that, now gushing from mossy Rocks, now falling in Cascades, and now spreading into a calm Length of Water, forms the most natural and pleasing Scene imaginable. At the Source of this Water, composed of some pretty Rills, that purl from beneath the Roots of Oaks, there is as fine a retired Seat as a Lover's Heart could wish. There I often sit, and with a dear exquisite Mixture of Pleasure and Pain, of all that Love can boast of excellent and tender, think of you. But what do I talk of sitting and thinking of you There? Wherever I am, and however employed, I never cease to think of my loveliest Miss Young. You are Part of my Being; you mix with all my Thoughts, even the most studious, and instead of disturbing give them greater Harmony and Spirit. Ah tell me, do I not now and then steal a tender Thought from you? I may claim that Distinction from the Merit of my Love. Yes I love you to that Degree as must inspire into the coldest Breast a mutual Passion. So look to your Heart, for you will scarce be able to defend it against my Tenderness—Nor is the Society here inferior to the Scene. It is gentle, animated, pleasing. Nothing passes but what either tends to amuse the Imagination, improve the Head, or better the Heart. This is the truly happy Life, this Union of Retirement and choice Society: it gives an Idea of that which the Patriarchal or golden Age is supposed to have been; when every Family was a little State by itself, governed by the mild Laws of Reason, Benevolence, and Love. Dont however imagine me so madly rural as not to think those who have the Powers of Happiness in their own Minds happy everywhere. The Mind is it's own Place, the genuine Source of it's own Happiness; and, amidst all my Raptures with Regard to the Country, I would rather live in the most London Corner of London with you, than in the finest Country Retirement, and that too enlivened by the best Society, without you. You so fill my Mind with all Ideas of Beauty, so satisfy my Soul with the purest and most sincere Delight, I should feel the Want of little else. Yet still the Country Life with you, diversifyed now and then by the Contrast of the Town, is the Wish of my Heart. May Heaven grant me that favourite Happiness, and I shall be the happiest of men. And so much the happier as the Possession of you will excite me to deserve my Happiness, by whatever is virtuous and Praise-worthy.

'Let me now, my dearest Miss Young, bespeak your Goodness. I shall soon, I am afraid, have Occasion for all your Friendship; and I would fain flatter myself that you will generously in my Absence speak of me more than you ever owned to me. If I am so happy as to have your Heart,

I know you have Spirit to maintain your Choice; and it shall be the most earnest Study and Purpose of my Life not only to justify but to do you Credit by it—Believe me, tho' happy here as the most beautiful Scenes of Nature, elegant Society and Friendship can make me, I languish to see you, and to draw every thing that is good and amiable from your lovely Eyes. Without you there is a Blank in my Happiness which nothing else can fill up. I will not be so extravagant as to hope to hear from you, but I will hope to hear of you or rather from you by the Means of our Friend. Think with Friendship and Tenderness of him, who is with Friendship and Tenderness inexpressible all yours James Thomson.'[1]

It would appear from the enigmatical second paragraph of this letter that the poet had written to Mrs. Young to ask her daughter's hand in marriage; at least the remark, 'If I am so happy as to have your Heart, I know you have Spirit to maintain your Choice', lends weight to this interpretation. Mrs. Young's reply was either an emphatic or conditional negative, and, if her character has not been maligned, it was most likely to be the first.

The visit to Hagley, however, was not entirely spent in pleasure. The poet carried down with him a copy of the 1738 edition of *The Seasons* interleaved with blank pages,[2] and while he stayed at Hagley he continued with his thorough revision of that work. He was inspired not only with an artistic desire to correct its earlier infelicities and to make some significant additions, but with the hope of raising money. If Andrew Millar owned the copyright of *The Seasons*[3] the poet could only expect from him in the way of

[1] This letter has been printed by earlier biographers but the present text is taken from the holograph in the possession of Lady Gordon Cumming.
[2] This copy is now in the British Museum, C.28. e.17.; the corrections in the hand other than Thomson's were once imagined to be Pope's (see Morel, *op. cit.*, pp. 146–150), but Macaulay (*James Thomson*, 1908, pp. 243–4) showed conclusively that they were Lyttelton's.
[3] Thomson apparently sold *Sophonisba* and *Spring* to Millar for £137 10s. 0d., and *Summer*, *Autumn*, and *Winter*, and other poems, to Millan for £105, in 1729. Millan sold out to Millar in 1738 for the price he had originally paid Thomson. See also p. 95, *n* 2.

additional payment, as successive editions of the poem were called for, what he chose to give; but a new and revised edition, considerably enlarged, would be the poet's own property to dispose of as he pleased. He could either print it for himself or he could sell the copyright to Millar for a good price. Millar would obviously be anxious to purchase it both as a friend eager to oblige and as a business man frightened lest the publication of so improved an edition should destroy the value of his property in the earlier editions. If the main obstacle to his marriage with Miss Young was his lack of fortune, Thomson would naturally set a high price on the new edition, which Millar would be willing enough to pay. Thomson had written in an earlier letter to Miss Young, 'Should my Name live, and I be mentioned hereafter, I shall be ambitious to have it said of me, that when seduced by that most fatal Syren Indolence and false Pleasure, to the very Brink of Ruin, the Angel of Love came in your form and saved me': and certainly posterity owes to her influence the revised edition of *The Seasons*.

Thomson's host himself helped with the revision. Lyttelton suggested emendations and, with remarkable self-confidence, even wrote some passages in imitation of Thomson's style, whose addition to the poem he thought would greatly improve it. Among the corrections written out on the blank leaves in Thomson's broad, impetuous hand there are some in Lyttelton's spidery, meticulous holograph. Thomson—who had earlier remarked upon William Aikman's suggested improvements that they did not regard the turn of his genius enough—generally disregarded Lyttelton's suggestions, and preferred his own style to the neat, impersonal diction that his host would have foisted on to him. Lyttelton may have been disappointed that his opinion should have been so little valued, because after the poet's death, while never failing to roundly praise his character and genius, he was always ready to condemn his diction. 'He painted Nature exactly,' he wrote, 'and with great strength of Pencil. His imagination was rich, extensive, and sublime: but his Diction was frequently *obscure* and *affected*.'[1]

The poet, however, paid Lyttelton the compliment of writing an admirable description in verse of Hagley Park, which he included in the revised edition of *The Seasons*, and the scene he chose to describe was the one he had already written about in his letter to Miss Young.

> There along the Dale,
> With Woods o'erhung, and shag'd with mossy Rocks,
> Whence on each hand the gushing Waters play,
> And down the rough Cascade white-dashing fall,
> Or gleam in lengthen'd Vista thro' the Trees,
> You silent steal; or sit beneath the Shade
> Of solemn Oaks, that tuft the swelling Mounts,
> Thrown graceful round by Nature's careless Hand.

Thomson found Hagley Park a suitable subject for his pen, but neither Hagley, nor the many other parks which were being laid out at this time all over the country, would perhaps have been so easily conceived had it not been for his genius. It was he who showed his contemporaries the beauty of landscape. His childhood observation of the Border country had trained him to appreciate the beauty of prospects rather than of particular scenes, and this general vision, this landscape view, of Nature was adopted by his contemporaries. His friend William Kent, who with peculiar appositeness had designed the plates for the subscription edition of *The Seasons*, simply carried into practice the implicit rules for landscape gardening which he found in that poem. Kent laid out a park in such a manner that Nature was shown to the best advantage. By planting woods, levelling hills, diverting streams, and turning valleys into lakes, he forced the observer's eye to follow the direction in which the landscape most subtly evolved its particular harmonies. He had learnt to appreciate what pictorial effects were inherent in any estate, and Thomson had taught him,

---

[1] Lyttelton, *Dialogues of the Dead*, 1760, p. 129.

and the other landscape gardeners, that lesson. It is strong confirmation of this opinion, that Kent cannot be shown to have laid out any estate before 1730, the year in which he illustrated *The Seasons*.[1] Thomson had also planted in the minds of many estate owners the wish to have their grounds so designed that they might derive the greatest pleasure from them; and as they stood on some eminence and looked over the prospect, they could see in reality a scene similar to those which the poet had described. The credit for landscape gardening does not, of course, belong to Thomson alone: many of his contemporaries were as quick to appreciate Nature as he was, but his works were so widely read, and had so persuasive an influence upon taste, that he must be allowed the credit for greatly encouraging that delightful art.

The letter Thomson wrote to Miss Young from Hagley is calmer and more confident than his earlier letters to her. He was too far away to be continually distressed by the hope of having, or the fear of losing, her company upon his walks; away, too, from the unmistakable reality of her refusal to give him the slightest encouragement. At Hagley he had pleasant company to distract his attention when his grief became unbearable, and he could retreat alone to the mossy oak trees at the stream's source to rehearse his dreams of rural retirement and wedded love when his imagination flattered him with a bright future. He could not prolong his visit indefinitely however; even had he been able to stay on at Hagley, he would soon have felt compelled to return to London and make another attempt to win her consent; by the 28 September he was once more at his cottage and writing to her another hopeless letter.

She had apparently asked to borrow his copy of Gay's comedy of *The Distress'd Wife*, which had been published that year, and his accompanying letter was a long and unfavourable criticism of the play. 'The Perusal of it gave me more Disgust than Pleasure,' he wrote, 'it presents so vile

[1] See Margaret Jourdain, *Works of William Kent*, 1948, pp. 74-81.

and perhaps so natural a Picture of a Town-Life. There are no Animals in the whole Creation that pass their Time so idly, and in my Opinion so miserably, as they who compose what they call the gay World do. With Regard to them it is Virtue to be a Misanthrope; and instead of the gay they should be called the gayly-wretched World. It is a World not of God's making, but a true Limbo of Vanity, made up of ridiculous shocking Phantoms of Folly, Affectation, and Vice. One Hour of virtuous Retirement, consecrated to Love Friendship and the Study of Nature, is worth an Age of it. I would have it an Article in the Litany—And from the dull, tiresome, vain, tattling, impertinent, unfeeling, and utterly worthless gay World, good God deliver me!' Thomson's detestation of the town and its artificial, shallow society was, of course, obvious enough before he met Miss Young, but this forceful anathema, which is quite irrelevant to the criticisms of *The Distress'd Wife* which followed it, and the attack on Bath, which he had included in his letter to Mrs. Robertson when she was convalescent there, suggest that his original dislike had been heightened into fear by Miss Young's presence in that society. He suspected perhaps that she enjoyed witty and fashionable company, that she preferred drawing-rooms to country lanes, and that, unless he could woo her away from society, in which he appeared to great disadvantage, or at least persuade her of its utter worthlessness, he would stand little chance of winning her hand. This suspicion is reinforced by a remark which he passed on one character, Miss Friendless, in Gay's comedy. 'And poor Miss Friendless', he exclaimed, 'how came the Author too to be so little her Friend, as to make her a matrimonial Prostitute to the most foolish of all foolish Lords. I expected, from her sensible serious Turn, that she would have disdained the Proposal, and rather lived in a Cottage with some Person she loved.'

Either Thomson did not write to Miss Young again in 1743, or she did not keep his letters—which is very unlikely since she so scrupulously preserved the others—, and

Q

there is nothing to show how he passed the early winter. He would of course continue to revise *The Seasons*, and to plan a new tragedy, which he designed to produce in the following season. But Miss Young had not yet finally rejected him, and he had the unhappy task of writing to her on 21 January 1743/4 to console her on the death of her sister, Mrs. Robertson. He enclosed in his letter, which set out in detail his attitude to death, a copy of the epitaph he had written for Elizabeth Stanley. It is a remarkable composition and deserves to be quoted in full.

'Give me Leave, my dearest Miss Young, from the most sincere and Heart-felt Sympathy, to condole with you upon your Sister's Death. Besides the Friendship and high personal Regard I had for Her, I deeply feel this melancholy Occasion upon your Account; for I must intimately partake of whatever affects you. Yes, I claim it as one of the sweetest Priviledges of Love, to mix my Tears with yours. Why am I not now with you? By what cruel Considerations of Prudence am I thus debarred free Access to your Company? That I might, by all which my Reason can suggest, by all the Arts of Tenderness in my Power, share and lighten your Affliction.

'Grief is it's own best Consolation. Nature has given Tears as a Balm to heal the Wounds of Sorrow. Then weep, my dearest Love, weep a gentle and amiable Sister; your chearful Companion, and tender Friend, from infant Years; with whom you have had so long an Intercourse, and mutual Participation of the same kindred Cares and Joys; with whom been of so many agreeable Parties, and passed so many soft and happy Hours. But, alas, how was the Scene altered for the last Months of her Life! You saw her gradual Decay; you saw Her dying daily, with full Time to contemplate all the Terrors of that awful Change; you saw her former Gaiety and Spirits, that used to make Her the Joy of Company, by Degrees gone; you saw her sprightly Features sunk to mournful Paleness; you saw (I remember it was your own affecting Expression) the piteous Looks she

PLATE III

No 10

January 21, 1743-4.

Give me Leave, my dearest Miss Young, from
the most sincere and Heart-felt Sympathy, to
condole with you upon your Sister's Death. Besides
the Friendship and high personal Regard I had
for Her, I deeply feel this melancholy Occasion
upon your Account; for I must intimately partake
of whatever affects you. Yes, I claim it as one
of the sweetest Priviledges of Love, to mix my
Tears with yours. Why am I not now with you?
By what cruel Considerations of Prudence am
I thus debarred free Access to your Company? that I
might, by all which my Reason can suggest, by
all the Arts of Tenderness in my Power, share and
lighten your Affliction.

Grief is it's own best Consolation. Nature has
given Tears as a Balm to heal the Wounds of
Sorrow. Then weep, my dearest Love, weep
a gentle and amiable Sister; your chearful Companion
and tender Friend, from infant years; with whom
you have had so long an Intercourse, and mutual
Participation of the same kindred Cares and Joys;
with whom been of so many agreeable Parties,

THOMSON'S LETTER OF 21 JANUARY 1743/4
TO MISS YOUNG

cast; and, at last, you saw Her, tho' blest with Patience, Resignation, and well-grounded Hope, I will also add Assurance of a happy Futurity, yet struggling to hold what Nature has made so dear to the human Heart, pierced with the sharpest Sting of Death, the being torn from Those we love.

'But after the first Sallies of Grief are past, consider, that when we lament upon these Occasions, it is ourselves we lament. Consider, that the dark and dreadful Passage from this to a higher and more exalted State, which yet abides us, is over with Her. Consider, She is escaped (as Shakespear calls it) from Life's fitful Fever, now warmed with Hope, now chilled with Disappointment; while we are still toiling here below, deluded Day after Day with false Views and vain Appearances of Things; for true Happiness is not the Growth of this mortal Soil, but of those blessed Regions where she now is. Sometimes indeed a few Seeds of that heavenly Plant fall below, and flourish in Love and Virtue. But what ought to settle our Hearts into perfect Peace, and joyful Serenity, is, the Consideration that Infinite Wisdom and Goodness, who made and rules all, does, cannot but do every Thing for the best. His Works are continually going on from Excellence to Excellence, from Bliss to Bliss, and will thro' eternal Ages ever be disclosing new Scenes of inexhaustible Wisdom and Goodness. There is no real Evil in the whole general System of Things; it is only our Ignorance that makes it appear so; and Pain and Death but serve to unfold his gracious Purposes of Love. The Dead, when we lament, may be supposed to address us thus.

—Grieve not like Those
Who have no Hope: we yet shall meet again;
We still are in a kind Creator's Hand:
Eternal Goodness reigns.—

'Permit me here, upon this serious Occasion, to mention to you another Source of Comfort, if I may fondly flatter myself it can be of any. Think, my dearest Miss Young, that there is one alive, who loves you with unequalled Tenderness, who loves you more, greatly more, than all Friends, all Relations, all the World besides can do; who lives alone, and could dy, for you. Oh come to my Soul, and let me hush your Tears with everlasting Fondness! Alas, that Fortune should put it so much out of my Power to prove, by more than Words, what a boundless Desire I have to make you happy. But I will hope that Love like mine cannot pass quite unrewarded. Tho', however That be, let us cherish this best of Passions, and at least be happy in conscious Love itself. I here devote my faithful Heart to you, and am, with perfect Friendship, inviolable Truth, and unexpressible Tenderness, all yours

'James Thomson.

'P.S. If I cannot properly see you soon, yet consider you owe me something. Tell me, by a Line, that my Love is at present of some Consolation to you. The Inclosed Epitaph, which I wrote on a young Lady, at the Request of her Mother who is my particular Friend, may perhaps be of some Amusement to your present Thoughts.'

This letter was the last he wrote to Miss Young for almost two years, but he still saw her in London and continued, although it must have been apparent that his suit was hopeless, to press her to marry him. He may have attempted to seduce her from society by holding out his offer of 'an elegant sufficiency', but she must be excused for doubting whether he was really in a position to provide her with even decent comfort. He was desperately hard up in 1744 and on 24 July he had to ask his prosperous friend, John Sargent the linen-draper, for a loan. His letter to Sargent is curious because it shows how tenaciously he clung to the ideal of harmony in spite of Miss Young's repeated rebuffs.

'Dear Sargent, After what passed betwixt us some Time ago, I will not use any farther Preamble with a Friend; but if you can spare me twenty Guineas for five or six Months you will oblige me. I propose to myself the Pleasure of calling on you about Thursday next: you will tell me if This be convenient for you; and I hope you will tell it me with all the friendly Freedom I ask you. If I was not thoroughly perswaded of your Friendship, I could not have asked it.

'I take it a little amiss of you, that you have not yet been so good as your Word of riding out this Way. You suffer the fine Weather to pass; but Charlton has greater Beauties to you than Richmond. If I was Sargent I should think so too; but at present I think London has greater Beauties than both, even London in the Depth of Summer, and all these Contradictions like the various Harmony of Nature, arise from one and the same Cause—Divine Attraction, the Energy of Heaven. It pleases me, my Friend, to think that you in the Height of Life—and the right Taste is yours— will be able with an elegant Sufficiency to enjoy those best Pleasures of the retired philsophical social Life. It is not so with all your Friends; but I hope it soon will be our Lot.'[1]

Sargent eventually won the hand of the beauty at Charlton, and enjoyed 'those best Pleasures', in the intervals of business, which were repeatedly denied to his correspondent. Twenty years later he was living in New Broad Street, a 'handsome street inhabited by merchants and other gentlemen'.[2]

A week or so before this letter was written, the revised and enlarged edition of *The Seasons* had been published. It was not a large edition; only one thousand five hundred octavo copies were printed; and it was seen through the press only after the author had made 'divers and repeated alterations', which cost Andrew Millar two pounds, four shillings.[3] The proofs must have been hurriedly read and Millar had also to pay for errata slips. The plates Kent had made for the subscription edition of 1730 were still used, but one, the frontispiece to *Summer*, had to be altered. It showed Musidora bathing under the secret gaze of the hidden Damon, and in the earlier version of the plate she was shown with three attendants about her. Thomson, however,

---

[1] Bodleian MS. Eng. Misc. C.1. The letter is published for the first time.
[2] Dodsley, *London and its Environs*, 1761, v, 26.   [3] *N. & Q.*, I Ser., xii, 218.

in the revised story made her bathe alone, and the plate had
to be altered to show only one naked girl seated pensively
on the river bank. If the plate is closely examined, it will be
seen that the attendants have not been completely erased,
and that they are still represented by a foot, a hand, and a
curve. Millar was very anxious to promote the sale of the
new edition, and, writing on 10 October to a friend travelling in Flanders, he mentioned 'our friend Thomson's new
edition of his Seasons, to which he has added above a 1000
new lines, the goodness of them I need not mention to you,
nor desire if it lies in yr way that you'll forward the sale of
them'.[1] Millar clearly underestimated the popularity *The
Seasons* would achieve in its revised form, and two years later
he printed a duodecimo edition of no less than four thousand copies.

The poet sent a copy of the revised edition to Miss
Young with these verses inscribed on the fly-leaf:

> To Miss Young, my dearest Amanda.
>
> Accept, lov'd Young! this Tribute due
> To tender Friendship, Love, and You;
> But with it take what breath'd the Whole,
> O take to Thine the Poet's Soul!
> If Fancy here her Power displays,
> And if a Heart exalts these Lays;
> You fairest in that Fancy shine,
> And all that Heart is fondly thine.
>   JAMES THOMSON.[2]

The publication of this edition in 1744 brought back into
Thomson's life his old friend, Aaron Hill. The poet forwarded a presentation copy to him through their mutual
friend, Samuel Richardson, the novelist and bookseller, and
Hill thanked him for his gift through the same channel. His
letter to Richardson shows that he considered Thomson's
neglect of him during the previous six years or so a slight

---

[1] *More Culloden Papers*, ed. Duncan Warrand, 1927, iii, 233.
[2] A facsimile of these verses is printed in *Works of Thomson*, ed. Cunningham,
1862, i, ix. A copy of *The Seasons*, inscribed by Thomson to Miss Young, was in the
possession of Lady Gordon Cumming until it was stolen in 1948.

that could not easily be forgiven. 'To the Author of the Seasons,' he wrote to Richardson on 24 July, 'will you be so good as to return my thanks, for his remembering an old friend; who though he had still been forgotten, would, not withstanding that, have yearly traced him round with new delight, from Spring quite down to Winter. And, because I find myself obliged to another writer for his present, through such a hand as your's, pray please to let him know, I thank him for the favour. But, indeed, the more I read these blank verse eruptions, the more beautifully necessary I perceive the yoke of rhyming.'[1] With this nicely barbed acknow-ledgement, Hill took his leave of Thomson, and they seem to have had no further communication. Hill had met Thomson when he had first arrived in London unknown and friendless; he had helped to establish him in literature; he saw him now on the crest of his contemporary fame; and it is a pity that their relations were not as cordial at the close as they had been at the beginning of their acquaintance.

Another old friend, Alexander Pope, had died just before the publication of the new edition of *The Seasons*, and it is to be wished that he was able to read in manuscript the affec-tionate lines written to him as he lay on his sick-bed. 'Which way, AMANDA, shall we bend our Course?' Thomson had asked in 'Summer', and continued,

Slow let us trace the matchless VALE OF THAMES;
Fair winding up to where the Muses haunt
In *Twit'nam*'s Bowers, and for their POPE implore
The healing GOD.

The friendship between Pope and Thomson may appear to be ill-assorted, but it was confirmed by their mutual respect for each other's genius and character.

Thomson spent the autumn of 1744 upon his new tragedy of *Tancred and Sigismunda*, but he also continued his pro-longed and ineffectual courtship of Miss Young. Her birth-day fell on 1 January and he presented to her on that occa-

[1] Richardson, *Correspondence*, 1804, i, 103.

sion in 1744/5 some verses which hitherto have not been published. There is no definite evidence to suggest to what year they belong, but 1744/5 is the most probable. They clearly set out all his claims to her affection and the attractions of the life that he could offer her.

> Hail to the Day! hail to the smiling Skies!
> That first unseal'd my lov'd Amanda's Eyes.
> Blest Day! thou still my Annual Voice shall hear,
> Thou joyous Leader of the brightening Year!
> How dead to Mine the Laureat's venal Lyre!
> How faint his Ardor! and how forc'd his Fire!
> While to the *Sovereign of my Heart* I pay,
> At once, a *Natal* and a *New-Year's* Lay:
> Dull Sack and Pensions prompt his Muse to sing;
> From Love and Beauty my glad Numbers spring.
>
> Come Source of Joy! come from thy Southern Goal,
> O Phoebus come! and chear my drooping Soul!
> Come, with the Loves and Graces in thy Train,
> Whate'er inspires the Bard or charms the Swain:
> The dancing Hours, the rosy-finger'd Dews,
> The gentle Zephirs, and the vernal Muse.
> Thou com'st! thou com'st! I see thee from afar,
> Nearer and nearer, roll thy golden Car;
> Each Day, still something, from oppressive Night,
> Thy Empire gains, some Minutes more of Light;
> The lucid Sky, all Nature, feels thy Power,
> And Spring shines out in every brighter Hour.
>
> Father of Love, come on! and, as along
> Thy Pomp proceeds, I first begin the Song.
> Soon will th' awaken'd Groves their Chorus join,
> And amorous Nature mix her Joy with Mine;
> The Blackbird soon will, from the Hawthorn Bush,
> Chaunt his gay Notes, and soon the mellow Thrush;
> Thro the soft Gleamings of a milder Day,
> Soon will the Woodlark tune his various Lay.
> Then fast they follow: *Valentine* will rise;
> They chuse their Mates; rous'd by the genial Skies,
> They sing what Beauty and what Love inspire,
> Till Philomel compleats the charming Quire,
> Till his unrival'd Song enchants the Grove,
> And Heaven and Earth are Harmony and Love!

Wilt thou, Amanda, *then*, give up thy Charms,
And yield thee to a faithful Lover's Arms?
Wilt thou forsake the City-Throng for me,
Whose Heart so long has imag'd None but thee?
For thee my Cares shall never cease to watch;
I, while it springs, thy rising Wish will catch;
I will explore each Motion of thy Eye;
Join Soul to Soul, and mingle Sigh with Sigh;
I to thy Pains, if Pains there be, will sing,
And Love shall give us an eternal Spring.

Fear not: We shall return, when Wintry Storms
Rise, and their Rage the pining Year deforms;
Then, in thy much-lov'd Scene, we shall again,
Annual, rejoin the chearful friendly Train.
It matters not, my Dearest! where we be,
In Town or Country; 'tis the same with thee:
Thy powerful Presence Time and Place beguiles,
And everlasting Eden round thee smiles.

What tho by Friends forgot? tho Fortune frown?
Great Love can make a Fortune of his own.
Love bade Heaven-breath'd Ambition first aspire,
And thro' the Bosom pour'd a generous Fire;
Love first to Labour rous'd the quicken'd Heart,
The lively Source of every Human Art;
By Love first Cities rose, and Nations throve,
And Wealth and Fame the Bounty are of Love.
Even Nature's Commoners, to whom is given
No Stores but Those of Providential Heaven,
See how, by Love incited, they supply
The Wants each of his little Family.
Nor is to meer Necessities, alone,
Their Care confin'd; it takes a higher Tone;
To bless their Brides they finer Arts employ,
And rise to Grace, to Elegance, and Joy:
And hast thou then less Confidence in me?
Think'st thou, my Soul! I will do Less for thee?

Come then! let no cold Fear thy Kindness curb,
No poor desponding Thought our Love disturb;
To Trust in Heaven yield an unbounded Scope:
'Tis nobler far to give a Loose to Hope.
Enough for me, if sacred Hymen join

Our Fates in One, and I can call thee Mine.
I ask no more but to possess thy Charms,
And fold thee in a tender Husband's Arms;
Still by thy winning Virtues to improve,
To read thy Eyes, the Devotee of Love;
Attun'd to Thine, my Passions to controul,
And in thy lovely Person clasp thy Soul.
What more I crave of Fortune to bestow,
Is all for thee: no Bliss but thee I know!

This poem—which never falters in the tenderness and forthrightness of its sentiments, although the rhymes occasionally jingle and the metre lapses into formlessness—was as ineffectual as the earlier letters, and the poet failed in his hopeless attempt to persuade her to marry him in the spring. It is a pity that Miss Young must remain such an enigmatical figure. It may be unfair to judge her behaviour without knowing her reasons, but she must have given the poet some encouragement or else he could not have persevered in his suit for so long. Had she never intended to marry him from the first, she should have been kind enough to act upon his warning—'To a Passion like mine a *little* Kindness is only Oil thrown upon the Flame, it only makes it consume me with fiercer Rage'—and forbidden him her presence absolutely. She seems at least to have concurred with her mother's opinion to refuse Thomson because of his lack of fortune, and her prudence, which her lover was always reprobating, was perhaps really heartlessness. But the human heart is so veiled and various that it would be unjust to condemn her entirely on the evidence of the poet's letters.

Thomson had asked his friend John Sargent to lend him the twenty guineas for a time of five or six months, and he must have intended to repay the loan out of the profits he expected to make from his new tragedy of *Tancred and Sigismunda*. He worked on this play throughout the autumn and winter of 1744, and it was put into rehearsal in the first months of the following year. The play was most painstakingly rehearsed, and the poet's friends, George Lyttelton and William Pitt, undertook its supervision. 'These two great statesmen, Pitt and Lyttelton, attended the rehearsal of Tancred and Sigismunda with great assiduity; they had a sincere value for the amiable author. Their instructions were heard by the players with great respect, and embraced with implicit confidence.'[1] It is a pleasant conceit that William Pitt, who was one of the noblest patriots to govern this country, should manage the rehearsals of a play by the most patriotic of all poets. Thomson, however, did not need his friends' help only to produce the play; they had also to prune and alter the text before it was suitable for the stage. The poet was far too discursive and descriptive to be a great dramatist, and his friends had to show him where to cut the lengthy speeches he allotted to his characters. Andrew Mitchell told James Boswell twenty years later, that 'the Drama was not his [Thomson's] province. He was too descriptive. When a sentiment pleased him he used to extend it with rich luxuriance. His friends used to prune very freely, and poor Thomson used to suffer. Mr. Mitchell said now and then, "This is fine, but it is Misplaced. *Non est hic locus*."'[2] Mitchell must have had *Tancred and Sigismunda* in mind when he made this remark, because an announcement was prefaced to the published play to the effect that 'This play is considerably shortened in the performance; but I hope it will not be disagreeable to the reader to see it as it was at first written; there being a great difference betwixt a play in the closet, and upon the stage'. Thomson clearly deferred to his friends' opinion as to what was good theatre but he preferred his own opinion as to what was good poetry.

It was announced in the *General Evening Post* for 14–16 March 1745 that 'We hear, that on Monday next there will be represented at Drury-lane Theatre, a new Tragedy, written by Mr. Thomson, call'd Tancred and Sigismunda'. An advertisement for the first performance duly appeared in the *General Advertiser* for Monday, the 18 March: 'DRURY LANE. *Never Acted before. By His Majesty's Company of*

---

[1] Davies, *op. cit.*, i, 78–9.   [2] Boswell, *Private Papers*, iii, 37.

Comedians, At the Theatre-Royal in Drury-Lane, this Day will be presented a New Tragedy, call'd TANCRED and SIGISMUNDA. The principal Parts to be perform'd by Mr. GARRICK, Mr. Sheridan, Mr. Delane, Mr. Harvard, Mr. Bridges, Mr. Mozeen, Miss Budgell, and Mrs. CIBBER. The Characters new Dress'd. Boxes 5s. Pit 3s. First Gallery 2s. Upper Gallery 1s. Places to be taken of Mr. Hobson, at the Stage-Door. To begin exactly at Six o' Clock.'

The tragedy was immediately a great success. 'Last Night a new Tragedy, call'd Tancred and Sigismunda,' announced the newspapers, 'was acted at the Theatre-Royal in Drury-lane, and was receiv'd with universal applause.' Even if the tragedy had not been the best of all the poet's dramatic works, it would certainly have succeeded through the efforts of the extraordinarily brilliant cast. Thomas Sheridan, who played Matteo Siffredi, the Lord High Chancellor of Sicily, was one of the foremost actors of his day, and he was able to show his notable elocutionary skill in his weighty and impassioned speeches. The other supporting actors were all competent performers who would not be completely over-shadowed by the two great principals, David Garrick and Susanna Maria Cibber, playing together for the first time. Garrick was quickly being recognized as the first actor of his day, and the new style he had developed, lighter and more natural than that of the older players, was changing the whole conception of acting. He found that Mrs. Cibber had an equal but complementary genius, and their playing of Tancred and Sigismunda was among the finest of eighteenth-century performances. Thomson, however, did not like Garrick as a man, although he probably approved of his playing. He disliked him primarily because he threatened to overthrow James Quin's theatrical supremacy. Quin's action and deliberative declamation appeared studied and laboured beside Garrick's impressionistic gestures and spon-taneous delivery. But Quin was a far greater man than the insincere and conceited Garrick, and his personal qualities would bias Thomson in his favour.

The story of *Tancred and Sigismunda* has a much larger human interest than the stories Thomson had used in his earlier plays. Tancred, a prince of royal blood, has been educated in the family of Matteo Siffredi, the Lord High Chancellor of Sicily, and has fallen in love with, and plighted his troth to, Siffredi's daughter, Sigismunda. Upon the death of the King of Sicily, it transpires that by the terms of his will Tancred, who until now has been kept in ignorance of his high destiny, is to succeed to the throne on condition that he marries the rival claimant, the Princess Constantia. Tancred will not agree to renounce Sigismunda, but Siffredi—whose only ambition is to prevent the civil war that will inevitably break out between the partisans of Tancred and Constantia if the terms of the late king's will are not obeyed—tricks Tancred into signing a paper by which he binds himself to marry Constantia. His signature of the document is publicly proclaimed, and Sigismunda, disgusted by his desertion and obedient to her father's wishes, marries Earl Osmond, the leader of Constantia's faction—a marriage which her father hopes will promote civil peace. Tancred is enraged by Siffredi's trickery, and seeks out Sigismunda to protest his undying love for her. They are surprised at an interview by Osmond, who, suspecting that his wife is unfaithful, fights with Tancred. Tancred kills him, but before he dies Osmond has strength enough to slay the unsullied Sigismunda. The play concludes with Tancred broken down by grief, and Siffredi horrified by the effect of his guile, which he had only practised to secure the noblest political ends.

The interest of the play is divided between two issues. The second in importance is Siffredi's sacrifice of a dearly loved daughter for the imagined good of his country; the first is the mutual and passionate love-affair of Tancred and Sigismunda, which is brought to disaster by Siffredi's unimaginative and unsympathetic interference. The conclusion is unavoidable that the poet was dramatizing his own love-affair with Elizabeth Young, who he believed, or persuaded himself to believe, would have married him, as Sigismunda would have married Tancred, had a parent not interposed her authority. Siffredi's concluding address to the audience is, in effect, Thomson's warning appeal to Mrs. Young. Siffredi, looking towards the dead Sigismunda, says:

> Behold the fatal work of my dark hand,
> That by rude force the passions would command,
> That ruthless sought to root them from the breast;
> They may be rul'd, but will not be opprest.
> Taught hence, ye parents, who from nature stray,
> And the great ties of social life betray;
> Ne'er with your children act a tyrant's part:
> 'Tis yours to guide, not violate the heart.

Because the play is inspired by the poet's own disastrous passion, and drawn from his own experience, it is immeasurably more affecting than his earlier political plays, which depended for their success upon their epitome of popular indignation with the administration. *Tancred and Sigismunda* escapes from an unreal, statuesque world, where patriot kings preside in immobile state and marmoreal queens utter noble but cold injunctions, into the real world of human passions. Because it could move an audience and allowed the players to show their skill, the play maintained its popularity beyond the close of the eighteenth century.

Tancred and Sigismunda was played nine times, and the author was given benefits on the third, sixth, and eighth nights, being the 21st and 26th March and the 1st April respectively. The Prince and Princess of Wales, the poet's tried patrons, attended his second benefit, and he dedicated the published play to the Prince. Andrew Millar printed five thousand ordinary and fifty fine royal copies of the play: sufficient testimony to its immediate and remarkable popularity.

While *Tancred and Sigismunda* was enjoying its successful run at Drury Lane, Thomas Arne took the opportunity to produce a revised version of *The Masque of Alfred*, for which

he had originally composed the music when it had been performed at Cliveden in 1740. The *Masque*, which was
grandiloquently classed as an 'Historical Musical Drama',
was renamed 'The Distresses of Alfred the Great, King of
England, With his Conquest over the Danes'; and Arne,
considering the original musical part to be 'too short for a
Night's Entertainment', added to it considerably. The ode,
Rule, Britannia, had already become famous, and Arne
advertised it among the *chef-d'œuvres* of the production; the
Masque was to conclude 'with a celebrated ODE in Honour
of GREAT-BRITAIN, in Imitation of those formerly sung
at the Banquets of Kings and Heroes'. The first performance
was given at Drury Lane Theatre on 20 March, and the
second on 3 April, and those who subscribed for both performances were to pay half a guinea for their tickets. Those
attending only one performance had to pay rather more than
they would have paid to see a play, and Arne carefully
explained the reason for this increased price in a disarming
footnote to his advertisements: 'Mr. *Arne* humbly hopes
the Town will not be offended at this small Advance of the
Price to those who don't subscribe, this Performance being
exhibited at extraordinary Expence, with regard to the
Number of Hands, Chorus Singers, building the Stage, and
erecting an Organ; besides all other Incidents as usual.'[1]

Fanny Burney understood that her father, the celebrated
Dr. Charles Burney, who was at this time a young pupil of
Arne's, set part of the *Masque* to music for this production.
She wrote that her father 'had the advantage of setting to
music a part of the mask of Alfred, which brought him into
close contact with the author [Thomson] and rivetted good
will on one side by high admiration on the other'.[2] It must
have been at this time that Burney paid his well-known visit
to the poet. Burney, calling on him 'one day at two o'clock
in the afternoon, found him in bed, with the curtains closed

---

[1] *General Advertiser*, 13 March 1745.
[2] Quoted Percy Scholes, *The Great Doctor Burney*, 1948, i, 24-5.

and the windows shut', and on asking the poet why he stayed so long in bed, received the answer, 'Why, Mon, I had not motive to rise'.[1]

The spring and summer of 1745 passed, and Thomson wrote on 9 August to another old friend, David Mallet, who, like Aaron Hill, was apparently upset by Thomson's neglect of their friendship. Although the days when Mallet and the players had spent convivial nights at the cottage in Kew Foot Lane were over, Thomson assured him in his letter of his continued friendship. 'You will do me great injustice', he wrote, 'if you judge of my friendship by the external forms of it, or by my regular observance of those regards, which I own it is a fault to omit. But I hope in time to amend in this instance, among the many other things we all have and ever will have to correct. It is one of the most endearing qualities of friendship for friends to have a mutual indulgence for one another's faults, yet not to harden themselves in them for that reason. I shall be sincerely glad to sustain and cultivate our old friendship, and I think I dare engage for my heart, that it will not in this be deficient in fully answering to yours.'[2] It is impossible not to feel the sadness underlying these remarks.

Although Thomson had at last realized the hopelessness of his suit, he could not resign himself to losing Miss Young. His protestations of undying love had not been false; he loved her beyond reason and almost more than life. He wrote her a despairing letter on 23 October, which he must have known she would not answer:

'You will very likely be suprized to see this Hand, after so long a Silence. Perhaps too your Heart may be moved at the Sight of it, as Mine is in the Writing; the Occasion whereof was This. A little While ago I happened to light upon some imperfect Scrawls of Letters I formerly wrote to you. What Effect they had upon me the following Lines will shew.

[1] Seward, *op. cit.*, ii, 341. [2] Cunningham, *op. cit.*, pp. 39-40.

O thou! for whom these Letters speak a Flame,
Than which from Heaven a purer never came;
Where every Line with genuine Passion glows,
While from the Heart the full Effusion flows;
Where endless Proofs of Love unequal'd reign,
That cordial Spirit Falsehood cannot feign;
Where highest Friendship holds the smallest Part,
Lost in the tender Transports of the Heart.
The restless Wish that sought thy Good alone,
And center'd in thy Happiness my own:
How couldst thou ever form so fell a Thought,
To lose the Lover who these Letters wrote?
Ah for some Moments quit the giddy Fry,
And o'er them cast again thy melting Eye.
Then thus, perhaps, a stealing Sigh will say:
What Pity! Love like This should pass away.

Still, as I read, the various Scenes arise,
And fond Remembrance fills my gushing Eyes.
I wander where the Thames his mazes leads,
I walk the Gardens, and I trace the Meads;
Our Parties, Quarrels, I recal again,
And think on all that gave me Joy, or Pain.
Is This, my Heart, a Sign thy Wounds are whole?
Ah no! they only fester in my Soul.

Love's Annals this undoubted Maxim prove:
They who have truly lov'd ne'er cease to love.
Interest or Vanity may mix Mankind,
May knit new Friendships and the old unbind:
But his eternal Empire Love maintains;
He binds the Soul in adamantine Chains;
He the wide Waste of Time itself can brave,
Out lives even Death, and triumphs o'er the Grave.
Then let—once dear! oh dearest still!—a Line
Revive the Heart that ever must be thine!'

His verses awoke no response. Even had Elizabeth Young
wished to reply, she was perhaps by now too deeply
committed to someone else to risk a consolatory answer.
She was silent, and Thomson sent her his last letter, the last
cry of a broken heart.

R

'Monday Night, Novr. 4th, 1745.

'My dearest charming Miss Young!—but Words cannot express how dear you are to me—have Pity on me, have Pity on a Heart that feels for you every thing that is good and tender in Love and Friendship. Think what I suffer during this Neglect and Silence of yours. I muse forever on you, not with that pleasing Joy as formerly, but with a Dejection that could not but move your Compassion if you knew it. O if you saw the Tears that often rush into my Eyes at the Thought of your Unkindness, That would be instead of all I can write to you! Is there any thing in Nature so prevailing as the Tears and Intreaties of Love like mine? You surely cannot be so barbarous as to reject them. Give me Leave to cite two Lines of a Work I am at present engaged in.

> Art thou above the Gods, who joy to shower
> Their doubled Goodness on repenting Mortals?

'It is late, and I will urge the Matter no farther with you in this Letter. Let me only beg you, conjure you by all the Tenderness and Endearments that have past betwixt us, to give me an Opportunity of seeing you if it were but for half an Hour. If I do not then intirely satisfy you, and put our future delightful Intercourse upon a better Footing than it ever was, I solemnly promise never to sollicite you more, but to be unhappy by myself in Silence. For unhappy must I be without. Without you I cannot live. You are truly the Life of my Life, the Soul of whatever is excellent good and desireable to me. I wish to live only to live with you; I wish for the Goods of Fortune only to bestow them on you; I wish to excel only to deserve your Love. Let us, my dearest Love! be reconciled, and I will never hereafter give you the least Shadow of Offence; neither will I take any from you. I will contend with you in nothing but uninterrupted Love and Kindness. Soon too, I hope, we shall be in a State which will afford no Foundation for these Love-Quarrels: for we shall then be sure that we love one another; we shall avow it to the World, and be forever blended together by a nuptial Tenderness that is above all Picques fears and Jealousies. Before next Spring I flatter myself I shall be the happiest of Husbands, and I dare also promise to be the kindest and best. O with what Ardor will I pursue your Good, and seek in your dearest Happiness my own! In the meantime, put an End to the Sufferings of him who so much wishes to give you Pleasure, and who is with unequaled unalterable Tenderness your James Thomson.'

Elizabeth Young in obedience either to her own or her mother's wishes married a young sailor, John Campbell, the son of the Rev. John Campbell, minister of Kirkbean in Dumfriesshire, and therefore a near neighbour of the Young family at Gulyhill. John Campbell had had an adventurous career in the Navy, and had returned to England in 1744 with the squadron which had sailed round the world under the command of Lord Anson. He was at the time of this voyage either a master or a lieutenant, and he was certainly promoted a master and commander upon his return. It is hardly necessary to make the comparison that Miss Young must have made between the young, adventurous sailor and the corpulent, retiring poet. Campbell was promoted post captain on 23 November 1747, and, after serving in all the major actions of the century, he rose to be vice-admiral of the Red. 'He was undoubtedly a very great naval character; being a man of undaunted courage, almost unrivalled as a seaman, and, among seamen perhaps wholly so, as an Astronomer and Navigator. His integrity was unimpeachable . . . He preserved his original simplicity of manners till his death, notwithstanding he lived among, and mixed with, the first people in the kingdom: but he had, withal, a dry, sarcastic mode of expression, as well as manner.'[1]

Did Elizabeth Young regret her choice? Did she remember Thomson and his broken heart? She carefully kept his

---

[1] *Gent. Mag.*, lxi, 100.

letters, but whether as trophies of her youth or as mementoes of happier days, it is impossible to tell. Was she happy as the wife of a vice-admiral? happier than she would have been with her devoted poet? There is only one anecdote told about her married life, from which the reader may draw his own conclusions. 'In the war which broke out in 1756 . . . Campbell was generally Admiral Hawke's Captain, and was sent home, by that gallant Commander, with the news of his victory over the French fleet in November, 1759. On this occasion it is said, that Lord Anson, as they were going in his coach to carry the news to the King, said, "Captain Campbell, the King will knight you, if you think proper."— "Troth, my Lord," said the Captain, who retained his Scotch dialect as long as he lived, "I know of no use that will be to me."—"But your Lady may like it," replied his Lordship. "Well then," rejoined the Captain, "his Majesty may knight her, if he pleases."'[1]

---

[1] *Ibid.* George Chalmers, the antiquary, told John Taylor, the gossip, who faithfully recorded it in *Records of My Life*, 1832, that an old housekeeper of the poet's had asserted that the poet was secretly married. Morel (*op. cit.*, pp. 159–60) pointed out that none of the poet's friends knew of this marriage, and it was impossible that it could have been kept so close a secret. Thomson's letters to Miss Young finally dispose of the lie.

CHAPTER IX

THE CASTLE OF INDOLENCE AND LAST YEARS

For ever running an enchanted Round
Passes the Day, deceitful, vain, and void.

JAMES THOMSON had passed the climacteric. He had
been physically older than his forty-two years when he
had first met Elizabeth Young; his body had been burdened
by its own weight and enervated by indolence; but his intellectual vitality had been that of a young and ambitious man.
He woke up from his dreams of love to discover how he had
been aged by his experience. His imagination was tired and
no longer inspired by the poetic enthusiasm that had so
distinguished his youth. He himself realized his changed
condition. When George Lyttelton in 1747 pressed him to
marry, he replied: 'I am too much advanced in life to venture to marry, without feeling myself invigorated, and made
as it were young again, with a great flame of imagination.'[1]
Elizabeth Young had kindled such a flame, and it had con-
sumed him. A melancholy languor cast its shadow over him,
a longing to withdraw from the world possessed him, and
his later years, irradiated still by friendship and delight in
Nature, assumed the regretful mood of his favourite season,
autumn.

He enjoyed, however, much greater security during these
last years than had hitherto been his lot. Sir Robert Walpole's
long political domination was broken in 1742, and the
triumphant opposition could at last reward their loyal supporters with the fruits of office. George Lyttelton, upon the
formation of the Pelham ministry in 1744, was appointed a
Lord of the Treasury, and he secured for Thomson the

---

[1] Quoted *Works of Thomson*, ed. Nicolas, i, xcii.

appointment of Surveyor-General of the Leeward Islands which, after he had paid his deputy in the office, brought him in about three hundred pounds a year.[1] The Prince of Wales immediately dismissed Lyttelton as his secretary when he accepted office under Pelham, but he continued to pay Thomson his annual pension of a hundred pounds until 1747 when, much to the poet's chagrin, it was stopped.[2] His position, therefore, can certainly be described as comfortable if not as affluent, but his good fortune came too late to be fully enjoyed.

Thomson had quoted in his last letter to Miss Young of 4 November 1745 two lines from a new tragedy upon which he had been engaged. 'Give me Leave', he had written, 'to cite two Lines of a Work I am at present engaged in.

> Art thou above the Gods, who joy to shower
> Their doubled Goodness on repenting Mortals?'

The tragedy was to be entitled *Coriolanus*, and the two lines occurred in a speech by Cominius in the third scene of the third act, which shows how far he had already advanced in the new work by the end of that year. His dramatic work had, of course, been inspired by the hope of marrying Miss Young, and when he realized at last that that was an impossibility, he no longer felt a need for money and finished the tragedy slowly and casually. It is the poorest of all his dramas. Shakespeare himself, from whom Thomson borrowed his plot, failed to animate the chill and statuesque Coriolanus into activity, or to make his brutal pride plausible to an audience, but at least he put some poetry into his mouth and sowed in the crevices of this hard play a few seeds of tenderness and pity. Thomson's Coriolanus is a hero of sounding brass, whose verbal clangour is continuous and unconvincing, and never once is a thought or a line pointed with a human passion. The whole play is cold, heartless, immobile, and removed from life. His handling

---

[1] *Memoirs and Correspondence of Lyttelton*, ed. Phillimore, 1845, i, 111–13.
[2] See letter to Paterson, April 1748; quoted *Works of Thomson*, ed. Nicolas, i, c.

of the action is an improvement on Shakespeare; his scenes
are more neatly connected and the dramatic unities are
more closely observed; but mere mechanical business
cannot save from failure a play which is lacking in spirit.

During 1746 he probably finished *Coriolanus*, and he
appears to have spent some weeks of the summer as the
guest of George Lyttelton at Hagley, but, apart from a slight
remark of Alexander Carlyle, we know nothing about his
movements or condition in this year. Alexander ('Jupiter')
Carlyle visited London in 1746, and met Thomson by
arrangement in a tavern. 'Of all the literary people I met
with at this time in London,' wrote Carlyle, 'I must not
forget Thomson the poet and Dr. Armstrong . . . A party
was formed at the Ducie Tavern at Temple Bar, where the
company were Armstrong, Dickson, and Andrew Millar,
with Murdoch his friend. Thomson came at last, and disappointed me both by his appearance and conversation. Armstrong bore him down, having got into his sarcastical vein
by the wine he had drunk before Thomson joined us.'[1] The
poet, however, had never shone in general company, and
his quietness on this occasion would be increased not only
by Armstrong's sarcasm but by dislike of visiting London.
He no longer left Richmond willingly, and particularly
objected to meeting his friends in London taverns. When
David Mallet invited him to one to read and criticize his
new poem of *Amyntor and Theodora*, he kindly but firmly
refused. 'I received yours', he replied on 31 March 1747,
'and am extremely glad to hear that we shall have one good
poetical entertainment this year. Your offer is very kind and
friendly; but I shall relish the pleasure which I know I must
have in reading your poem infinitely better here than in a
damned London tavern.

'The evenings are now too short for reading there a poem
of any length; and I am besides much of the humour of
Sancho. I love to munch a good morsel of that kind by
myself in a corner. There cannot be a more delightful corner

[1] Carlyle, *op. cit.*, pp. 196–7.

than Love Lane is at present wherein to munch a poetical morsel; and should you send me your song for a night or two, the nightingales will strike up at the same time. But if the advanced season of the year makes that inconvenient, with regard to the printing, I will suspend my curiosity till it is published, putting the reading of it to the account of the pleasures of this spring. When the good genius of the season delivers you from the demon of the town I will desire you as a friend to read "Coriolanus". Tho' pretty much indifferent whether ever he appear upon the stage or no, yet I am far from being so with regard to his having your approbation.'[1] This was the last letter from Thomson to Mallet that has been preserved, and it well illustrates his mood at the time.

Thomson's friendship with George Lyttelton became much closer during these years. Lyttelton's first wife, Lucy Fortescue, to whom he had been married for only four years, died in January 1747, and perhaps his loss, so like to Thomson's, quickened the understanding and affection between the two men. Thomson condoled with him and sent him a copy of *The Seasons*, in which these verses were inscribed:

> Go, little book, and find our friend,
>   Who nature and the muses loves,
> Whose cares the public virtues blend
>   With all the softness of the groves.
>
> A fitter time thou canst not choose,
>   His fostering friendship to repay;
> Go then, and try, my rural muse,
>   To steal his widow'd hours away.

Lyttelton found consolation in his religious beliefs. He was a most devoted Christian and an adherent of the extraordinary group of converts who gathered around Selina, Countess of Huntingdon. He not only introduced the poet into this society but attempted to convert him to Christianity. It will have been apparent from both his poetry and

---

[1] Cunningham, *op. cit.*, p. 42.

his correspondence that the poet, although a deeply religious man, was not a Christian, and Lyttelton, perhaps taking advantage of his friend's mental lassitude after his unfortunate affair with Miss Young, set out to erase this one blot in his character. He had written during a visit to Thomson at his cottage in Kew Lane in 1746 a treatise entitled *Observations on the Conversion of St. Paul*; 'to which', wrote Dr. Johnson, 'infidelity has never been able to fabricate a specious answer.[1]' The work enjoyed great popularity, and was reprinted many times as one of the most effective evangelical works of the century. The treatise was designed for a wide audience but it seems to have been particularly intended by its author to convert the poet from his errors. A copy was at once sent to him, and Lyttelton wrote in the accompanying letter: 'My refuge and consolation is in philosophy—Christian philosophy, which I heartily wish you may be a disciple of, as well as myself. Indeed, my dear friend, it is far above the platonick. I have sent you a pamphlet upon a subject relative to it, which we have formerly talkt of. I writt it in Kew Lane last year, and I writt it with a particular view to your satisfaction. You have therefore a double right to it, and I wish to God it may appear to you as convincing as it does to me, and bring you to add the faith to the heart of a Christian.'[2] It may be doubted if the pamphlet achieved this desired effect, but the poet would welcome it as a touching instance of Lyttelton's deep friendship.

Thomson passed the autumn of 1747 on a visit to Hagley Park. Lyttelton wrote to his colleague in the ministry, George Grenville, on 21 September to persuade him to spend some time at Hagley in the following year: 'In the meantime,' he wrote, 'Mr. Pitt and I have been contriving some considerable new improvements to make you the more inexcusable if you do not visit us then; though, indeed, I think if there were no other reason to bring you to us, but the desire we all have of your company, that alone would

---

[1] Johnson, *op. cit.*, iii, 450.   [2] *Memoirs and Correspondence of Lyttelton*, i, 307.

leave you without excuse . . . Thomson is just come to us, and as he is very unwilling to leave this place soon, I wish, that instead of returning to town on the 7th of next month, as I intended to do, I could be allowed to stay 'till the 14th.'[1] The poet would pass his time pleasantly enough in the company of these old and tried friends, and he had also made another interesting friendship in the neighbourhood. This new acquaintance was the pastoral poet, William Shenstone, who lived on a small estate near Hagley, called the Leasowes. There he wrote his small, but extremely delicate and finished, verses, which have the ring of an echo in a summer twilight, and indulged his taste for landscape gardening, an art in which he showed the greatest ingenuity. Dr. Johnson reflected with amusement upon Shenstone's delight in gardening: 'Now was excited his delight in rural pleasures, and his ambition of rural elegance; he began from this time to point his prospects, to diversify his surface, to entangle his walks, and to wind his waters, which he did with such judgment and such fancy as made his little domain the envy of the great and the admiration of the skilful: a place to be visited by travellers, and copied by designers. Whether to plant a walk in undulating curves, and to place a bench at every turn where there is an object to catch the view; to make water run where it will be heard, and to stagnate where it will be seen; to leave intervals where the eye will be pleased, and to thicken the plantation where there is something to be hidden, demands any great powers of mind, I will not enquire: perhaps a sullen and surly spectator may think such performances rather the sport than the business of human reason. But it must be at least confessed that to embellish the form of nature is an innocent amusement, and some praise must be allowed by the most supercilious observer to him who does best what such multitudes are contending to do well.'[2]

Thomson was no 'sullen and surly spectator', and he had at once won Shenstone's affectionate regard. After his visit

[1] *Grenville Papers*, 1852, i, 68–9.   [2] Johnson, *op. cit.*, iii, 350–1.

to Hagley in 1746, Shenstone had written enthusiastically about him to his friend Richard Graves: 'I have had little company since I saw you. One day indeed I was suprized by a visit from Mr. Thomson, Author of the Seasons.— Mr. Lyttelton introduced him. I have not room to tell you all that passed.—They praised my place extravagantly;— proposed alterations, &c. Thomson was very facetious, and very complaisant; invited me to his house at Richmond. There were many things said worth *telling*, but not *writing* to you.'[1] Shenstone dined at Hagley a few weeks before Thomson's arrival in 1747, and learnt then that 'that right friendly bard', as he called him, was expected. He was clearly anticipating the pleasure of showing Thomson his recent improvements to his estate, and their meeting was not long delayed. 'As I was returning last Sunday from Church,' he wrote to Richard Graves on 21 September, 'whom should I meet in my way, but that *sweet-souled* bard Mr. James Thomson, in a chaise drawn by two horses lengthways.—I welcomed him into the country, and asked him to accompany Mr. Lyttelton to the Leasows . . . which he promised to do. So I am in daily expectation of them and all the world this week. I fancy they will lavish all their praises upon *nature*, reserving none for poor *art* and *me*.'[2] Shenstone's two complementary phrases, 'right friendly' and 'sweet-souled', reveal how distinct and amiable an impression Thomson made upon his younger contemporaries.

Lyttelton's kindness to Thomson extended farther than a sinecure and hospitality; he even tried to find a wife for him. A willing young lady, whom he considered suitable to the task of caring for the poet, and talented enough to make him forget Miss Young, was at last discovered, and through an intermediary, a Mr. Gray, Lyttelton urged the poet to propose to this lady. Thomson kindly but firmly turned down the impossible suggestion in a memorably phrased letter of 14 December 1747 to Lyttelton:

[1] *Letters of Shenstone*, ed. Williams, 1939, p. 106.   [2] *Ibid.*, p. 116.

'Dear Sir,

'I should have answered your kind, and truly friendly
letter some time ago. My not having answered it hitherto
proceeded from my giving it mature and deep consideration. I have considered it in all lights and in all humours, by
night, by day, and even during these long evenings. But the
result of my consideration is not such as you would wish.
My judgment agrees with you, and you know I first
impressed yours in her favour. She deserves a better than
me, and has as many good and worthy qualities as any
woman: nay to others and I hope to men of taste, she has
charming and piquant ones: but every man has a singular
and uncontrollable imagination of his own: now as I told
you before she does not pique mine. I wonder you should
treat that objection so lightly, as you seem to do in your last.
To strike one's fancy is the same in love that charity is in
religion. Though a woman had the form, and spoke with
the tongue of angels; though all divine gifts and graces
were her's; yet, without striking the fancy she does nothing.
I am too much advanced in life to venture to marry, without
feeling myself invigorated, and made as it were young again,
with a great flame of imagination. But we shall discuss this
matter more fully when I have the happiness of seeing you
at full leisure. What betwixt judgment and fancy, I shall run
a great risk of never entering into the holy state, in the mean
time I wish to see you once more happy in it. Forgive me if
I say, it would be an ungrateful frowardness, to refuse the
bounty of providence, because you have been deprived of
former enjoyments. If you cannot again love so exquisitely
as you have done, so much the better; you will not then
risque being so miserable. To say that one cannot love twice
is utterly unphilosophical, and give me leave to say contrary
to my own experience. Can there not be more objects than
one for the same passion? If so, why cannot the passion be
renewed, when it finds a new object? The flame of any love
was never so strong yet, as to burn out the heart. So far
from that, the powers of the mind rather grow by exercise.

The truth is, it is not a former passion that prevents a second: it is only the hardening of the heart from years and harsh untender business. If you could get so much master of your just grief as to think of a second match, I may be tempted also to try to be happy along with you. I wish you joy of the sun's now turning his all-enlivening and beautiful face towards us. May the genial spirit of the returning year animate and cheer you, and yet again make you happy! than which nothing can give greater pleasure to yours, J. Thomson.

'P.S. Mr. Gray discharged his commission faithfully, and with very decent gravity; to whom I gave the same answer I send you.'[1]

Other matters concerned with marriage had earlier engaged the poet's attention. His favourite sister, Elizabeth, had married the Rev. Robert Bell, minister of Strathaven, in 1740, and before the marriage Bell had asked the poet for his permission. Thomson had written a kindly and understanding letter to his sister on the occasion. 'I entirely agree to this marriage,' he wrote, 'as I find it to be a marriage of inclination, and founded upon long acquaintance and mutual esteem. Your behaviour hitherto has been such as gives me very great satisfaction, in the small assistance I have been able to afford you. . . . I must chiefly recommend to you to cultivate, by every method, that union of hearts, that agreement and sympathy of tempers, in which consists the true happiness of the marriage state. The economy and gentle management of a family is a woman's natural province, and from that her best praise arises. You will apply yourself thereto as it becomes a good and virtuous wife. I dare say I need not put you in mind of having a just and grateful sense of, and future confidence in, the goodness of God, who has been to you a "Father to the fatherless". Though you will hereafter be more immediately under the protection of

---

[1] Quoted *Works of Thomson* ed, Nicolas, i, xcii–xciii.

another, yet you may always depend upon the sincere friendship, and tenderest good offices of your most affectionate brother.'[1] Elizabeth, however, did not live long after her marriage, and her husband, who wished to remarry, asked Thomson if he had any objection. The poet referred to this matter in a letter of 4 October 1747 to another sister, Jean, who had married Robert Thomson, the master of Lanark Grammar School. Dr. Johnson first printed this letter, which Boswell found for him, in his life of the poet, and he wrote that he communicated it 'with much pleasure, as it gives me at once an opportunity of recording the fraternal kindness of Thomson, and reflecting on the friendly assistance of Mr. Boswell, from whom I received it'.[2]

'My dear Sister,
'I thought you had known me better than to interpret my silence into a decay of affection, especially as your behaviour has always been such as rather to increase than to diminish it. Do not imagine, because I am a bad correspondent, that I can ever prove an unkind friend and brother. I must do myself the justice to tell you, that my affections are naturally very fixed and constant; and if I had ever reason of complaint against you, of which, by the by, I have not the least shadow, I am concious of so many defects in myself, as dispose me to be not a little charitable and forgiving.
'It gives me the truest heartfelt satisfaction to hear you have a good kind husband, and are in easy contented circumstances; but were they otherwise, that would only awaken and heighten my tenderness towards you. As our good and tender-hearted parents did not live to receive any material testimonies of that highest human gratitude I owed them, than which nothing could have given me equal pleasure, the only return I can make them now is, by kindness to those they left behind them. Would to God poor Lizy had lived longer, to have been a farther witness of the truth of what I

1 Quoted *Works of Thomson*, ed. Nicolas, i, cxxiv. 2 Johnson, *op. cit.*, iii, 295.

say; and that I might have had the pleasure of seeing once more a sister, who so truly deserved my esteem and love. But she is happy, while we must toil a little longer here below: let us, however, do it cheerfully and gratefully, supported by the pleasing hope of meeting yet again on a safer shore, where to recollect the storms and difficulties of life, will not, perhaps, be inconsistent with that blissful state.

'You did right to call your daughter by her name; for you must needs have had a particular tender friendship for one another, endeared as you were by nature, by having passed the affectionate years of your youth together, and by that great softener and engager of hearts, mutual hardship. That it was in my power to ease it a little, I account one of the most exquisite pleasures of my life. But enough of this melancholy though not unpleasing strain.

'I esteem you for your sensible and disinterested advice to Mr. Bell, as you will see by my letter to him. As I approve, entirely, of his marrying again, you may readily ask me why I do not marry at all. My circumstances have hitherto been so variable and uncertain in this fluctuating world, as induced me to keep from engaging in such a state; and now, though they are more settled, and of late, which you will be glad to hear, considerably improved, I begin to think myself far too advanced in life for such youthful undertakings, not to mention some other petty reasons that are apt to startle the delicacy of old bachelors. I am, however, not a little suspicious, that was I to pay a visit to Scotland, of which I have some thoughts of doing soon, I might possibly be tempted to think of a thing not easily repaired if done amiss. I have always been of opinion, that none make better wives than the ladies of Scotland; and yet, who more forsaken than they, while the gentlemen are continually running abroad all the world over? Some of them, it is true, are wise enough to return for a wife. You see I am beginning to make interest already with the Scotch ladies. Pray let me hear from you now and then: and though I am not a regular correspondent, yet perhaps I may mend in that respect.

Remember me kindly to your husband, and believe me to be your most affectionate brother, JAMES THOMSON.'[1]

During these last years of his life, the poet was putting the finishing touches to a poem, *The Castle of Indolence*, which had intermittently engaged his attention for a long time. He mentioned the work in a letter of April 1748 to William Paterson: 'Now that I am prating of myself,' he wrote, 'know that, after fourteen or fifteen years, the "Castle of Indolence" comes abroad in a fortnight ... You have an apartment in it as a night pensioner; which you may remember, I filled up for you during our delightful party at North Haw. Will ever those days return again? Do not you remember eating the raw fish that were never caught?'[2] *The Castle of Indolence* was, at first, wrote Patrick Murdoch, 'little more than a few detached stanzas, in the way of raillery on himself, and on some of his friends, who would reproach him with indolence; while he thought them, at least, as indolent as himself. But he saw very soon, that the subject deserved to be treated more seriously, and in a form fitted to convey one of the most important moral lessons.'[3]

The first canto, which is by far the finer of the two, describes how the wizard Indolence entices into his castle the unwary passers-by, among whom Thomson's friends prominently figure. The reader is not told in what part of the country this castle stands, but the opening stanzas clearly and felicitously depict the rich Thames valley in which the poet had made his own home:

> In lowly dale, fast by a river's side,
> With woody hill o'er hill encompassed round
> A most enchanting wizard did abide,
> Than whom a fiend more fell is no where found.
> It was, I ween, a lovely spot of ground;
> And there a season atween *June* and *May*,
> Half prankt with spring, with summer half imbrown'd,
> A listless climate made, where, sooth to say,
> No living wight could work, ne cared even for play.

[1] Quoted *ibid.*, pp. 295–7. [2] Quoted *Works of Thomson*, ed. Nicolas, i, ci.
[3] *Works of Thomson*, 1762, i, xiv.

Was nought around but images of rest:
Sleep-soothing groves, and quiet lawns between;
And flowery beds that slumberous influence kest,
From poppies breath'd; and beds of pleasant green,
Where never yet was creeping creature seen.
Mean time unnumber'd glittering streamlets play'd,
And hurl'd every-where their waters sheen;
That, as they bicker'd through the sunny glade,
Though restless still themselves, a lulling murmur made.

Join'd to the prattle of the purling rills,
Were heard the lowing herds along the vale,
And flocks loud-bleating from the distant hills,
And vacant shepherds piping in the dale:
And now and then sweet Philomel would wail,
Or stock-doves plain amid the forest deep,
That drowsy rustled to the sighing gale;
And still a coil the grasshopper did keep;
Yet all these sounds yblent inclined all to sleep.

These stanzas, and indeed the whole canto, are an evocation
of a high summer's day, when the grasses bend beneath the
heat, the cattle crowd under a sycamore's shade, and the
waters twist slowly below their brilliant sheen, and an
invocation to the memory of those many parties which the
poet had once made with the friends at whom he gently
railed in the poem. These summer excursions, to North
Haw and to other hamlets along the Thames, must have
been delightful. Thomson referred to them nostalgically in
his letter to Paterson, and they were mentioned several
times in his correspondence with Elizabeth Young; indeed,
his penultimate letter to her touched directly and sorrow-
fully upon their memory:

> Still, as I read, the various Scenes arise,
> And fond Remembrance fills my gushing Eyes.
> I wander where the Thames his mazes leads,
> I walk the Gardens, and I trace the Meads;
> Our Parties, Quarrels, I recal again,
> And think on all that gave me Joy, or Pain.

He shut out from *The Castle of Indolence*, however, the recol-
s

lection of pain, and introduced only the joyousness of those distant days.

The wizard Indolence waylays the travellers as they pass by his gates, and wooes them to enter with an entrancing song. The sleepy richness of the language and the speciousness of the thought are most attractive. Who could have resisted this appeal?

> Come ye, who still the cumbrous load of life
> Push hard up hill; but as the farthest steep
> You trust to gain, and put an end to strife,
> Down thunders back the stone with mighty sweep,
> And hurls your labours to the valley deep,
> For-ever vain: come, and, withouten fee,
> I in oblivion will your sorrows steep,
> Your cares, your toils, will steep you in a sea
> Of full delight: O come, ye weary wights, to me!

The most specious stanza, and one which shows how clearly and easily Thomson could write on occasions, is that in which the wizard reflects upon virtue:

> What, what, is virtue, but repose of mind,
> A pure ethereal calm, that knows no storm;
> Above the reach of wild ambition's wind,
> Above those passions that this world deform,
> And torture man, a proud malignant worm?
> But here, instead, soft gales of passion play,
> And gently stir the heart, thereby to form
> A quicker sense of joy; as breezes stray
> Across th' enliven'd skies, and make them still more gay.

The interior of the castle, its groves and gardens, its furnishings and decorations, are richly described, and the poet ransacked his imagination for every luxuriant image, and his memory for gleanings of travel literature and Oriental fable, to heighten the scene. At last, after introducing the phantoms which appeared in the seduced travellers' dreams, he had exhausted his full store:

> No, fair illusions! artful phantoms, no!
> My Muse will not attempt your fairy-land:

She has no colours that like you can glow:
To catch your vivid scenes too gross her hand.
But sure it is, was ne'er a subtler band
Than these same guileful angel-seeming sprights,
Who thus in dreams, voluptuous, soft, and bland,
Pour'd all th' *Arabian Heaven* upon our nights,
And bless'd them oft besides with more refined delights.

Another of the poet's characteristics, which is not apparent in either his other poetry or his correspondence, is very marked in this poem; his humour is always alive and pointed. Patrick Murdoch wrote that the poet's 'wit flowed freely, but pertinently, and at due intervals',[1] in conversation, but only in *The Castle of Indolence*, which was originally intended to amuse his friends, did he make any literary use of this quality. It lends a gaiety to his descriptions of the exaggerated comforts within the castle:

Soft quilts on quilts, on carpets carpets spread,
And couches stretch around in seemly band;
And endless pillows rise to prop the head;
So that each spacious room was one full-swelling bed.

The portraits of those friends, whom he imagined to be victims of the wizard's guile, have generally been identified. James Quin was the 'Esopus of the age', whose 'well urged sense th' enlighten'd judgment takes'; George Lyttelton was the guest 'of sense refin'd' who occasionally visited the castle; and Patrick Murdoch was the hero of this delightful stanza:

Full oft by holy feet our ground was trod,
Of clerks good plenty here you mote espy.
A little, round, fat, oily man of God,
Was one I chiefly mark'd among the fry:
He had a roguish twinkle in his eye,
And shone all glittering with ungodly dew,
If a tight damsel chaunc'd to trippen by;
Which when observ'd, he shrunk into his mew,
And strait would recollect his piety anew.

[1] *Works of Thomson*, 1762, i, xviii.

Nor did the poet spare himself; he described his own
appearance in the famous line,

> A bard here dwelt, more fat than bard beseems,

and Lyttelton, it is said,[1] completed the stanza:

> Who, void of envy, guile, and lust of gain,
> On virtue still, and Nature's pleasing themes,
> Pour'd forth his unpremeditated strain:
> The world forsaking with a calm disdain.
> Here laugh'd he careless in his easy seat;
> Here quaff'd encircled with the joyous train,
> Oft moralizing sage: his ditty sweet
> He loathed much to write, ne cared to repeat.

Among the remaining portraits there are three stanzas
describing a poet which are perhaps the most beautiful
verses in the poem; they anticipate the tenderness, melancholy, and romanticism which Matthew Arnold was to
display in *The Scholar Gypsy*:

> Of all the gentle tenants of the place,
> There was a man of special grave remark:
> A certain tender gloom o'erspread his face,
> Pensive, not sad, in thought involv'd not dark,
> As soot this man could sing as morning-lark,
> And teach the noblest morals of the heart:
> But these his talents were yburied stark;
> Of the fine stores he nothing would impart,
> Which or boon Nature gave, or nature-painting Art.

> To noontide shades incontinent he ran,
> Where purls the brook with sleep-inviting sound;
> Or when Dan *Sol* to slope his wheels began,
> Amid the broom he bask'd him on the ground,
> Where the wild thyme and camomoil are found:
> There would he linger, till the latest ray
> Of light sat trembling on the welkin's bound;
> Then homeward through the twilight shadows stray,
> Sauntering and slow. So had he passed many a day.

> Yet not in thoughtless slumber were they past:
> For oft the heavenly fire, that lay conceal'd

[1] See Fawkes and Woty, *Poetical Calendar*, 1763, xii, 106.

Beneath the sleeping embers, mounted fast,
And all its native light anew reveal'd:
Oft as he travers'd the cerulean field,
And markt the clouds that drove before the wind,
Ten thousand glorious systems would he build,
Ten thousand great ideas fill'd his mind;
But with the clouds they fled, and left no trace behind.

These stanzas are generally accepted as a portrait of William
Paterson; the poet told Paterson in his letter to him of April
1748 that he had an 'apartment' in *The Castle of Indolence*,
'as a night pensioner'; but there has always been a suspicion
that the verses are in fact a portrait of William Collins, to
whose appearance and character they are so exactly fitted.
Collins's countenance was 'o'erspread' with a 'tender
gloom' of thought; he particularly loved the sun's 'latest
ray', and his *Ode to Evening* is the matchless evocation of
that hour; and he too built 'ten thousand glorious systems'
which 'left no trace behind'. His friend, Dr. Johnson,
reflected upon this last fault: 'He designed many works,
but his great fault was irresolution . . . He planned several
tragedies, but he only planned them.'[1] We know nothing
about Paterson to suggest that he was possessed of a genius
comparable to that described in these verses, and if they
were intended for him, the poet must have exaggerated his
quality.

Collins was the latest of Thomson's friends. He apparently
took lodgings in Richmond in order to be near to him,
giving them up when Thomson died.[2] This is sufficient
proof of his love and admiration for the elder poet. They
were entirely matched in temperament, and their conversations must have strayed into remote regions of the imagination. Collins, wrote Dr. Johnson, 'had employed his mind
chiefly on works of fiction and subjects of fancy, and by
indulging some peculiar habits of thought was eminently
delighted with those flights of imagination which pass the
bounds of nature, and to which the mind is reconciled only

[1] Johnson, *op. cit.*, iii, 335.   [2] See *Works of Thomson*, 1762, i, xvi.

by a passive acquiescence in popular traditions. He loved
fairies, genii, giants and monsters; he delighted to rove
through the meanders of inchantment, to gaze on the
magnificence of golden palaces, to repose by the water falls
of Elysian gardens.'[1] He must have delighted in *The Castle
of Indolence*, and particularly in this stanza, which illustrates
how quickly and secretly the guests dispersed throughout
the castle's grounds to enjoy in privacy their illusionary
pleasures:

> As when a shepherd of the *Hebrid-Isles*,
> Plac'd far amid the melancholy main,
> (Whether it be lone fancy him beguiles;
> Or that aerial beings sometimes deign
> To stand embodied to our senses plain)
> Sees on the naked hill, or valley low,
> The whilst in ocean *Phoebus* dips his wain,
> A vast assembly moving to and fro:
> Then all at once in air dissolves the wondrous show.

The second canto of *The Castle of Indolence* tells how the
antic Knight of Arts and Industry, whose strenuous efforts
have spread civilization throughout the world, learns of the
enchanted castle's existence. He resolves to destroy the
wizard's power, and to free those whom he has enticed
within from the tyranny of false pleasures. He accomplishes
his purpose. The canto is moral enough but very dull compared with the gaiety and felicity of the first. Thomson
wrote the first canto from the heart, and his friends were
quick to recognize that it gave a true and vivid impression
of his character: 'His Castle of Indolence', wrote Lady
Luxborough to Shenstone, 'I have read at last, and admire
several parts of it. He makes the Wizard's song most engaging: but, as Lady Hertford observes, it is no wonder; for

> "He needs no Muse who dictates from the Heart;"

and Thomson's heart was ever devoted to the Archimage.'[2]
He wrote the second canto from the reason, and its moral

[1] Johnson, *op. cit.*, iii, 337.
[2] *Letters written by Lady Luxborough to Shenstone*, 1775, pp. 56–7.

exhortations, so similar to those resolutions of better behaviour which he had avowed in his letters to Miss Young, are meagre fare for the imagination. The poem was begun in the hey-day, and concluded in the saddened autumn, of his life. The second canto, however, contains one beautiful stanza which fully expresses Thomson's inspiration:

> I care not, Fortune, what you me deny:
> You cannot rob me of Free Nature's grace;
> You cannot shut the windows of the sky,
> Through which *Aurora* shews her brightening face;
> You cannot bar my constant feet to trace
> The woods and lawns, by living streams, at eve:
> Let health my nerves and finer fibres brace,
> And I their toys to the *great Children* leave:
> Of fancy, reason, virtue, nought can me bereave.

The Castle of Indolence is an avowed imitation of Edmund Spenser, and it is remarkable how completely Thomson caught all his master's swiftness, sweetness, and purity of diction. The influence of the most natural of our poets made him throw off at once all those obscurities, complexities, and infelicities of style which irritate and distract the reader of *The Seasons*, and inspired him to write directly and un-affectedly. Also, because the poem was so intimate in its origin, he did not attempt those flights into high serious-ness which had strained his style in the earlier poetry, and, contented with a lower achievement, he moved more naturally and easily. William Shenstone, whose opinion, as the author of an admirable imitation of Spenser, *The School Mistress*, is to be respected, wrote about *The Castle of Indolence*: 'It is I think a very pretty poem, & also a good *Imitation* of *Spenser*: which latter Circumstance is the more re-markable, as Mr. Thomson's diction was not reckon'd the most *simple*.'[1]

Thomson told William Paterson, in his letter of April 1748, that *The Castle of Indolence* 'comes abroad in a fort-night', and he also gave him some news about his tragedy

[1] *Letters of Shenstone*, p. 170.

of *Coriolanus*: 'Coriolanus has not yet appeared on the stage', he wrote, 'from the little, dirty jealousy of Tullus towards him who alone can act Coriolanus.' The tragedy had been finished in March 1747, when the poet asked Mallet to read it critically, and it had been submitted to Drury Lane Theatre in order that it might be produced during the season of 1747/8. It is apparent from Thomson's remark to Paterson, that the poet's fixed intention was that David Garrick should take the part of Tullus and James Quin should play the hero, Coriolanus. Unfortunately, Garrick refused to play the subsidiary part, and his refusal prevented the production of the tragedy until after Thomson's death, when Quin played Coriolanus as the poet had originally intended. This incident is another example of Thomson's unshakeable loyalty towards his old friends.

While Thomson lived quietly at Richmond and drew his salary as Surveyor-General of the Leeward Islands, William Paterson, who succeeded him in the office after his death, was in the Barbadoes acting as his deputy. The poet sent this kindly friend a long letter in April 1748, and included some news about their mutual friends. John Sargent, the prosperous linen-draper, who had married his Charlton beauty by this time, 'turns out one of the best men of our youthful acquaintance,' he wrote, '—honest, honourable, friendly, and generous. If we are not to oblige one another, life becomes a paltry, selfish, affair,—a pitiful morsel in a corner. Sargent is so happily married, that I could almost say,—the same case happen to us all.' Other friends were also mentioned, and it is pleasant to see how the poet delighted to sing their praises. Andrew Mitchell, he continued, 'is in the house for Aberdeenshire, and has spoke modestly well; I hope he will be something else soon; none deserves better; true friendship and humanity dwell in his heart . . . Peter Murdoch is in town, tutor to Admiral Vernon's son, and is in good hope of another living in Suffolk, that country of tranquillity, where he will then burrow himself in a wife and be happy. Good-natured, obliging Millar, is as usual. Though the Doctor [Armstrong] increases in business, he does not decrease in spleen, but there is a certain kind of spleen that is both humane and agreeable, like Jacques in the play: I sometimes, too, have a touch of it.' This is the last letter of the poet's which has survived, however, and because it illustrates the melancholy of his last months, it deserves to be quoted more fully.

'That I have not answered several letters of yours, is not owing to the want of friendship and the sincerest regard for you, but you know me well enough to account for my silence, without my saying any more upon that head; besides I have very little to say that is worthy to be transmitted over the great ocean. The world either futilises so much, or we grow so dead to it, that its transactions make but feeble impressions on us. Retirement and nature are more and more my passion every day; and now, even now, the charming time comes on: Heaven is just on the point, or rather in the very act, of giving earth a green gown. The voice of the nightingale is heard in our lane.

'You must know that I have enlarged my rural domain much to the same dimensions you have done yours. The two fields next to me, from the first of which I have walled—no, no—paled in about as much as my garden consisted of before, so that the walk runs round the hedge, where you may figure *me* walking any time of the day, and sometimes of the night. For *you*, I imagine you reclining under cedars, and there enjoying more magnificent slumbers than are known to the pale climates of the north; slumbers rendered awful and divine by the solemn stillness and deep fervours of the torrid noon. At other times I imagine you drinking punch in groves of lime or orange trees, gathering pineapples from hedges, as commonly as we may blackberries, poetising under lofty laurels, or making love under full spread myrtles. But, to lower my style a little, as I am such a genuine lover of gardening, why do not you remember me in that instance, and send me some seeds of things that might succeed here during the summer, though they cannot perfect their seed sufficiently in this, to them, uncongenial climate to propagate? in which case is the caliloo, which, from the seed it bore here, came up puny, rickety, and good for nothing. There are other things certainly with you, not yet brought over hither, that might flourish here in the summer time, and live tolerably well, provided they be sheltered in a hospitable stove, or green-house during the winter. You will give me no small pleasure by sending me, from time to time, some of these seeds, if it were no more but to amuse me in making the trial. With regard to the brother gardeners [his nephews] you ought to know that, as they are half vegetables, the animal part of them will never have spirit enough to consent to the transplanting of the vegetable into distant, dangerous climates. They, happily for themselves, have no other idea but to dig on here, eat, drink, sleep, and kiss their wives.

'As to more important business, I have nothing to write to you. You know best. Be, as you always must be, just and honest: but if you are unhappily, romantic, you shall come home without money, and write a tragedy on yourself . . . if you are not infected with a certain Creolian distemper, whereof I am persuaded your soul will utterly resist the contagion, as I hope your body will that of the natural ones, there are few men so capable of that unperishable happiness, that peace and satisfaction of mind, at least that proceeds from being reasonable and moderate in our desires, as you. These are the treasures dug from an inexhaustible mine in our own breasts, which, like those in the kingdom of heaven, the rust of time cannot corrupt, nor thieves break through and steal . . . Let us have a little more patience, Paterson; nay, let us be cheerful; at last all will be well, at least all will be over,—here I mean: God forbid it should be so hereafter! But, as sure as there is a God, that will not be so . . . May your health, which never failed you yet, still continue, till you have scraped together enough to return home and live in some snug corner, as happy as the corycius senex, in Virgil's fourth Georgic, whom I recommend both to you and myself as a perfect model of the truest happy life.'

He had little time left to enjoy his new garden and his snug corner at Richmond; within five months of writing this letter to Paterson he was dead. The occasion of his fatal illness is best told in the words of his friend and biographer, Patrick Murdoch. 'He had always been a timorous horseman; and more so, in a road where numbers of giddy or unskilful riders are continually passing: so that when the weather did not invite him to go by water, he would commonly walk the distance between *London* and *Richmond*, with any acquaintance that offered; with whom he might chat and rest himself, or perhaps dine, by the way. One summer evening, being alone, in his walk from town to *Hammersmith*, he had overheated himself, and in that condition, imprudently took a boat to carry him to *Kew*; apprehending no bad consequence from the chill air on the river, which his walk to his house, at the upper end of *Kew-lane*, had always hitherto prevented. But, now, the cold had so seized him, that next day he found himself in a high fever, so much the more to be dreaded that he was of a full habit. This however, by the use of proper medicines, was removed, so that he was thought to be out of danger: till the fine weather having tempted him to expose himself once more to the evening dews, his fever returned with violence, and with such symptoms as left no hopes of a cure.'[1] Two days after this relapse, Dr. John Armstrong and Andrew Mitchell were warned of their friend's condition, and 'posted out at midnight to his assistance: but alas! came only to endure a sight of all others the most shocking to nature, the last agonies of their beloved friend. This lamented death happened on the 27th day of *August*, 1748.'

Andrew Mitchell at once scribbled a note to Murdoch:

'My dear P.

'Our dear friend Thomson died this morning about four o' Clock, after a very short illness. His distemper appeared

[1] *Works of Thomson*, 1762, i, xv.

first in the shape of a tertian; but soon ended in a continued fever. I am here to see the last duties fairly paid. I am almost sunk w^t this last stroke.

'Your's, affect^y, A.M.'[1]

Armstrong wrote at length to Murdoch on 30 August: 'You must have seen a piece of News, by this time, that could not fail to suprise and shock you. Poor Thomson died last Saturday morning of a fever, which at first appeared to be an intermittent; but in a short time degenerated from a fever, which I hoped would do him a great piece of service, by scouring his habit, into the low nervous malignant one which soon proved fatal to him, as it has to many. This blow makes a hideous gap; and the loss of such an agreeable Friend turns some of the sweetest scenes in England into a something waste and desolate; at least for the time: it will be so for a long time with me; for I question whether I shall ever be able to see Richmond again without sorrow and mortification.'[2] Armstrong gave some further details of the progress of the poet's illness in a letter of 3 September to a Scottish friend of Thomson, John Forbes: 'The loss of such an agreeable friend as poor Thomson', wrote Armstrong, 'is so much the more shocking, that it was unexpected by every body. He died of a malignant nervous fever, that came upon the back of a tertian; and I had no notice of his being in any danger till I saw it in the most formidable shapes. It is certain, nature was oppressed in him with a great load of materials for a disease, not to be easily thrown off by a constitution so much worn as his was; and if he had struggled thro' that Fever, there are many reasons to believe, that it must almost unavoidably have been followed by some lingering disease, much worse than a speedy death: this is the most comfortable light in which I can view this shocking loss.'[3]

Patrick Murdoch was heartbroken at the news, and he wrote to John Forbes on 2 September: 'You will have had the most unwelcome news of the death of our dear friend.

---

[1] *Culloden Papers*, 1815, p. 306.   [2] *Ibid.*   [3] *Ibid.*, p. 307.

I received it only this morning; and must own that nothing
in life has ever more shocked and afflicted me: it makes such
a gap, as the D^r in his Letter to me calls it, in the circle of
our acquaintance, as nothing can repair; yet we must bear
this and every thing else in life, till we ourselves are released
. . . and all we have to do is, to unite closer, and cherish his
memory, and each other, till we are called where he is gone.'[1]
Only six days later, Murdoch again wrote to Forbes: 'We
have lost, my dear F., our old, tryed, amiable, open, and
honest-hearted Thomson, whom we never parted from but
unwillingly; and never met, but with fresh transport; whom
we found ever the same delightful Companion, the same
faithful depository of our inmost thoughts, and the same
sensible sympathising adviser. To pretend to be stoical on
such a loss, would be an impertinent belying our characters; our tears must flow, and time alone can dry them.'[2]

Thomson had intended to visit Hagley Park in the first
week of September, and the news of his death cast a gloom
over the party which had assembled there to await his
arrival. Lady Luxborough described the effect of the news
in a letter to Lady Hertford: 'At Hagley we learn'd the
Death of Mr. Thomson, which Mr. Lyttelton was grieving
at under one Tree, and Mr. Shenstone under another as we
walk'd in the gloomy part of the Park.'[3] Although Shenstone had had only a slight acquaintance with the poet, he
felt that his death was a deep personal loss: 'Poor Mr.
Thomson, Mr. Pitt tells me, is *dead*', he wrote to a friend on
3 September. 'He was to have been at Hagley this week,
and then I should probably have seen him *here* . . . I was
really as much shocked to hear of his death, as if I had
known and loved him for a number of years.'[4] George
Lyttelton was very distressed but he sought consolation, as
he had done after the death of his wife, Lucy, in the Christian
religion: 'God's will be done!' he wrote to his clerical
friend, Dr. Doddridge, 'it has pleas'd his Providence to

---

[1] *Ibid.*   [2] *Ibid.*, p. 308.   [3] Quoted Hughes, *op. cit.*; *Mod. Phil.*, xxv, 465.
[4] *Letters of Shenstone*, p. 163.

afflict me lately with a new stroke in the sudden death of poor Mr. Thomson, one of the best and most beloved of my friends. He loved my Lucy too, and was loved by her. I hope and trust in the Divine goodness that they are now together in a much happier state. That is my consolation, that is my support.'[1] Lyttelton was very anxious to learn whether Thomson had accepted Christianity before his death, and he was able to send this reassurance to Dr. Doddridge on 7 November: 'Thomson I hope and believe died a Christian. Had he lived longer I don't doubt but he would have openly profest his faith; for he wanted no courage in what he thought right, but his mind had been much perplexed with doubts which I have the pleasure to think my book on St. Paul had almost entirely removed. He told me so himself, and in his sickness declared so to others. This is my best consolation in the loss of him, for as to the heart of a Christian he always had that, in a degree of perfection beyond most men I have known.'[2]

This chorus of private grief was taken up by the public, and the obituaries which appeared in the newspapers echoed the *Penny London Post* for 26–29 August: 'Last Saturday Morning at four o' Clock died of a violent Fever at his House in Kew Lane, the celebrated Mr. James Thomson, Author of the Seasons, &c. an honest Man, who has not left one Enemy behind him. His Abilities as a Writer, his Works sufficiently witness to all the World, but the Goodness of his Heart, which overflowed with Benevolence, Humanity, universal Charity, and every amiable Virtue, was best known to those who had the Happiness of his Acquaintance; by every one of whom he was most tenderly beloved, and now most sincerely and most deservedly lamented.'

Patrick Murdoch complained that Thomson's 'brother poets' did not 'at all exert themselves' on the occasion of his death, but it was his love for his friend that made him exaggerate their silence. William Shiels, a fervent admirer of the poet and his first biographer, published a competent,

---

[1] *Memoirs and Correspondence of Lyttelton*, i, 406.   [2] *Ibid.*, i, 409.

Plate V

HAGLEY PARK IN 1749

if uninspired, elegy entitled *Musidorus: A Poem sacred to the Memory of Mr. James Thomson*. Two poems on his death were also printed in the *Scots Magazine* for September and October 1748, and the first contained this appropriate image:

> Gen'rous, sincere, sublimely simple man!
> Thy nervous sense, in music softly breath'd,
> Joins with the sweet, the strong; thy scenes
> With all Imagination's colours glow,
> Yet still distinguish Truth's unspotted white.

Other and better poets, however, paid tribute. William Shenstone raised an urn to his memory in a part of his grounds called Virgil's Grove,[1] and wrote some charming and plaintive verses:

> Though Thomson, sweet descriptive bard!
>   Inspiring Autumn sung;
> Yet how should we the months regard
>   That stopped his flowing tongue?
>
> Ah! luckless months, of all the rest,
>   To whose hard share it fell!
> For sure he was the gentlest breast
>   That ever sung so well.
>
> He! he is gone, whose moral strain
>   Could wit and mirth refine;
> He! he is gone, whose social vein
>   Surpass'd the power of wine.
>
> Fast by the streams he deign'd to praise
>   In yon sequester'd grove,
> To him a votive urn I raise,
>   To him and friendly Love.
>
> Yes, there, my Friend! forlorn and sad,
>   I grave your Thomson's name,
> And there his lyre, which Fate forbade
>   To sound your growing fame.

[1] See *Letters of Shenstone*, p. 163.

There shall my plaintive song recount
    Dark themes of hopeless woe,
And faster than the dropping fount
    I'll teach mine eyes to flow.

There leaves, in spite of Autumn green,
    Shall shade the hallow'd ground,
And Spring will there again be seen
    To call forth flowers around.

But no kind suns will bid me share,
    Once more, his social hour;
Ah! Spring! thou never canst repair
    This loss to Damon's bower.

The absolute expression of Poetry's grief was given by
William Collins, and his *Ode on the Death of Mr. Thomson*
is among the most moving and melodious of all elegies:

In yonder grave a Druid lies
    Where slowly winds the stealing wave!
The year's best sweets shall duteous rise
    To deck its Poet's sylvan grave!

In yon deep bed of whisp'ring reeds
    His airy harp shall now be laid,
That he, whose heart in sorrow bleeds,
    May love thro' life the soothing shade.

Then maids and youths shall linger here,
    And while its sounds at distance swell,
Shall sadly seem in Pity's ear,
    To hear the Woodland Pilgrim's knell.

Remembrance oft shall haunt the shore
    When Thames in summer wreaths is drest,
And oft suspend the dashing oar
    To bid his gentle spirit rest!

And oft as Ease and Health retire
    To breezy lawn, or forest deep,
The friend shall view yon whitening spire,
    And 'mid the varied landscape weep.

But Thou, who own'st that earthy bed,
    Ah! what will every dirge avail?
Or tears, which Love and Pity shed
    That mourn beneath the gliding sail!

Yet lives there one, whose heedless eye
    Shall scorn thy pale shrine glimm'ring near?
With him, sweet bard, may Fancy die,
    And Joy desert the blooming year.

But thou, lorn stream, whose sullen tide
    No sedge-crown'd Sisters now attend,
Now waft me from the green hill's side
    Whose cold turf hides the buried friend!

And see the fairy valleys fade,
    Dun Night has veil'd the solemn view!
Yet once again, dear parted shade,
    Meek Nature's Child, again adieu!

The genial meads assign'd to bless
    Thy life, shall mourn thy early doom,
Their hinds, and shepherd-girls shall dress
    With simple hands thy rural tomb.

Long, long, thy stone, and pointed clay,
    Shall melt the musing Briton's eyes,
O! vales, and wild woods, shall He say,
    In yonder grave Your Druid lies!

The poet had died intestate, but on 25 October 1748 George Lyttelton and Andrew Mitchell were declared his executors in the name of Mary Craig, the poet's eldest surviving sister.[1] Their first action was to persuade the manager of Covent Garden Theatre to produce the tragedy of *Coriolanus*, and the first performance was given on 13 January 1749, with James Quin playing the title role. The prologue was written by Lyttelton and spoken by Quin.

[1] Mary Thomson married William Craig, merchant, Edinburgh, and died in 1790 (see Scott, *op. cit.*, ii, 139). Mary and Jean Thomson assigned *Coriolanus, Alfred,* and fifteen poems to Andrew Millar on 7 February 1751 for £200 (see *Poetical Works of Thomson*, ed. Nicolas, revised by Peter Cunningham, 1862, i, cxxiii).

T

Quin, dressed in black, advanced before the curtain and spoke these lines:

> I come not here your candour to implore
> For scenes, whose author is, alas! no more;
> He wants no advocate his cause to plead;
> You will yourselves be patrons of the dead.
> No party his benevolence confin'd,
> No sect—alike it flow'd to all mankind.
> He lov'd his friends (forgive this gushing tear:
> Alas! I feel I am no actor here)
> He lov'd his friends with such a warmth of heart,
> So clear of int'rest, so devoid of art,
> Such generous friendship, such unshaken zeal,
> No words can speak it, but our tears may tell.—
> O candid truth, O faith without a stain,
> O manners gently firm, and nobly plain,
> O sympathizing love of others bliss,
> Where will you find another breast like his?
> Such was the man—the poet well you know:
> Oft has he touch'd your hearts with tender woe:
> Oft in this crowded house, with just applause,
> You heard him teach fair Virtue's purest laws;
> For his chaste muse employ'd her heav'n-taught lyre
> None but the noblest passions to inspire,
> Not one immoral, one corrupted thought,
> One line, which dying he could wish to blot.
> Oh, may to-night your favourable doom
> Another laurel add to grace his tomb:
> Whilst he, superior now to praise or blame,
> Hears not the feeble voice of human fame.
> Yet if to those, whom most on earth he lov'd,
> From whom his pious care is now remov'd,
> With whom his liberal hand, and bounteous heart,
> Shar'd all his little fortune could impart;
> If to those friends your kind regard shall give
> What they no longer can from his receive,
> That, that, even now, above yon starry pole,
> May touch with pleasure his immortal soul.

Quin's striking delivery made the Prologue more moving to the spectators than it could ever be to future readers, and William Shiels, who attended the performance, has left a description of the scene on that first night: 'Mr. Quin was the particular friend of Thomson, and when he spoke the following lines, which are in themselves very tender, all the endearments of a long acquaintance, rose at once to his imagination, while the tears gushed from his eyes.

> He lov'd his friends (forgive this gushing tear:
> Alas! I feel I am no actor here)
> He lov'd his friends with such a warmth of heart,
> So clear of int'rest, so devoid of art,
> Such generous freedom, such unshaken zeal,
> No words can speak it, but our tears may tell.

The beautiful break in these lines had a fine effect in speaking. Mr. Quin here excelled himself; he never appeared a greater actor than at this instant, when he declared himself none: 'twas an exquisite stroke to nature; art alone could hardly reach it . . . A deep-fetch'd sigh filled up the heart felt pause; grief spread o'er all the countenance; the tear started to the eye, the muscles fell, and,

> The whiteness of his cheek
> Was apter than his tongue to speak his tale.

They all expressed the tender feelings of a manly heart, becoming a Thomson's friend. His pause, his recovery were masterly; and he delivered the whole with an emphasis and pathos, worthy the excellent lines he spoke; worthy the great poet and good man, whose merits they painted, and whose loss they deplored.'[1]

The executors' next duty was to sell up all the poet's effects and a catalogue was duly printed. The title-page read: 'A CATALOGUE Of all the Genuine Houshold Furniture, Plate, China, Prints and Drawings, &c. OF Mr. *JAMES THOMSON*, (AUTHOR of the *Seasons*) Deceased. Which will be SOLD by AUCTION, By Order of the *Executrix*, On *Monday May* the 15th, and the two Following Days, at his late Dwelling-house in *Kew-Lane, Richmond, Surrey*. CONSISTING OF Morine, Harrateen, Cheney Beds and good Bedding, with Window Curtains and Chairs

---

[1] Cibber, *op. cit.*, v, 215-16.

suitable to the Same, Sconces and Chimney Glasses in gilt Frames, and a Parcel of very good Kitchen Furniture, together with His compleat Library of Books. The Whole to be viewed till the Time of SALE; which will begin each Day at half an Hour after Eleven o'Clock precisely. *Catalogues* to be had, the Days of Viewing, at the Place of Sale, and of Mr. Millar's, Bookseller in the *Strand.*' His library cannot have been complete because this appeal is printed in the catalogue: 'N.B. *Such Gentlemen as have any Books of Mr.* Thomson's, *are desired to return them to* A. Millar, *Bookseller in the Strand.*'

George Lyttelton made an independent and mistaken attempt to heighten the poet's posthumous reputation. He had been closely associated with the poet when he was revising *The Seasons* for the edition of 1744, and had suggested at that time many changes which he believed would have generally improved the quality of the verse. The poet had adopted a few of his suggestions but disregarded the majority. After Thomson's death, Lyttelton published in 1750 an edition of his works, and, unembarrassed by the poet's presence, he liberally edited, or, more correctly, interfered with, the texts. He was very pleased with this performance, and a copy of the edition was sent to Mrs. Doddridge: 'By the Northampton coach of next week, I shall send Mrs. Doddridge a new, compleat and correct edition of Mr. Thomson's works made under my care, which I beg the favour of her to accept', he wrote to the Doctor on 22 March 1750. 'You will find this edition much preferable to any of the former, though not entirely free from false prints. Great corrections have been made in the diction and many redundancies have been cut off . . . so that upon the whole I am persuaded you will think Mr. Thomson a much better poet, if you take the trouble to read over his works in their present form, than you ever thought him before.'[1] One can only marvel at Lyttelton's self-confidence. Luckily for the poet's reputation,

[1] *Memoirs and Correspondence of Lyttelton*, i, 322.

Lyttelton's revised edition did not become the established text.

The poet's remains had been buried in the church of St. Mary, Richmond, two days after his death, on 29 August, and the service had been attended by a few of his friends. It is uncertain whether any stone or monument was immediately erected over the vault where he was buried. Richard Crisp, the historian of Richmond, imagined that such a stone or monument had been erected soon after his burial, but that it had been destroyed later in the century when it became necessary to increase the pew accommodation.[1] The phrase Collins used in his *Ode*, 'thy pale shrine glimm'ring near', would suggest that some memorial had been erected in the church, but there is no other evidence that it ever existed. His friends may originally have intended to raise a memorial and Collins may have anticipated their intention. Before this could be done, however, it was decided that the only appropriate place for a memorial to such a poet was in Westminster Abbey, and Patrick Murdoch was responsible for its accomplishment. He agreed to edit the poet's works and to write a prefatory memoir, and Andrew Millar, with characteristic generosity, offered to devote the profits of this edition to defray the cost of a monument to the poet in the Abbey.

Murdoch wisely and scrupulously refused to print the texts which Lyttelton was anxious to foist on to the world, and he set out in a letter to Millar the reasons for his refusal. 'With regard to the alterations proposed to be made in Mr. Thomson's Seasons,' he wrote, 'having now fully considered that matter, and seen how few and inconsiderable his own last corrections were, I am confirmed in my first opinion—so much, that I shall retract most of my concessions, and even some of the alterations which I had thought I had made for the better. In a word, I can have no hand in any edition that is much different from the small one of 1752 . . . It is a pity indeed that Mr. T. aided by my lord

[1] See Crisp, *op. cit.*, p. 19.

L[yttelton]. did not correct and alter many things himself; but as that went no further than a bare intention, it is too late to think of it now, and we can only say "Emendaturus, si licuisset, erat" . . . What if after all some of my Lord's alterations should prove bad? . . . this would produce a second edition and then a third, which would end in a total contempt of Mr. Thomson's works, or in a restitution of them from the copies published by himself (and with so much deliberation and care, that his printer were tir'd to death, as you well remember) . . . As to Mr. Th.'s diction, of which my Lord's acquaintances so much complain, I would recommend to these gentlemen to read Milton with care, and the greatest part of that objection would vanish . . . Certain it is that Mr. Thomson's language has been well-received by the publick, excepting those my Lord speaks of, who are more disposed to find blemishes than capable of feeling beauties . . . His numbers and manners have been adopted by good authors, and, since he began to write, our poetry is become more nervous and rich.'[1] This edition was published in two noble quarto volumes, illustrated by frontispieces to each separate work, in 1762, and the list of subscribers was headed by the young king, George III. The monument to his memory in the Abbey was also unveiled the same year, and a brief announcement was made in the *London Chronicle* for 8–11 May: 'This morning was opened in Westminster Abbey a monument, erected to the memory of JAMES THOMSON, Author of the Seasons, and other poetical Works. It is situated between Shakespear's and Rowe's, and executed by Michael Henry Spang, Statuary, after a design of Mr. Adam, Architect to his Majesty. There is a figure of Mr. Thomson sitting, who leans his left arm upon a pedestal, and holds a book with the cap of Liberty in his other hand. Upon the pedestal is carved a bas-relief of the Seasons, to which a boy points, offering him a laurel crown as the reward of his genius. At the feet of the figure, is the tragick mask, and ancient harp. The whole is sup-

[1] Quoted John Wooll, *Biographical Memoir of Joseph Warton*, 1806, p. 252.

ported by a projecting pedestal, and in a pannel, is the following inscription.

JAMES THOMSON,

Ætatis 48, Obiit 27 August, 1748.

Tutor'd by thee, sweet Poetry exalts
Her voice to ages; and informs the page
With music, image, sentiment, and thoughts,
Never to die!

This monument was erected 1762.'

Every poet of reputation inspires after his death some enthusiasts to form themselves into a society to celebrate his memory, and various meetings were held in honour of Thomson throughout the eighteenth century. These were probably decorous affairs until David Stewart, Earl of Buchan, a member of the lunatic fringe, suddenly took it into his wild head to interest himself in the poet's reputation. He decided that a monument should be erected to Thomson on Ednam Hill, and that an anniversary celebration should be held on the Hill on 22 September 1791. He announced his intention in a broadsheet: 'The Earl of Buchan,' it read, 'as Chairman of the Society for the erection of a Monument to the Memory of THOMSON, and for the celebration of his Anniversary, gives notice, That the Festival will be held at KELSO that day [22 September], and that the Dean and Chapter of Westminster having allowed a GESS to be moulded from the Statue of Thomson in Westminster Abbey, which is to be presented to the Earl of Buchan by Thomas Coutts, Esq. Banker at London, he proposes to crown Thomson's Bust on Ednam Hill, at two o'clock afternoon, if the day proves favourable, with a Garland of Laurel and Civic Oak, from Wallace's Tree in the Torwood of Stirling; if not, to perform the same in the Great Room, at Horsington's, at the same hour of the day ... N.B. It is proposed that the Ladies shall be invited, and that there shall be a BALL in the evening.'[1] Robert Burns

1 *Forster Coll.*, 48 E.4; V. & A.

was invited to attend and write some verses on the occasion, but ill health prevented his attendance and a modest consciousness that he could never hope to excel Collins's *Ode* prevented his contribution from rising above mediocrity. Buchan's enthusiasm ran away with him at the ceremony, and he crowned not only Thomson's bust with a wreath but also a copy of the 1730 quarto edition of *The Seasons*, and delivered an extraordinary address, largely devoted to an attack upon Dr. Johnson for his unsympathetic reflections on Thomson's genius, which he subsequently published. Later he presented this fortunate copy of *The Seasons*, and some other Thomsoniana, to Edinburgh University Library, where it is still displayed.

It was not enough, however, for Buchan to project only one memorial; he determined to place a plaque to the poet's memory in St. Mary's Church, Richmond, and this was duly erected in the following year. The inscription reads:

In the earth, below this tablet,
are the remains of
JAMES THOMSON
Author of the beautiful Poems entitled
'The Seasons', the 'Castle of Indolence' etc.
who died at Richmond
on the 27th of August
and was buried
on the 29th O. S. 1748
The Earl of Buchan
unwilling that
so good a Man, and sweet a Poet
should be without a memorial,
has denoted the place of his interment,
for the satisfaction of his Admirers,
in the year of our Lord
M. DCC. XCII.

It would be unfair to disparage Buchan's efforts to honour the poet, but this brass tablet is a paltry fixture which should have been augmented long ago by a worthier monument. Nor does it fulfil its claim to denote the place of the poet's interment. Richard Crisp, the historian of Richmond, examined the vaults below the tablet in 1866, when the church was being restored, and found no remains that could possibly correspond to the poet's. 'Many old Richmond persons', continued Crisp, 'recollect hearing it said that his coffin was buried partly inside and partly outside. If there is any truth in this tradition, so singular a circumstance may be accounted for in this way. It is just probable that he was buried outside the church, and that during some extension and enlargement of the north aisle the wall of the building might have been erected over the vault in which he lay; but it is not unlikely that in the making of the vault described as a modern one, his remains were removed and deposited elsewhere, there being perhaps at that time no memorial over his grave indicative of him whose bones may have thus been so ruthlessly disturbed.'[1]

The proposed monument to the poet on Ednam Hill was delayed for several years, but at last the foundation stone was laid in 1819. It is a sturdy obelisk, fifty feet high, and any one who visits it in the summer, when the fields of ripening corn brush at its grey base, will recognize that it is an appropriate edifice. The Cheviots lie far away low-backed on the horizon, the larks ride high on the buoyant silence, and the vital peace of the countryside presses up to the monument, which marks the source not only of the poet's birth but of his inspiration.

The best memorial to the poet is, however, more firmly founded than any monument. It is English poetry. There are poets whose imaginative flights still command the attention of all eyes; there are others who have colonized some strange region of the mind to which they alone can grant admittance; and there are some whose greatness is as universal as the sky; but there is none whose genius is as natural and as persuasive as Thomson's. He sensibly affected the whole temperament of poetry, and could often claim as his own those praises which are lavished on his successors. His

[1] Crisp, *op. cit.*, pp. 206–7.

genius is only fully recognized when we attempt to imagine what would have been the course of English poetry and sensibility had he not written. We are for ever meeting the shadow of his presence as we read, or look out upon Nature.

NOTE TO p. 27.

The entry in the minutes of the Presbytery of Jedburgh for 1 Jan. 1724 reads: "The Presbyterie unanimously appoints Mr James Thomson to be their Lowland Burser in Divinity for another year, and appoints him to return Certificates of his attendance upon the Profession, and likewise appoints the said Burse to be paid unto him by all the Sessions accordingly." I am indebted to the Rev. John Campbell, librarian of the General Assembly Library, for this extract from the minutes.

APPENDIX A

James Thomson's Correspondence with Elizabeth Young

I

This first letter, dated, 'March 10th, 1743', is printed in the text, pp. 203–6.

II

This letter is quoted in part in the text, pp. 208–9; it is here printed in full.

'Kew-Lane; April 19th, 1743.

'Miss Young, my Love, my Soul! it is impossible to speak the Agitation of my Heart ever since I parted from you. All that an absent Lover can feel I feel in it's most exquisite and charming Distress. I would not wish you had a better and more affecting Picture of my Love than to have been Conscious to what passed in my Mind as I returned. Then you could never doubt it more; never tell me again that it will be transitory, and that there is no such thing as undecaying Love in the World. Mine will not only last but grow forever. Yesterday, to the last Moment I was with you, I discovered numberless new Beauties, and felt Emotions that had not pierced my Heart before.

Still as I gaz'd new Beauties met my Sight,
Your serious Eyes grew still more sweetly bright;
I still perceived some secret dawning Grace,
And Heaven, methought, fair-open'd in your Face.

'What Pity is it that Lovers (would I could say of us both Lovers) should part! Life is too short, to pine away so many lonely Days, to see so many Suns rise and set in vain, unblest with her Company who gives Light and Joy to their Beams, and who spreads Beauty over all they show. Ah when shall I be always with you, always under the divine Influence of your Eyes, that look Virtue, Love and Happiness? May Heaven, Parent of Love, grant me That, and grant it soon! It is all I ask: let the tasteless joyless Sons of Interest take the Rest. But, in the meantime, how shall I support this Absence? how quiet this busy, doubting, hoping, delighted, tortured Heart? Every thing I see puts me in Mind of you. Here you sat; there you walked; there Love first unloosed his Tongue, and with faultering Accents could scarce articulate his Words.

'O my better Angel! let me thank you for the Change you have made in my Mind, for the Virtue and determined good Purposes you have inspired it with. Your Eyes are to me the Source of all that is good and lovely, and Wisdom from your Lips is doubly beautiful. Were not those Hints with Regard to Regularity and Temperance, which you now and then so prettily insinuated, meant for me? Yes, I will interpret them so; for it most exquisitely flatters my Heart to think that you would wish all Objections removed that may ly betwixt us. And shall such low, such vile, such false Pleasures ever stand in the least Competition with that Happiness, that darling Happiness, I shall enjoy with you? with you, whose every Look gives infinitely more Delight than Ages of these can give? Believe me most firmly, they have not the smallest Temptation for me; I hate, I loath, I detest them; and if ever I indulge them more may you utterly abandon me! the worst Imprecation I can call upon my Head. Do not rally me then, that I shall do myself Violence by this Change. So far from That, it is to me the Luxury of Virtue, of more than Virtue of virtuous Love. No, my dearest dearest Miss Young! (I must call you mine) our Ways of thinking are not so different as you supposed, but I hope did not believe. I can answer for my Heart: and I will flatter myself my Head is more reasonable than to differ from Her who is good Sense and right Judgment itself.

'As to Objections from unkind Fortune, which you are too generous to make, and I too much concerned for your Happiness not to give them their full Force; they may, they shall be removed. It is saying nothing to say, that the largest Fortune, if in my Power, would seem poor to what my Heart wishes to lay at your Feet. By this I know I love you, love you with the highest Passion that can actuate the human Breast, that infinite Desire I have to make you happy. I feel for you the Kindness of creating Nature. But Heaven has constituted Things so graciously, that Happiness does not consist in Fortune, or those external Advantages that are out of our own Power. Competency with Contentment, a virtuous improved well-ordered Mind, right Affections, Friendship and Love, these give the truest Happiness, and these we may command. Encouragement from you will inform me with a new Soul, will inspirit me to the Pursuit of all that can be agreeable to you, and that can promote your dearest Welfare. Yet, o Miss Young!

(for I love to repeat your Name) I cannot recover any tolerable
Degree of Peace without still more Encouragement, more Assurance from you. The Hope you permitted me to indulge is not
enough. There are Remains of Doubt and Anxiety that still distract my Mind, that render me incapable of performing what I
have promised my Friends, the Public, and above all my own
Heart upon your Account. If you have any Regard, any Tenderness, or even any Pity for me, bless me with a Line. And can you
think it much to give him a Line who loves you as I do, who lives
alone for you, whose Cheeks are now bathed with the sincerest
Tears Love can shed, who continually thinks of you, and could for
ever pour forth his Soul into your Bosom? You cannot refuse me
one Line. If a few kind Words will soften this Anguish that con-
sumes my Heart, and restore my Mind to Harmony; if they will
enable me to exert myself, and with Spirit perform my Part in
Life, can you be so cruel as to refuse them? Will you do nothing
for one who could dy for you with Pleasure?—I cannot long support this Absence; I must see you soon; and oh that then I may
have an Opportunity of begging an Alms from you of one encouraging Word, one tender Look, to live upon till I see you
again. Is there no Method for me to know when I can find you
at home, or abroad in some Walk? There is, there is—And shall
it not be put in Practice?

'This Letter, I am afraid, grows tedious; but I know not how to
part from you even in a Letter. Yet tho' I cease from writing to
you, I can never cease from thinking of you. O that you would
teach me to think with less Pain on so charming a Subject! This
you easily, with one reviving Word, can do. Speak then the dear
the generous Word, make use of the Priviledge of your excellent
good Sense, and if I can have your Heart tell me so. Let not my
Days be miserable when they may be happy. What Arguments
shall I use to perswade you? I can use none, but that I love you
with perfect Esteem, with unspeakable Tenderness; and, whatever be the Fate of my Passion, in Life and Death, while I am
conscious of this Being, I must always be unalterably your's James
Thomson.'

III

This letter has been quoted in part in the text, p. 211; it is here
printed in full.

'My dearest Miss Young! it is now ten long long Days since I
saw you, since I was blest with a Look from those Eyes where all
Beauty all Sweetness and all Excellence shine. Pardon me then if I

cannot resist writing. My Heart o'erflows, and can find no Consolation but in pouring itself forth to Her who has confirmed it in right Sentiments, and Virtues, which I have often felt but never truly possessed before. I wish you was conscious to whatever has passed in my Mind since I saw you last: you would find the Whole but one fond Letter, one continued Effusion of Soul devoted to you and Virtue. You would then have a Picture of Love, sincere, pure, disinterested, tender, passionate; such as you yourself could not but approve of. You would then see how busy my Thoughts are about you, how pierced with your Beauties, that strike me particularly as the full Expression of an excellent Mind: you would see how incessantly they are employed in studying to please you, in planning your Happiness, in renouncing all Happiness without you; and, above all, how zealously they resolve upon acquiring and exerting whatever can recommend me to your Heart. Sometimes indeed you would find them upbraiding you, calling you unkind, cruel, for making me so faint so doubtful a Return, or if your Sentiments are really kinder for concealing them. Yet I will hope; you gave me Leave so to do. Your Words, your dear Words, the most charming I ever heard in my Life—I know not what Time may produce—are engraved on my Heart. How critically I consider these Words! I examine them in all Manner of favourable Lights; I draw all possible pleasing Consequences from them, with the utmost Subtilty of refining Love. She whom I love, whom I love for the Virtues of her Mind even more than for the matchless Beauties of her Person, whatever her Sentiments are with Regard to me, she is too just, too generous, ever to do or say any thing that may hereafter aggravate my Misery; she will never permit Hopes which she has no Purpose, in certain Circumstances, of realizing. Such and numberless more are my Reasonings upon this Occasion; but, alas, they are only Reasonings. Without further Encouragement and Assurances, I must still fluctuate in miserable Uncertainty, I must still think of you with too great a Mixture of Pain, I cannot recover Temper and Peace of Mind enough to perform what should entitle me to this inestimable Blessing which Time may bestow. It is one distinguishing Characteristic of Love, never to be satisfyed, neither with receiving nor giving Assurances. By this last Mark you may be convinced how much I love—Ah tell me, is the First to be found in you?

'I am going, if I can, to put a finishing Hand to the Description of a Season now in high Song and Beauty, but to which I am dead. You alone I hear, you alone I see: all Harmony and Beauty are comprized in you. Those Parts, however, will be obliged to you

which attempt a Picture of virtuous happy Love. O Miss Young!
thou loveliest of thy Sex, and the most beloved! as you have
taught me the Virtue, so teach me the Happiness of this best
Passion! O let the Picture be ours!—Here one who has little agreeable to me but his Sirname, and you may guess what that is, comes
in and interrupts me. I can only add that I hope soon to see you.
Another Week will be insupportable without that dearest Happiness. Permit me to subscribe myself, with perfect Esteem, unalterable Truth, and unexpressible Tenderness all yours

' James Thomson.

   ' April 28th, 1743.'

IV

   This letter has been quoted in part in the text, pp. 213–14; it is
here printed in full.

   'My dearest Miss Young! let me pour forth my Soul in Gratitude to you, for the Peace and Harmony of Mind you have at last
given me. Yes, I will now exert myself, and perform the Promises
I have made my own Heart; I will keep your enlivening Image
ever in my View, and endeavour to render myself worthy not
only of your Esteem but of your Love and Tenderness. Virtue
was always my determined Choice; I always loved it with my
warmest Approbation, and resolved upon a more attentive and
regular Practice of it: but now I love it doubly, it is doubly beautiful, as proceeding from you. Should my Name live, and I be mentioned hereafter, I shall be ambitious to have it said of me, that
when seduced by that most fatal Syren Indolence and false
Pleasure, to the very Brink of Ruin, the Angel of Love came in
your Form and saved me.

   'I cannot enough admire, upon cool Reflection, your Behaviour, during those happy miserable Days I last saw you. What
Grace, what Decency, what Dignity, what amiable Prudence it
displayed. It has charmed me to such a Degree, that my Reason
is as much enamoured of you as my Heart, and my Friendship for
you ventures even to rival my Love. What an invaluable Treasure
is such a lovely Friend, who while by gentle Insinuations she
teaches Wisdom makes it at the same Time charming! The pompous Lessons of Philosophers, of all your proud Moralists, are
insipid, and void of Power, compared to the slightest Hints from
the Lips of those we love. They take immediate Possession of the
Heart, and intimately move it in it's most active Springs. They
cannot so properly be said to teach as to inspire Virtue. I could
write a whole Treatise on the moral the divine Influence of vir-

tuous Love. And would you have me destroy such a Passion? I should look upon it as a Crime, an Outrage, to whatever is good and excellent. But indeed how much in vain would the Attempt prove! I can as soon cease to be, as cease to love you.

'Will you pardon me, if, from the Violence of my Passion, I was perhaps unreasonable in expecting Assurances which you did not think proper to give. I ought to have been satisfyed with several finely judged encouraging Expressions you from Time to Time threw kindly out, with those dear Hopes you allowed me to indulge; I ought to have been thankful, I ought to have been happy. Nor think I was insensible to the Value of what you said, if I asked more. No, you cannot lose one Word one Look upon me. They are all treasured up in my inmost Heart, and my Thoughts make many a fond Comment on them. I must, however, plead in my own Excuse, that you said things which might very justly and highly distress one who loves like me, and some things you said on Purpose to pique me. That Answer particularly which you gave me, when I enquired about the Subject of a certain Picture, was levelled at me with the utmost Keeness. I remember your Words—Sir, it is a serious View of an ill-concerted Marriage—And the Manner with which you spoke them made them keener still. How could you give it such a wicked Turn, when you knew the Marriage represented in that Picture was a vile Marriage of Fortune? Afterwards you made a malicious Comparison betwixt Painters and Writers, in which you could not be in earnest: you have too good Taste and Judgment for That. But these pretty *Malices* (as the French call them), with which your Sex loves to pique ours, and of which you have your Share, please more than they hurt. Give me your Heart, and I care not how much you plague me with your Wit.

'You must by this Time wish my Letter at an End, you who desired me not to write at all; and yet I should be unhappy to believe that such was your real Desire, for that were desiring me not to love. When will that dear unkind Heart of yours, which in a tender Moment you said you would consult, permit you to bless me with a few Lines? Sollicitation takes off from the Merit of a Favour: it would be generous then to suprize me, now that I neither hope nor sollicite it more. All that the finest Writers ever wrote cannot give me half the Pleasure I shall have in reading a few Lines from your lovely Hand——

'Ah, my charming Miss Young! I am afraid I deceive myself— I feel this Moment a sweet Anguish stirring in my Breast, which tells me my Peace is far from being secure—Remembrance bleeds afresh. Alas! you are too sparing of the Balm of kind Words and healing Hopes—A thousand things crowd upon me, and pierce me in every Thought—did ever Love triumph so much in any Bosom as mine? But I must conclude here, or I shall undo all again. O my dearest Miss Young! think kindly of him who is, with perfect Esteem, and the most Heart-flowing Tenderness, unalterably yours

'James Thomson.

'Kew-Lane, Richmond, Surrey,
  'May the 14ᵗʰ 1743.'

V

This letter has been quoted in part in the text, p. 215; it is here printed in full.

'Kew-Lane, May 26ᵗʰ, 1743.

'My dearest Miss Young! I was contriving how to see you to-day, but, alas, am disappointed. This comes to beg I may have that Happiness soon. Methinks I long more to see you than ever, to lose my Soul again, with unspeakable Pleasure, in your beauteous Eyes. What sensible Softness, what lively Sweetness do they contain! The last Time I saw them they looked with a particular Loveliness, for they looked kinder. To gaze upon, or rather to look into, the tender Eyes of those we love is a pure and exalted Pleasure; it resembles the Love of Angels, which Milton calls—mixing Irradiance—There is a Light shines from them that charms, refines and nourishes the Soul. When long absent from you, mine droops and decays, is famished as it were, for want of this etherial Nourishment. But to return to what I was going to intreat of you—the Bearer of this tells me, that you have been for some time proposing to take a Walk to Chealsey. If it does not interfere with the Party to Richmond, you will make me truly happy by doing this on Saturday or Sunday next; and he will let me know when and where I shall find you—for it would be Madness in me to think you will write yourself. I might as well hope to hold a Correspondence with superior Beings. Do you know, Madam, that I shall begin to put a vain Interpretation on your obstinately refusing to write? "You think it improper to write kindly, and your Heart will not permit you to write indifferently." Thus will I turn your very Silence into a Love-Letter. I remember you threatened me with a Letter, which, you said, perhaps I would not like, and I rashly dared you to it. Upon second Thoughts my Courage fails me. No, dont write unless the Spirit of the Letter be kind; however you season it with those pretty Piquancies with which you can agreeably vex a Lover. Remember the Condition

U

upon which I gave you full Freedom to plague me. Let all the little Darts of Raillery be thrown by Love, and they will please. You may plague, but o take Care of hurting me. I am infinitely tender, and the least Shadow of a real Unkindness would kill me, would make me more miserable than I have ever yet been, for I hope more.

'Give me Leave to send you Inclosed a Song I have lately writ. Whatever the Writing be I maintain the Sentiment to be just, and desire you would seriously peruse it. Tell me, thou lovely Critic, shall I not correct—my—into—our—in the following Line?

And too much Prudence starve my Passion.

If you agree to it, I shall think it one of the happiest Corrections that can possibly be made. I shall value it more than all I have writ in my Life.

'Here I am interrupted. O thou best Treasure of my Soul! my ever dearest Miss Young! think kindly of me. Think that Love like mine deserves to be cherished, deserves to be returned. Think how fondly I am always thinking of you; and with what perfect Friendship, and unequaled Tenderness, I am unalterably your's James Thomson.'

VI

This undated letter has been quoted in part in the text, pp. 215–16; it is here printed in full.

'Monday Morning.

'Unkind, yet ever dearest Miss Young! did you but know what I suffered yesterday, and still suffer, you must pity me even from common Humanity. Indifference itself would pity me. To one who loves as I do every Disappointment pierces the Heart, but when it carries a Look of Unkindness it is Torture, it is Agony. If your good Sense (which is excellent) told you that as you was circum-stanced it was improper to come, could you not have contrived how to prevent my miserable Walk? Was there no Method to give me a Hint of your Intention to walk in Kew-Lane, that I might have had the Pleasure of walking with you—any way? The only Opportunities almost I have of conversing with you are during the little Time you are here, and these too are lost! I begin to fear I am utterly undone—It is impossible for me to live at this Distance from you; and yet I have no Hopes of seeing it other-wise. You have, I most gratefully own, been good to me; you have done and said several dear encouraging things, which I treasure up in my Heart as what alone in this World can give it

Joy. But ah! that Joy is mixed with a far far greater Share of Pain, and if you will not do more for me you do nothing. To a Passion like mine a *little* Kindness is only Oil thrown upon the Flame, it only makes it consume me with fiercer Rage. Miss Young! my charming Miss Young! let me tell you in plain Words, and with the strictest Truth, if you do not give me an Opportunity of talking with you before you go to Town, if you will not settle my Mind into some Peace and Harmony, I am the most miserable Man alive, as the most in Love. I shall see I shall converse with no Body, I shall do nothing—but break my Heart. This very Moment it labours under a terrible Oppression, it bursts from my Breast in Sighs, it flows from my Eyes in Tears, and I must hasten to conclude before David comes down and finds me in this Disorder. If you will not take Compassion on me, then conclude me lost, undone; I shall not be able to support it, I shall dy with excessive Love. As you do not go to Town this Day (a Circumstance you attempted cruelly to conceal from me) may not I flatter myself with the Hopes of walking with you this Evening? O then, if you have any the least Regard for me, let me know when and where I may have an half Hours Conversation with you! Cannot you put it down on Paper, in Case you have not an Opportunity of telling me by Word of Mouth? I live in Hopes of it—If you neglect to do it you will kill him who is fondly and unalterably your's, however you use him, James Thomson.'

VII

This letter is quoted in part in the text, pp. 218–19; it is here printed in full.

'Kew-Lane.

'Wedensday [*sic*], August 17th, 1743.

'Unkind yet ever dearest Miss Young, You who have so much Compassion in your Nature, how can you thus torture him who loves you? Words cannot express how exquisitely I suffer from your least Unkindness, for they cannot express how much I love. It is, besides, a cruel Time you take to exercise the Tyranny of your Power over me: for by that Means you will disappoint me in the most essential Views and Purposes of my Life. Have you a Mind intirely to ruin me? I am at present utterly unfit to go any where, or to execute any Scheme I may have formed. Let me once more conjure you either to treat me with frank open generous Kindness, or to dismiss me for ever. In this last case, it is true, I shall be undone and miserable, but then I shall be more calmly so, and I will retire to enjoy my Misfortunes out of the Eye of the

U*

World. O say, my dearest Miss Young! where and when shall I
have a Meeting with you, here or in Town? I have taken a Place
in the Worcester Stage-Coach, that sets out on Friday Morning
early; but if you do not restore my Mind to Peace, I lay aside the
Thoughts of That, and of every thing else. If you stay here to-day,
I beg to have a Walk with you in Twitnam-Park Meadows before
Dinner: if you go to Town, give me Leave to wait upon you to-
morrow Evening in Lancaster Court. And may not I have the
Happiness of walking with you to Mortlake? But as there will
probably be Company with you to Town, let that be as you please
—Ah tell me, did not you take Pains to pique and make me un-
easy on Monday Night? And was it not a cruel Neglect, not to
walk in the Meadows with me so fine a Day as yesterday was? The
whole Day was lost without seeing you! and you on other Parties!
But it was a most miserable Day to me. Think seriously, consult
your Heart, does Love like mine deserve such usage? Not to say
generous, is it Just to use me so? Remember that your Conduct
towards me must determine of my Welfare, and the future Happiness of my Life. Can you neglect the Happiness of him whose
only Wish is to make you happy? Yet I must always be, however
you treat me, with unshaken Friendship and the most affectionate
Tenderness all yours J. Thomson.'

VIII

This letter, dated 'Hagley, August 29, 1743', is printed in the
text, pp. 219–21.

IX

This letter is quoted in part in the text, pp. 224–5; it is here
printed in full.

'Sep^{tr}. 28, 1743.

'My dearest Miss Young!

'I would have sent you the Distressed Wife before now, but I
had mislaid it and only found it again yesterday. The Perusal of it
gave me more Disgust than Pleasure, it presents so vile and perhaps so natural a Picture of a Town-Life. There are no Animals
in the whole Creation that pass their Time so idly, and in my
Opinion so miserably, as they who compose what they call the
gay World do. With Regard to them it is Virtue to be a Misanthrope; and instead of the gay they should be called the gayly-
wretched World. It is a World not of God's making, but a true

Limbo of Vanity, made up of ridiculous shocking Phantoms of
Folly, Affectation, and Vice. One Hour of virtuous Retirement,
consecrated to Love Friendship and the Study of Nature, is worth
an Age of it. I would have it an Article in the Litany—And from
the dull, tiresome, vain, tattling, impertinent, unfeeling, and
utterly worthless gay World, good God deliver me! The Design
of the Play is very good, to satirize this Life so unworthy of a
reasonable Creature, but I dont think it so well executed. Barter is
the best Character in it; but there are few such Citizens as he:
they are still more vile, by their Imitation of the Luxuries of this
End of the Town. S^r. Thomas Willit is a weak Man, and if he had
a Heart could not possibly bestow it on such a Woman as his
Lady. For Her, she is detestable, and past all Reformation. Besides
her Affectations are drawn so monstrous, they are not the Affectations of a Woman of Sense and Wit but of a Fool. Miss Sprightly's
Wit is affected, and has not that amiable Softness and gentle
Character which ought to recommend the Sprightliness of your
Sex. And poor Miss Friendless how came the Author too to be so
little her Friend, as to make her a matrimonial Prostitute to the
most foolish of all foolish Lords. I expected, from her sensible
serious Turn, that she would have disdained the Proposal, and
rather lived in a Cottage with some Person she loved. Pardon
these Criticisms on a Play you seemed to like: but I like several
Things in it as much as you, and am greatly pleased with the
honest Intention and Moral of the Piece.

'Ah my dearest Miss Young! I can have no other Idea of happy
Life but with you. How miserable is it then that I should be so
much absent from all that is dear and lovely to me in the World?
It is impossible, I cannot support Life with out at least your
Presence. How can I live at a Distance from my Heart, especially
as you will not directly assure me that I have all yours in Return?
But remember I will have it, if the highest Friendship, the most
exalted Love and everlasting Tenderness can gain it. Could you
refuse me your Heart, I will not have my own again, for it would
then be fit for no human Purpose. Dont how ever take any Advantage over my too-much tortured Heart already, from my making
this frank Declaration that I am wth unconquerable Love all yours
'James Thomson.'

X

This letter, dated 'January 21, 1743–4', is printed in the text,
pp. 226–8.

XI

This letter, dated 'Wedensday, [*sic*] Octr. 23rd, 1745', is printed in the text, pp. 240–1.

XII

This letter, dated 'Monday Night, Novr. 4th, 1745', is printed in the text, pp. 242–3.

APPENDIX B

*Three Songs given to Elizabeth Young by James Thomson, and kept by
her among his letters*

I

SONG

1

Come, dear Eliza, quit the Town,
    And to the rural Hamlets fly:
Behold, the wintry Storms are gone,
    A gentle Radiance glads the Sky.

2

The Birds awake, the Flowers appear,
    Earth spreads a verdant Couch for thee;
'Tis Joy and Music all we hear,
    'Tis Love and Beauty all we see.

3

Come, let us mark the gradual Spring,
    How peeps the Bud, the Blossom blows;
Till Philomel begin to sing,
    And perfect May to swell the Rose.

4

Let us secure the short Delight,
    And wisely crop the blooming Day;
Too soon our Spring will take it's Flight:
    Arise, my Love, and come away.

II

SONG

1

Come, gentle Power of soft Desire,
    Come and possess my happy Breast!

Not Fury-like, in Flames and Fire,
　　In Raptures, Rage, and Nonsense drest.

2

These are the vain Disguise of Love,
　　And only speak dissembled Pains;
Or else a fleeting Fever prove,
　　The frantic Passion of the Veins.

3

But come in Friendship's Angel-Guise:
　　Yet dearer thou than Friendship art;
More tender Spirit in thy Eyes,
　　More sweet Emotions at thy Heart.

4

O come, with Goodness in thy Train,
　　With Peace, and Transport void of Storm:
And wouldst thou me for ever gain?
　　Put on Eliza's winning Form.

III

SONG

1

One Day the God of fond Desire,
　　On Mischief bent, to Damon said:
Why not disclose your tender Fire?
　　Not own it to the lovely Maid?

2

The Shepherd mark'd his subtle Art,
　　And, softly sighing, thus reply'd:
'Tis true you have subdued my Heart,
　　But shall not triumph o'er my Pride.

3

In private yet he only bears
　　Your Bondage, who his Love conceals;
But when his Passion he declares,
　　You drag him at your Chariot Wheels.

4

Till I perceive some pleasing Ray
   Of finding the Return I seek,
Whate'er my tell-tale Eyes betray,
   My Heart may burst but shall not speak.

INDEX

The numerals in italics refer to footnotes.